Suitcase to Heaven

A Traveler's Collection of Life's Souvenirs

Emilia En L'air

WESTBOW
PRESS®
A DIVISION OF THOMAS NELSON
& ZONDERVAN

Scripture quotations taken from the Holy Bible, New Living Translation, Copyright © 1996, 2004. Used by permission of Tyndale House Publishers, Inc., Wheaton, Illinois 60189. All rights reserved.

Scripture taken from the Holy Bible, NEW INTERNATIONAL VERSION®. Copyright © 1973, 1978, 1984 by Biblica, Inc. All rights reserved worldwide. Used by permission. NEW INTERNATIONAL VERSION® and NIV® are registered trademarks of Biblica, Inc. Use of either trademark for the offering of goods or services requires the prior written consent of Biblica US, Inc.

Scripture taken from the King James Version of the Bible.

Scripture quotations taken from the New American Standard Bible®, Copyright © 1960, 1962, 1963, 1968, 1971, 1972, 1973, 1975, 1977, 1995 by The Lockman Foundation. Used by permission. (www.Lockman.org)

WestBow Press books may be ordered through booksellers or by contacting:

WestBow Press
A Division of Thomas Nelson & Zondervan
1663 Liberty Drive
Bloomington, IN 47403
www.westbowpress.com
1 (866) 928-1240

Because of the dynamic nature of the Internet, any web addresses or links contained in this book may have changed since publication and may no longer be valid. The views expressed in this work are solely those of the author and do not necessarily reflect the views of the publisher, and the publisher hereby disclaims any responsibility for them.

Any people depicted in stock imagery provided by Thinkstock are models, and such images are being used for illustrative purposes only. Certain stock imagery © Thinkstock.

ISBN: 978-1-5127-0098-5 (sc)
ISBN: 978-1-5127-0100-5 (hc)
ISBN: 978-1-5127-0099-2 (e)

Library of Congress Control Number: 2016900673

Print information available on the last page.

WestBow Press rev. date: 02/09/2016

Contents

Dedication

I dedicate this book with profound gratitude to
GOD, who is the Greatest! He directed my steps, and
restored my tears into an oasis of blessings.

To my mom, Linde, who believed that I could write
this book. She gave me the confidence that God will
use it, and the prayers to keep me going.

To my dad, Sezefredo, with loving memory, who shan't
be forgotten for the fingerprints left in my life.

To my wonderful children, Laura, Mike and
Anna, for their daily encouragement,

As well as Max and Trenton, for being a special part of my life.

Acknowledgement

Thank you to the following people who without their contributions, this book would not have been written:

My son Mike, for the love and valuable input.

My daughter Anna, for the love, book cover design, careful editing, and nudges to do better.

My mom's daily prayers.

Lyssete's inspiring life.

Zaki, who has asked about "the book" each week of every month.

"If I find in myself desires which nothing in this world can satisfy, the only logical explanation is that I was made for another world...I must keep alive in myself the desire for my true country, which I shall not find till after death; I must never let it get snowed under or turned aside; I must make it the main object of life to press on to that other country and to help others to do the same." — C.S. Lewis, Mere Christianity

Introduction

Have you noticed that everything in this planet is volatile?

Everything rapidly changes, just like the sun is suddenly covered by clouds and daylight suddenly turns into nightfall. Nothing lasts, just like a freshly budded rose that soon loses its pedals, crumbles, and shrivels away. Nothing remains because everything in this world is unstable. Everything quickly comes and quickly vanishes away. Even our "weeping may stay for the night, but rejoicing comes in the morning." (Psalm 30:5)

One minute we are in despair, the next filled with laughter because even our emotions are never constant. We're like feathers blowing here and there with the wind. Our internal and external circumstances are constantly changing because our moments are continuously fading into new realities requiring adaptation. The lack of constancy causes emptiness inside us because humans crave for security and lasting joy. Our frustration with life's impermeability drives us to seek a cure to fill the void. We want to be full but are always running on empty. Our perpetuation for the fulfillment of our longings becomes infinite. We look into new dreams, hoping something will fulfill our hollowness. However, the results are always the same: an unceasing emptiness which remains unfulfilled. That's because we try to satisfy our internal needs through the things of this world. The problem is that our needs cannot be met with anything that exists in this planet, because this world only collects dust. This world and its things are not meant to satiate but to lead us to something greater and permanent.

Have you been placing your hopes in this world to fulfill your void?

We go from one dream to the next. We go from one relationship to another. If we are single, we want to be married. If we are married, we want to have children. If our children are young, we can't wait for them to grow up and move out. If we are working, we can't wait to retire, and when we become old, we wish we were young again. We want many things because current attachments can't satisfy the void. As a consequence, we seek new attachments. We're repetitively on the lookout for something new, beyond ourselves, but our desires are never satisfied (see Proverbs 27:20). There's no end to our longings until we realize that the emptiness can only be fulfilled by something bigger than ourselves.

We never arrive to our destination of fullness because all the dusty things of this world are a mirage of satisfaction. That's because "… the world offers only a craving for physical pleasure, a craving for everything we see, and pride in our achievements and possessions…" (1 John 2:16) Family, friends, careers, fancy cars are not meant to satisfy our void. This world promises billboards promoting bliss but they're false advertisements. We buy into the briberies of this planet, but are never truly quenched by its lures.

What are the first thoughts you have when you wake up? What are the last thoughts you have before you fall asleep?

We wake up thinking about the things that we are consumed by in this planet. We wake up thinking of our needs. We go to sleep trying to gain control over our befuddled lives. We make plans to acquire new attachments that will complete our emptiness. We are consumed by this world which interchangeably deceives us into believing that its attractions will embrace our souls. We make this planet our final destination by letting it occupy our hearts and desires. But the world deceives us with its illusion, keeping us slaves of commercialized fantasies.

Have you wondered why you were placed in this world if your longings are transformed into mirages?

We are obsessed with the things that our physical body desires, not realizing that our flesh is chasing illusory and unattainable fulfillments. If we "… love money will never have enough. How meaningless to think that wealth brings true happiness!" (Ecclesiastes 5:10) That's because this planet is not the answer to our fulfillments. This planet is not our final destination. We are here just for a few years and then we die. James 4:14 says: "Your life is like the morning fog—it's here a little while, then it's gone."

We're travelers in this world. This is not meant to be our permanent home because our flesh dies and our soul goes on. Worldly attractions don't provide everlasting joy. We want that which is finite to quench, dismissing the fact that only the infinite presence of God can fill our vacant souls. Jesus warned us to look towards Heaven instead of collecting treasures on earth: "'Don't store up treasures here on earth, where moths eat them and rust destroys them, and where thieves break in and steal. Store your treasures in Heaven, where moths and rust cannot destroy, and thieves do not break in and steal.'" (Matthew 6:20) Jesus knew that fulfillment on earth was futile by storing earthly treasures. Jesus warned us that we should let Him occupy our hearts more than worldly possessions. Treasures on earth are tantalizers that can't fulfill our souls. We simply borrow treasures from God to lead us into our journey towards His loving embrace.

God grant us gifts, such as treasures of loving relationships, smiles of children, and snow falling softly on the ground. His favors are blessings of having special talents, food and shelters, or cure for diseases. God's blessings are given to us for our use and spiritual enrichment, not to be consumed by them. Blessings are not meant to be our goal or obsessions. Blessings don't fulfill the void. Blessings are meant to lead into spiritual growth and closer to Jesus. But when we make blessings the fulfillment of our internal void, unhappiness settles in, and emptiness perpetuates. That's because we become consumed with the blessings instead of the Blessor. If we depend on the blessings to make us happy more than the Provider, we squeeze the Lord out of our hearts. Once that happens, the void grows deeper because we start loving the things of this world more than the Lord.

Our hearts were not created by God to be consumed by the world. God designed our hearts to enhance our walk towards His eternity. "He has made everything beautiful in its time. He has also set eternity in the human heart; yet no one can fathom what God has done from beginning to end." (Ecclesiastes 3:11 NIV) If we allow the Lord to occupy the center of our hearts, then the void will be filled as Jesus said: "'Anyone who is thirsty may come to me! Anyone who believes in me may come and drink! For the Scriptures declare, 'Rivers of living water will flow from his heart.'" (John 7:37-38)

Have you noticed that all humans are born and die with a void unless they choose to drink from the rivers of living water?

I remember when I was thirsty for the living water because I felt a great void. Nothing completed me and I found everything utterly meaningless (Ecclesiastes 1).

I was only thirteen years old when I looked out from the back porch of my parents' house and admired the day losing its strength. Beautiful shades of yellow, orange, and pink painted the sky against the silhouette of the hills of the Brazilian tropical Rain Forest. The sun descended below the horizon, as my heart fell into sadness and loneliness. I lived in the silence of my fears. I needed a sense of hope and safety. I needed something infinite, permanent, and dependable. I needed something stable and unchangeable. I needed an unbreakable love which could fill my emptiness.

I thought I was alone. I thought my void could not be filled. But God called me to a sunset. And that particular sunset was not like any other sunset. God enticed me to the beauty of His peace. God called my attention to His loving face. At that moment, something changed inside me. My emptiness was suddenly filled with His living water. That unexpected and unannounced moment rekindled me with God's loving Spirit. That extraordinary moment became rooted in my soul forever.

As my faith in the Lord grew, I began working my salvation (see Philippians 2:12). I realized I was just a traveler in this planet. During my travelling, I began filling my spiritual Suitcase to Heaven. Not with souvenirs of different cities, but heavenly souvenirs. Every experience and trial that Jesus allowed in my life became an opportunity to add more souvenirs into my suitcase to my permanent home, Heaven.

I share in this book, my transformations through tribulations, and how I turned to Jesus in hardships. Everything I gained, and everything I lost in this world brought me closer to Him by filling my void with spiritual gifts. Every heartbreak, pain, and sorrow became jewels in my path to God. I was of this world but never drowned by it, because I became not of this world (see Romans 12:2).

I share in this book some of the heavenly souvenirs I have been collecting throughout the years which are now inside of my spiritual Suitcase to Heaven.

Traveler, what souvenirs have you been collecting in your spiritual Suitcase to Heaven?

What Do I Have To Be Thankful For

"Rejoice always, pray continually, give thanks in all circumstances; for this is God's will for you in Christ Jesus." 1 Thessalonians 5:16-18

There is a question that I really don't enjoy answering, but inevitably, it's the first thing people ask me when they meet me: "Where are you from?" I tense up immediately. I answer the question as quickly as possible and try to change the subject.

How am I to answer such a question? I'm a TCK, known as third culture kid. I accompanied my parents into different societies because of my father's career as an airline pilot. Although it was fun to experience different places in the world, I didn't have full ownership in any culture. I became a global nomad.

I struggled to adjust to new environments, customs, and people. Experiencing culture shock was routine. I was homesick many times, not knowing why, for I actually didn't know any particular place I called home on this vast planet.

"You will adapt," my parents used to say every time we moved.

One particular time relocating took a toll on me. It was a new culture, friends, school, community, weather, and food all over again. The unfamiliar place made me lose my identity. It was as if I had passed away. Nothing was predictable. I withdrew from the outside world.

Everything around me had changed, yet my home dynamics remained the same, and not to my comfort. Outside was a storm, and my home was not a shelter from the storm. My father constantly fought with my mother. He was always angry at something or someone. My mother was constantly crying, and my brother kept venting his frustrations on me.

I spent hours lying in the fetal position in my closet. Seclusion brought me closer to God and sheltered me from fear. My closet became my safe haven. However, sadness grew stronger, and hopelessness took over.

I listened to sad songs. The notes fed my grief. I lost desire to exist. I felt locked in my sadness with no way out. No one noticed me; no one heard my cry for help. During the full moon, I contemplated jumping from a high-rise building. However, as I gazed at the beauty of the moon God spoke to me. He showed me that every day was a miracle I was ignoring. He showed me that every day had something special worth appreciating. God shook the self-pity out of me. His light shone in my darkness and gave me strength to keep going.

My situation didn't change, but God changed me. During my struggles the Lord showed me what I had to be thankful for. I began counting my blessings and delighting myself in the Lord. Small things meant more than ever to me. Showering was one of them. It was a place where I was not disturbed by anyone. I loved the feeling of the water. It relaxed me and made me feel safe. A warm shower was my first offer of praise to the Lord.

After that, Jesus showed me many things to be thankful for. I could move, dance, see, and eat. I had a cozy bed and a closet to hide and pray. I had shelter from the cold. I had clothes to wear. Most of all, I had God's love.

Counting my blessing kicked away my hopelessness. I was able to feel peace and joy again. Praising God elevated me into intimacy with His presence. It provided a channel for His power to operate in me. It brought hope into my sadness. The more I centered myself in giving thanks, the bigger Jesus was magnified in my soul and the smaller my problems turned out to be. I was able to deal with life with a completely different approach, which brought light into my previous darkness.

All is a miracle Lord! You closed the door of sadness and unlocked the door of thanksgiving. You navigated my grievous heart out of misery and put a new song in my spirit. I praise you for the daily miracles you bestow in my life: eyes to see, ears to hear, hands to touch, a heart to love others. Most of all, I thank you for your love for me. Amen.

Additional reading: Psalm 28:7, Psalm 69:30, Psalm 95:1-6, Colossians 2:6-7, 1 Chronicles 16:34, Psalm 34:1, 1 Thessalonians 5:18.

Self-reflection: What do you have to be thankful for?

Give Forgiveness, Receive Forgiveness

"If you forgive those who sin against you, your heavenly Father will forgive you. But if you refuse to forgive others, your Father will not forgive your sins." Matthew 6:14-15

Finally, I became an adult. I was packed and ready to move out of my parents' house. My new home was four thousand miles away from everyone I knew. My mom cried and hugged me. My father was cold and distant. My brother was indifferent. I looked at them one last time. I felt relieved. My heart praised God because I was free at last from years of abuse. I left everything behind and started anew. Or so I thought!

An ocean separated my family and me. Their day was my night; my night was their day. Little did I know at the time, my address had changed, but not my pain. I had smuggled it into my luggage unknowingly. Pain crossed the world. I didn't leave it behind. I carried it within my soul.

My body remembered the marks of abuse. It was a poison circulating in my blood. I thought I was contaminated for life. Healing seemed impossible. Wounds echoed in my memories. Trauma impacted my existence. It shaped my self-worth in the worst possible way.

My soul needed mending. Night after night I lay in my bed ruminating thoughts of my past. I resented my father. I couldn't understand why he acted the way he did. "Why did he abuse me? Didn't he have compassion? Did anyone in my family see my pain? Didn't they care about me? Why is it that nobody heard me?" I asked myself.

As the years went by, my resentment deepened. I had children and advocated for them. "Why is it that no one advocated on my behalf?

Was I that insignificant?" I kept questioning. Some nights it would take hours to fall asleep because the past kept repeating itself in my brain. My mind was a prisoner of my aching thoughts. The spoiled resentment was my nightly companion.

One day the Lord spoke to me as clear as a bell: "Are you ready to forgive your father?" My negative emotions were so ingrained in me that I didn't know how to let go. I needed a miracle from God.

I honestly didn't think God could heal me from my resentment. It seemed too big of a miracle. How could years of brain junk just go away? But, God is a God of miracles!

It took two months and all the brain junk was gone, never to return. God showed me an open window to my past. He reminded me of His presence in my childhood. He was my safety, my refuge, and my Father of comfort. I offered my simple prayers to Him, and in return, I sensed His presence during my darkest hours.

God turned something that was meant to harm me into something good for me. He used my scars to help me understand others in similar situations. It became easy to empathize with those who had gone through childhood abuse.

The poisonous resentment finally left my heart once I found a new way to look at my father's abusive behavior. I changed my thinking from "poor me" to comprehending his personality and childhood. I began to understand that every unjust action he displayed toward me was rooted in an unjust action displayed towards him. It was a cycle of "hurting people- hurting others." He hurt me because he didn't know how to receive healing himself. He didn't know how to engage in healthy love because he had never received healthy love.

Once I understood my father's childhood, I was able to comprehend why he became who he was. My change in thinking released forgiveness. I stopped wanting him to be who I wanted him to be, and began praying that God would soften his heart to be the man He wanted my father to be.

The poison in my blood was gone. God lifted an incredible weight from my shoulders. I was miraculously free and healed from childhood abuse. Forgiving my father was my cleansing balm.

Finally, I was able to go to bed without overthinking the past. Within ten minutes, I'd fall asleep. Forgiveness set me free.

My God of miracles, you examined my heart and saw the dark thoughts that lived in me. You placed your miraculous blessings in my spirit and set me free from anger. You brought light into my nights and gave me peaceful dreams. Thank you for being with me. Cleansed, at last! Amen.

Additional Reading: Psalm 139, Psalm 71, Genesis 50:20, 1 John 1:9, Isaiah 43:25-26, Mark 11:25, Matthew 26:28.

Self-reflection: Do you believe God is going to use your trials for your good? Is resentment keeping you from being all that God wants you to be? Are you ready to let go of your past, forgive those who hurt you, and let God miraculously change you?

My Worth Comes From God

"Thank you for making me so wonderfully complex!
Your workmanship is marvelous—how well I know it."
Psalm 139:14

For many years, I struggled with issues of self-worth, even after I came to know Jesus. Echoes from the past fed my negative thinking as if I was watering my own rose thorns. I was hurting my own rosarium, which was my soul.

I felt unintelligent, unattractive, and unworthy. I was shy well into my adult years. I used to sit in corners, observing the world around me, thinking I had no right to be a part of it.

Asides from the abuse that occurred at home, bullying at school added to my low self-esteem. In high school, it escalated to a daily ritual to the point I had to be transferred to another school in order to alleviate my troubles.

During my time in Bible College, I continued to be a target for bullying. I thought I would be part of a group once being among Christians. After all, they were my brothers and sisters in Christ. But that was far from what happened. Some colleagues performed a theatrical play making fun of me because I was hard of hearing. My self-esteem plunged to zero by then.

I continued being plagued by identity issues even after having children. However, one blessed day changed my life. I gave a speech presentation during nursing school. A colleague said to me: "You have so much self-confidence!" I was shocked when I heard her say such a wonderful complement. She didn't notice the battlefield that my soul was fighting. In reality, I had zero self-confidence and my nursing school speech presentation was the fruit of prayers and leaning on Jesus. I didn't show on the outside the turmoil I was having in the inside.

My speech presentation helped me push my prayers further. I finally asked Jesus to heal me from my low self-esteem. And, He began working inside me by giving me new insights into a miraculous new healthy me.

I finally realized Jesus didn't die on the cross for me to feel worthless and ugly. I had to change my wrong thinking. As Proverbs 23:7 says: "For as he thinks in his heart, so is he." I was definitely following my stinking thinking. I desperately needed to change my thinking patterns and follow Christ's thinking.

My prayers turned into therapy sessions with Jesus. He actively listened as I emptied all my thoughts on Him. He gave me new insights, twenty-four hour daily consultations, a shoulder of true empathy to cry on and a healing balm. All free of charge!

I surrendered to Jesus a list of people that made me feel worthless. I grabbed a piece of paper and drew two columns. On top of the first column I wrote the names of the people that hurt me in the past. Underneath it, I wrote all the derogatory words and insults they described me and how they made me feel. On the second column I wrote Jesus name on top, and underneath it, I wrote all about His unconditional love and acceptance towards me. Every insult of the past began to be erased by the way Jesus looked at me. I carried that piece of paper in my pocketbook until I was completely healed.

I began to notice that the first column was nothing more, nothing less than a distorted mirror of me. It had no foundation on reality. People hurt me because they were hurting themselves. They lashed out their frustrations on me. I finally understood that the second column was the true representation of who I was- a child of God.

Today I still have that note tucked away somewhere but it's nothing more than a memorial. It's nothing short of a miracle that I finally see myself through God's eyes. The negative thoughts I once carried since childhood no longer impacted me. My worth and value finally originated from the One who died for me and lives in me.

I began to experience a complete new freedom I've never experienced before. I was no longer the timid frightened person I used to be. I continued being molded more and more into Christ's image. He gave me a supernatural assurance of who I was in Him.

People's opinion of me lost its relevance because I became more grounded in Christ. His opinion became my number one priority.

Through Christ, I became a new creature for I realized: I'm His child. I'm His temple. I'm His ambassador. I'm His witness. I'm His righteousness. I'm His workmanship. I am good and acceptable to Him. I'm His branch as He is my vine. I am complete and wonderfully made by His wonderful hands.

My Almighty Maker, you've made me out of your image. You've given me a brain that works in harmony with your will for my life. Yet, I sighed and said to myself and others I was not lovely or good enough. Surprisingly, you embraced my insecurities for I could not see the sunlight shining through my scars. Then, you've given me a mirror. I looked at myself and finally saw your sunlight radiating all around me. You live in me! At last, I said, "I am beautiful." Amen.

Additional Reading: Colossians 2:10, Romans 12:3, 1 Corinthians 15:10, 2 Corinthians 5:17, 1 Peter 1:3, Psalm 139:14, John 15:5, 2 Corinthians 5:17, Romans 8:1, 2 Corinthians 5:21, Romans 12:2.

Self-reflection: Do you suffer with identity crises, low self-worth, and comparison issues? Does your worth come from family, friends, society or God? Would you like to learn to see yourself as God sees you?

The Birth Of A Ministry

"Jesus knew that His hour had come to leave this world and return to His Father. He had loved His disciples during His ministry on earth, and now He loved them to the very end. Jesus knew that the Father had given Him authority over everything and that He had come from God and would return to God. So He got up from the table, took off His robe, wrapped a towel around His waist, and poured water into a basin. Then He began to wash the disciples' feet, drying them with the towel He had around Him…'And since I, your Lord and Teacher, have washed your feet, you ought to wash each other's feet. I have given you an example to follow. Do as I have done to you.'" John 13:1, 3-5, 14-15

It's remarkable that Jesus washed the disciples' feet. His humble action teaches us a lesson on love and servitude. Washing feet in Jesus' days was not like going to a spa nowadays, where pedicurists offer feet pampering. It was an extremely humbling job done by people of low-status, such as slaves or servants. People walked either barefooted or wore sandals. It was the lowliest of all services. The foot washers had to wash filthy feet with dust, dirt or dung trapped in between toes and nails.

Even though Jesus came as a King, He did not come to conquer. He came to serve and not to be served. Jesus humbled himself as one of the lowest servants. It was scandalous for Jesus to kneel down and wash sweaty dirty feet. The root of His actions was to love others at all cost. He conveyed His message through foot washing foreshadowing His supreme love on the cross.

As a follower of Christ, I desired to emulate His servitude. When I came to know Christ as a teenager, He washed my sins and I received His salvation. I wanted to serve Jesus by washing other's feet. But I didn't quite know how to serve Him during my youth, so I asked Him to give me a ministry.

One afternoon I was playing volleyball with the church youth group. A stranger by the name of John came to join our ball game. No one from church knew him. He came out of nowhere. We didn't know his history, but we welcomed him into our group. He joined the church services and Bible studies.

Mysterious John was part of our small church for approximately two months. Suddenly John disappeared. He left me a wooden hand crafted boat with a church member. "Give it to Emilia," he said. No one from church ever saw him again, including me.

Months went by, and unexpectedly, I received a letter addressed to the church, from an inmate incarcerated in Florida. His name was Thomas. I was puzzled! I didn't know anyone named Thomas. I didn't know anyone who had broken the law or had committed any crimes. Furthermore, prison was a faraway reality from my protective Christian social world.

Bewildered, I read the confusing letter twice and came to the conclusion that mysterious John was actually Thomas. He wrote me in his prison letter that he had escaped a New York State Prison after being sentenced for first degree murder. He made our Californian church his hidden fugitive adobe. I realized we played volleyball, prayed, and communed with a fugitive murderer who wanted to be my pen-pal!

My small naïve world was radically turned upside down upon receiving a letter from a killer. I knew there were no coincidences with God. I prayed for a ministry and God had just opened the door to wash someone's feet dipped in crime.

I began writing John/Thomas about the love of Christ. He was the first inmate I ever wrote about the Lord. After that, many other inmate letters followed. God provided an outlet to minister about His love and forgiveness. I began to spread the love and salvation of Christ. In the following four years I was led to visit several prisons, juvenile halls, and jails in California, and São Paulo, Brazil.

Jesus birthed me a ministry. He loved inmates through me. They wrote me about their crimes and I wrote them about the full extent of Jesus love, forgiveness, and cleansing. After all, Jesus did not give anyone preferential treatment. His love extends to all mankind. He even washed the feet of the one who He knew would betray him.

My humble King Jesus, you didn't come to conquer the world, but you conquered my heart. I want to echo everything you've done for me to others. I want to mirror your love, humility, kindness, and servitude. Help me to love and serve at least one person today. Amen.

Additional reading: Psalms 58:10, Song 5:3, 1 Samuel 25:41, John 13:1-16, Matthew 20:28, John 12:26, Luke 22:27, Romans 12:1.

Self-reflection: Are you following Jesus example on foot washing? Are you open to be used by Jesus even if it means washing someone's feet that you don't like? Are you willing to wash the feet of the one that hurt you the most?

Carandiru

"Those who live in the shelter of the Most High will find rest in the shadow of the Almighty.

This I declare about the Lord: He alone is my refuge, my place of safety; He is my God, and I trust him."
Psalm 91:1-2

During my late teenage years I attended Bible College in Brazil. As part of the school mission, I'd take two buses and the subway to visit inmates in prison in order to minister the Word of God. One time I walked in a penitentiary called Carandiru. It was a maximum security prison known for riots and massacres due to uprisings. One of the major problems they faced at the time was the massive AIDS epidemic.

Carandiru's courtyard smelled like open sewage. Inmates didn't have uniforms and wore only shorts. The building was a big block of gray concrete with no trees or flowers, which intensified the darkness of the place. The courtyard was surrounded by a three story high building with several cells. Inmate's legs and arms hung outside of the cells bars like chimpanzees inside zoo cages. Each cell was overcrowded. Hopelessness echoed the walls of the prison.

I was the only female among two other Christian males. We walked inside the prison courtyard. I really needed God's extra protection. I took one alert step in front of the other as inmates began to enclose me from each side. I walked towards the prison chapel located at the end of the courtyard. I should have been terrified for I was encircled by murderers, child molesters, rapist, and thieves, yet I felt protected by God's angels. I experienced an overwhelming sense of peace which transcended my understanding (see Philippians 4:7). God gave me grace to minister, sing, and love the unloved forgotten inmates.

The chapel was dark and infested with cockroaches. The bugs thrived because of the moisture in the building. They were crawling everywhere on and under the pews. There was an awful musty unpleasant odor. I realized it came from the roaches. It was hard to breathe. Meanwhile, inmates kept coming into the chapel. We sang and praised the Lord. The prisoners referred me as their sister in Christ. I was in God's protective bubble. I could have died that day, but God was my protector, and I lived in Christ to tell this story.

I was young and underqualified for the task of ministering to inmates, but somehow, God used me for His ministry. I was naïve, but God called me and gave me grace to love the unloved with radical faith.

I could have been terrified to go inside prisons but I could not have joined fear and trust simultaneously. Fear could have contaminated my faith.

God befallen a difficult ministry on my hands, but He made it easy to fulfill His task by His grace.

Lord of all grace, guide those who are struggling with fear to know the freedom that's in you. You bring light into darkness. You safeguard every path ahead. Thank you for your protection. Amen.

Additional reading: Matthew 28:18-20, 2 Thessalonians 3:3, Luke 12:32, Isaiah 41:10, Isaiah 54:17, Psalm 46:1.

Self-reflection: Do you have fear or faith?

Run To The Throne, Not The Phone

"The Lord says, 'I will guide you along the best pathway
for your life. I will advise you and watch over you. Do
not be like a senseless horse or mule that needs a bit and
bridle to keep it under control.'" Psalm 32:8-9

Years ago I was in love with the man that eventually became my husband. Dating Tom was painful because he kept giving me mixed messages. I spent hours crying because things were not working out between us. I was clueless to what direction to take. I would call my friend Sue on the phone and dump all my agony on her. At some point in time, she became sick and tired of my tears. She said I needed to find answers in God's promises because she didn't know how to comfort me. Her words made me feel somewhat rejected, but her thinking was correct.

I noticed that every time I poured my problems on Sue, I met more loss and confusion. She was not qualified to fix my problems. She didn't have a crystal ball. She couldn't change my situation or help me. On top of it all, I was driving her crazy by being a senseless mule that needed a bit and bridle to keep me under control.

I was so wrapped up in my longings for Tom, that my circumstances seemed like a vortex turning my thoughts around and around with no way out. I invited my closest friend into my problem and left the All-knowing God out.

I thought constantly of "he loves me, he loves me not," until my emotions became tortuous. I allowed Satan to play with my emotions. I asked Sue for advice hoping she'd have the solutions for my problems. However, when Sue said something I didn't want to hear, I rejected her advice. When Sue said something I wanted to hear, I was happy! But if what I wanted to hear wouldn't come to fruition, my frustrations would escalate.

The powerful Wayne Lawson's quote came to mind: "Run to the throne, not the phone." I finally gave up on the phone and poured all my insecurities, fears, and tears on the throne of God. I sought Jesus in everything, and I found all answers in Him.

I turned murmuring into faith by seeking God's wisdom: "If you need wisdom, ask our generous God, and He will give it to you. He will not rebuke you for asking. But when you ask Him, be sure that your faith is in God alone. Do not waver, for a person with divided loyalty is as unsettled as a wave of the sea that is blown and tossed by the wind." (James 1:5-6)

God answered my prayers. The man I loved returned my affection. Tom and I eventually got married. But, I also learned that marriage was not my final destination. Marriage was not my happily ever after. It was only the beginning of another great trial.

I understood that going to God's throne was the most secure way to be centered on His path. The Lord was the only one who could really guide me into His perfect plan.

My Shepherd, lead my troubled heart into peaceful pastures. Guide me out of mental turmoil. You answer all my questions. I empty my thoughts on you and miraculously you show me where to go. Amen.

Additional reading: Psalm 1:1-2, Proverbs 1:5, Proverbs 9:9, Proverbs 1:7, Proverbs 3:13-19, Ephesians 3:20, Jeremiah 33:3, Matthew 7:7.

Self-reflection: Have you been going to chat, texting, and phone or to the Throne? Do you ask everyone for advice? Does that make you more confused? Have you asked God to show you His path for your life? Have you invited the All-Knowing God into your troubled heart and asked for His wisdom?

Forgive

> "Then Jesus asked them, 'Would anyone light a lamp and then put it under a basket or under a bed? Of course not! A lamp is placed on a stand, where its light will shine. For everything that is hidden will eventually be brought into the open, and every secret will be brought to light. Anyone with ears to hear should listen and understand.'" Mark 4:21-23

When Tom and I were still married, we hiked on the trails of Point Toros Natural Reserve in California. It follows the shoreline and leads to hidden coves. It is a beautiful place with headlands and rolling meadows. The smell of the sea, seals, and otters made me feel close to God's natural wonders.

Point Toros' cypress trees have roots that spread out above the ground. I walked carefully not to trip. Tree roots are usually hidden, but due to rain and soil erosion, cypress roots are exposed. It reminded me of secrets. Souls conceal them, time exposes them. "For there is nothing hidden that will not be disclosed, and nothing concealed that will not be known or brought out into the open." (Luke 8:17)

Cypress roots reminded me of my ex-husband. Time exposed Toms' roots and his darkest secrets were bare for all to see. Soil erosion and rain uncovered his transgressions.

Tom lived the all American dream. He was loved by me and our children Laura, Mike, and Anna. He had a home on top of the mountain. He was a physician with two practices, chief medical staff of a hospital, and enough money to enjoy vacations.

Tom seemed like a wonderful father to all our children, especially to Laura. He took her to medical rounds since she was four years old. Mike and Anna lagged behind and didn't get as much attention from him as Laura. I remember Tom's truck approaching our driveway. We would run toward his direction and hug him.

Nevertheless, our picture perfect family disintegrated as Tom's façade melted when Laura was twelve years old. She told me Tom sexually abused her from age's four to ten. She kept the abuse as a secret in order to protect her siblings. But the day came when she finally made her pain known to me. I confronted Tom on the subject, but it didn't stop him from wanting to do our children harm. I left him behind in the West Coast and began life anew with our children in Brazil.

Everything I believed about Tom was a lie. His fatherhood was a lie. Our marriage was a lie. He robbed Laura from having a healthy childhood. We were living with a predator and an oppressor.

The foundation of Tom's life was based on deceits. All the skeletons in his closet fell on the ground. His incestuous behavior was put to an end after I sought help from the police and the child protective service, two years later upon returning to the United States.

Today Tom sits in a prison cell, facing fifty-eight years behind bars. He lost his dignity, family, medical license, and home.

It took years for our lives to be reconstructed. I sought God's guidance for each step I took and He set us free from oppression. My previous home fell apart, but Jesus rebuilt another one from bottom up with a new solid foundation.

I committed my ways to the Lord and He made our paths straight. Jesus brought justice by setting Laura free from abuse. The road towards healing continued, as Jesus balm touched us little by little. The Lord did not abandon us but led us to safety (see Psalm 37).

I focused on Jesus' promises instead of the storm that was going on in our lives. God allowed pain to produce in us a greater measure of faith, wisdom, forgiveness, and love.

In order to advocate for Laura, I chose to forgive Tom and teach forgiveness to my children. Jesus said: "If you forgive those who sin against you, your heavenly Father will forgive you. But if you refuse to forgive others, your Father will not forgive your sins." (Matthew 6:14-15)

I cleared my soul from bitterness, hatred, and resentment. Eventually my children forgave Tom as well. God's justice prevailed when love was offered in the face of injustice. Forgiving the oppressor opened the door for God to deliver Laura and us from oppression.

God gave me the grace to keep my heart and thoughts pure, which gave Him a platform to operate His miracles in our lives. Hatred only leads to more hatred. "Do not nurse hatred in your heart for any of your relatives. Confront people directly so you will not be held guilty for their sin." (Leviticus 19:17)

Forgiving Tom did not mean restoration of our relationship. It did not mean he would not serve time in prison. It meant choosing to have a healthy heart for the sake of God and my children.

I wanted a perfect father for my children but God had other plans. Tom was broken, as all of us are broken in this world. However, my role in the brokenness of our family was to follow Jesus' footsteps on forgiveness. I invited Him into our suffering and He led us out of bondage. He gave us grace out of our lack. The hardships of our lives made us yearn less for the things of this world and yearn more for the things of God.

In the end, Tom was the oppressor. Laura was the victim. God was the restorer. Forgiveness was the healer.

El-Roi, you are our Restorer, the strong one who sees all that is hidden in our hearts. You love the oppressed. You love the oppressor. Your love has no preferential treatment. Help us to love and forgive as you do. Bring healing and love to everything that is shattered. Amen.

Additional reading: Psalm 31:18, Genesis 16:13, Matthew 10:26-28, Matthew 12:36-37, Ephesians 4:25, Ephesians 4:29, Philippians 4:6-8, Romans 2:16, Luke 12:2, Galatians 6:7-8.

Self-reflection: Are you living in a web of secrets that eventually is going to hurt others and yourself? Would you ask Jesus to make things right in your life? Would you ask Jesus to help you forgive the ones that hurt you the most?

Angel Man

"Those who live in the shelter of the Most High will find rest in the shadow of the Almighty. This I declare about the Lord: He alone is my refuge, my place of safety; He is my God, and I trust him. For He will rescue you from every trap and protect you from deadly disease. Do not be afraid of the terrors of the night, nor the arrow that flies in the day...If you make the Lord your refuge, if you make the Most High your shelter, no evil will conquer you; no plague will come near your home. For He will order His angels to protect you wherever you go...The Lord says, 'I will rescue those who love me. I will protect those who trust in my name. When they call on me, I will answer; I will be with them in trouble. I will rescue and honor them. I will reward them with a long life and give them my salvation.'" Psalm 91:1-3, 5, 9-12, 14-16

While Tom and I were still married, we went for a hike with our children during a beautiful sunny day. Laura and Mike played with pinecones as we climbed uphill on the steep trail, while I carried Anna on a baby backpack carrier. The ground was slippery due to fog, moss, and pine cone needles. The hike was desolate with God, nature, and us. We were having fun and sang out loud to our hearts' content.

After a couple of hours of hiking we spotted the peak of the waterfall about twenty feet from where we were. Mike, who was four years old at the time, began running towards the cliff of the waterfall. I panicked and ran after him hoping to stop him. I shouted at the top of my lungs:

"Stop!!!" But Mike did not stop! I ran as fast as I could but I could not reach him. He kept on going just about an arms' length ahead of me, and at the same time an inch from falling down from a cliff to his death.

During our hike, I haven't seen one person. I thought we're entirely on our own. But not a moment too soon, not a moment too late, a man sat by the edge of the waterfall, with his legs criss cross applesauce. I thought he'd be gazing at the waterfall, but he was facing us running towards him and the cliff of the fall. Mike was going to take the plunge not realizing what he was doing. The man stared at my desperate eyes. He stretched his left arm and grabbed the back of Mike's t-shirt. He brought Mike back to land a second before falling to his death.

If that man wasn't there, Mike's life would have been lost. God provided a man to rescue him. The man was at the right place, at the right time, to save Mike from falling. He sat at the perfect spot. His arm was the perfect length to grab Mike's t-shirt. That was no coincidence. God supplied an angel to save Mike! That was the Almighty's miracle moment in the life of our family.

On the other hand, it's puzzling to understand God's refuge, safety, and shelter when we are not scooped out of a trap of suffering. Then, our human tendency is to question God. Our nature rebels against His ways and we ask: "Where were you, Jesus, when terror came my way?"

During that same week my young son Mike was rescued by God's angel, my oldest daughter Laura was being sexually abused by Tom. It seemed unfathomable that Tom would commit such a heinous crime. Tom was a doctor who advocated in behalf of victims of sexual abuse. Yet, he was the perpetrator himself! Laura kept her pain hidden from me to protect Mike and Anna from being abused.

Laura's refuge and safety came at the time she told me about the abuse. I left the country and upon my return to the United States, I contacted the police. After a lengthy difficult trial and trusting God for miracles, Tom was sentenced to fifty eight years in prison.

Laura lived years of sexual abuse in the silence of her pain until rescue arrived. Until then, she was vulnerable under an incestuous' ill mind. Where was God's angel during the years of her abuse? Why wasn't I able to catch Tom on the act? Why didn't God protect Laura and shelter her from Tom's traps? Laura was afraid of the terrors of the night and her loneliness turned into years of darkness.

It would seem that God protected my family at times and not others. It seemed as God did not pay attention to every possible danger in the life of our family. Was God taking a nap when Laura was being abuse? Was I blind or too trusting of the man I married? Did God allow suffering to enter Laura's life in order to satisfy a molester's sick desires?

I had to dig deeper in the Bible to understand God's nature and comprehend His rescuing modality. I finally learned that God swiftly scoops us out of trouble in miraculous ways once in a while. Other times, we have to go through longsuffering. However, He doesn't leave His faithful ones abandoned during suffering. He doesn't take a nap or turn His eyes away from us while we suffer. As a matter of fact, He does see us through our hardships by providing His grace during our storms. He guides us out of the furnace of affliction once our faith has been developed out of the trials. We gain "beauty from our ashes." (Isaiah 61:3)

At times we beg God to remove the pain but to our dismay, troubles linger from season to season. Paul speaks of this in 2 Corinthians 12:8-9: "Three different times I begged the Lord to take it away. Each time He said, 'My grace is all you need. My power works best in weakness.' So now I am glad to boast about my weaknesses, so that the power of Christ can work through me."

In our lingering pain, the Lord tests the fibers of our faith. The essence of God's plan was not to rescue Mike and Laura or anyone who puts their trust in Him from every hardship. Job 23:10 says, "But He knows where I am going. And when He tests me, I will come out as pure as gold." God test us in our trials and helps us through the trials so we may come out as pure as gold. He hand picks our tribulations so we may grow in Him. We must endure our trials in order to be purified from our imperfections. Our pain becomes a rescue from our self-centered sinful nature. That's a spiritual rescue, not necessarily a situational rescue.

Trials are meant to bring about fruits of purity in our souls. Some trials come and go quickly as samples of God's armor of protection such as Mike's miraculous angel man. Other trials linger on like Laura's abuse. She was finally free from it, but through her pain, she was able to collect much beauty. Both trials were a process to become more like Christ. Eventually, both trials ended, new ones began.

It's important to view trials as blessings and not curses (see James 1:2-4). Attempting to escape trials only postpones our growth in the Lord. By drinking the chalice of His will for our lives, we discover that His grace is truly sufficient for every situation, good or bad. Only then, we begin to live our heavenly life, yet in our earthly bodies.

El-Roi, you are my God who sees everything. Your eyes are everywhere, knowing my heart. My iniquities are no secret to you. Your power brings justice and sets me free. You defend me in my affliction. You are my strength during my troubles. In you there is no fear. Amen.

Additional reading: Genesis 16:13, Jeremiah 16:17, Jeremiah 23:24, Acts 1:24, 1 John 3:20, Psalm 82:3-4, Psalm 37:39, Philippines 4:13, Isaiah 61:1-3.

Self-reflection: Can you name times in your life when God miraculously rescued you? Have you had times of longsuffering in which God's rescue came through costly pain and suffering?

It's My Choice

"But if serving the Lord seems undesirable to you, then
choose for yourselves this day whom you will serve,
whether the gods your ancestors served beyond the
Euphrates, or the gods of the Amorites, in whose land
you are living. But as for me and my household, we will
serve the Lord." Joshua 24:15 (NIV)

Laura continued to heal her soul from sexual abuse during her teenage
years. She was seen by a therapist weekly. It was not an easy road and
due to her battle and confusion, she ended up pregnant while she was a
teenager. Little Max was the new addition to our small family. Through
the years she became a good parent, married, and continued on her road
to recovery.

Seven years before Laura met her husband, I co-raised her son Max.
I recall one such day when Mike, Anna, and I were up and ready to
begin our morning. I was unsuccessful in getting Max up and ready for
school. He whined to get up, eat breakfast, and get dressed for school.
He sassy me until he had a full temper tantrum.

By the time everyone was done with breakfast we were frail by
all of Max's commotion. I had my knees glued on the carpet with
supplications: "Help me Lord, Lord, Lord!"

It was not unusual for Max to be rumbustious. Everything was a
battle of wills. Nothing was ever smooth when it came to him. Not at
home nor at school. He liked to make his own choices for everything and
battled me with obedience. I constantly reiterated that he could make
any choice he wanted for every situation, as long as he was prepared to
live with the consequences.

By the time I drove Max to school I was discouraged. I talked to him about making good choices, yet I realized I could not chose who he was going to be and how he was going to act. I could only choose how I reacted when he disobeyed. But no matter what, I always reacted with love because I loved him unconditionally.

Adults get frustrated with young children whenever they disobey. We want them to wake up on time to go to school. We want them to eat a healthy breakfast so they grow up strong. We want them to use kind words so they grow up loving others. We want children to obey us because we know what's best for them. We think they understand that we are trying to help them, but they don't.

Discipline is no different when it comes from our Heavenly Father. He gives us guidelines in regards to obedience. It should be obvious that His path is better than our path; however, we think we know what's best and do things our own way. We are sassy towards God, take His name in vain, and blame Him for our choices. Then we get angry because we sinned and reap what we sow.

Just like regular parents, God does not chose who we are going to be. We have free choice to take any path we choose for our lives. This autonomy makes us accountable for our actions. The skies are unlimited for the choices we can make. God does not turn His back when we disobey. No matter what, He always loves us unconditionally.

God loves us by giving us freedom to choose whether we will follow His path or not. It would be unloving if He would dictate every step we would take. It would bind and restrain us to being His slave. God's freedom permits us to love Him with a heart of adoration and not of obligation.

God loves us because love is His nature. The essence of His love is everlasting. If we choose to obey Him our lives will be blessed forevermore.

My Way of Life, I chose to sin. You chose to forgive me. I chose to reject you. You chose to redeem me. Yet, I know that choosing you it's what's best. Give me grace to listen and obey all the words you say. Oh my Lord, I really love your divine way and truly wish to follow you wherever road you take. Amen.

Additional Reading: Romans 5:8, 1 John 4:8, 1 John 4:16, John 3:16, 1 John 3:16, Jeremiah 31:3, Ephesians 2:8, Romans 8:35.

Self-reflection: Do you choose to go God's way or your way? Romans 8:35 says there's nothing that can separate us from the love of Christ. Would you name situations in your life in which Christ poured His love in your distress even when you disobeyed Him?

Suffering

"We can rejoice, too, when we run into problems and trials, for we know that they help us develop endurance. And endurance develops strength of character, and character strengthens our confident hope of salvation. And this hope will not lead to disappointment. For we know how dearly God loves us, because He has given us the Holy Spirit to fill our hearts with his love." Romans 5:3-5

I was living an active life as a single mother of three and a toddler. After a long day, I was cozy in my bed trying to doze off to sleep but my thoughts kept me awake. I pondered on the many ways the Lord healed me from past emotional hurts and aided me in unusual situations. I realized God taught me wisdom in secret places. Many tests in my life have been completed and all was well with my soul.

Somehow, there was still a desire to go deeper in knowing the Lord. "Jesus, I still want to know you more! I still can't comprehend your pain on the cross. I have never really carried pain in my body. Jesus, give me a new insight so I can know you better," I prayed not realizing that God was about to answer my prayer in total.

One year later my prayer was answered and my life changed radically with the onset of my neuromuscular disease. Little did I know when I prayed that prayer, the only way to truly understand the cross was by living some of the pain of the cross.

Pain became my new cup of suffering. Thus, I've began to understand Jesus better. I'd wake up with my muscles rapidly contracting and relaxing involuntarily. The sudden movements felt like a shock sensation that went from my head to my toes. During the nights, I experienced sleep disturbances which kept me awake for hours. I dreaded going to sleep due to the horrible experiences. It became my nightly battle.

Day time was but affliction and my night was just as tortuous. My health was in complete disarray. I was trying to make sense of suffering. Why would a loving God make me go through this physical torture day after day? What have I done to deserve such pain?

It'd have been easy to think God had turned His back on me. But I knew deep inside, my pain was an answer to my prayers to know Jesus' cross better.

The truth of the matter is that God permitted suffering in my life. I prayed to know Him better, and I was! His back was not turned away from me when I came down with a neuromuscular disease. He was simple giving me a key to unlock His grace in order to showcase His power through my afflictions.

God permitted His only son Jesus to suffer immeasurable pain on the cross. His back was not turned away from His son. Salvation came to us because God allowed His son to suffer. If God permitted His son to suffer, why wouldn't He permit my suffering?

Much good came from my afflictions. I began to delight in my physical weakness and boast about Christ's power because He made me strong during my greatest difficulties. He was shining through my sickness and teaching me that I could be sustained by Him during my pain.

Roman 8:28 says: "And we know that God causes everything to work together for the good of those who love God and are called according to His purpose for them." All things worked together for my good. Not just the things that were fun for my life, but those things which were of great challenge as well.

I realized that my sleep disturbances were working for my own good. The Lord did not allow the night disturbances to happen in my sleep by mishap. He used every part of my disability for my good in order to accomplish the plan of molding me into His image.

His plan for my life was to produce something great out of suffering. Through His grace, He began to create greater endurance, character, hope, and steadfastness in me. He was making me complete and lacking nothing by filling His character into my feeble self.

My afflictions were a portion of the suffering Jesus endured at the cross. He did not have a temper tantrum or get angry at God for allowing pain to enter His life. He did not have a pity party during his physical suffering. Much the contrary, Jesus knew God had to accomplish the plan of salvation and He rested all the little details of His life into the Almighty's hand.

I continued suffering from a neuromuscular illness, but my sleep disturbances lasted for about a year. I was able to praise Him in my thunder and lightning nights and thank Him for healing my sleep problems.

Jehovah-Rapha, my great healer! I rejoice as I share in your suffering because your glory is magnified through my pain. Your life is manifested in my afflictions. In my sufferings you are with me, restoring and strengthening me. I felt your healing touch stretching forth during my nights. I praise you for putting your hand upon my hand. Amen.

Additional reading: James 1:2-4, 1 Peter 1:2-4, Romans 8:18, 1 Peter 4:12-19, John 16:33, 2 Corinthians 4:8-10, Revelation 21:4, Isaiah 43:2, 1 Peter 4:12-13, Luke 14:27, 2 Timothy 3:12.

Self-reflection: How do you reconcile God and suffering? How do you respond to suffering in your life? Do you get angry and bitter at God for your afflictions? Do you go into a temper tantrum when things don't go your way? Do you see God's restoring hands during the turmoils of your life?

Dependance On God

"In the thirty-ninth year of his reign Asa was afflicted with a disease in his feet. Though his disease was severe, even in his illness he did not seek help from the Lord, but only from the physicians. Then in the forty-first year of his reign Asa died and rested with his ancestors." 2 Chronicles 16:12-13

Neuromuscular illness sneaked up on me during the summer of 2009. I was cleaning the house just like any other day when suddenly my tongue became stiff and protruded. I couldn't swallow at all. Somehow I didn't think much of it. I made fun of myself and showcased my kids the bizarre symptom. As entertaining as it seemed, having a nursing education, I decided to head to the emergency room.

I waited for a few hours to be seen by an emergency room physician. But somehow, my tongue normalized by itself before the doctor showed up, so I ended up leaving the hospital without a diagnosis.

I wished that had been a onetime weird occurrence, but it was merely the beginning of my path through physical pain. It went from funny to outright scary. I've seen many different specialists, but always left their offices frustrated because no one knew what was wrong with my health.

My final stop was at Byington Hospital. I was seen by a neuromuscular specialist and a genetics liaison. I became a human guinea pig. My physicians couldn't find out what was wrong with me except that I was ill. After many tests and office visits, they stamped *mystery diagnosis* in my medical chart.

I was finally referred to the Office of Rare Diseases Research (ORDR). By that time, my medical chart was very thick. There was much paper work to be completed by my primary care physician in order for me to be accepted to the program. But he procrastinated, it never got done, and I was never able to be treated at the ORDR.

Meanwhile, my health kept on deteriorating without a concrete diagnosis. I had lost all faith in doctors. The small energy I had, I'd spend searching on the web for possible diagnosis so I could feel better. It was like finding a needle in a haystack. Nothing really matched my symptoms and I ended up nowhere.

I was praying for God to help fulfill *my* plan for my own health salvation. I wanted to fix my own problem my own way by controlling the situation. I was exercising independence because deep inside I thought I could figure out things. At the same time, God kept echoing in my ears to stop searching for a diagnosis. I kept ignoring Him and doing things my way.

Not only was I sick, but I was also stubborn like the King of Judah, Asa, who did not rely on the Lord and died of a disease. I carried my independent attitude towards Jesus, while He clearly wanted me to depend on Him because only He could meet my needs and guide me. As the Bible says: "I know, O Lord, that a man's life is not his own; it is not for man to direct his steps." (Jeremiah 10:23)

Searching for my diagnosis lead me to an endless road of unanswered questions. I finally put my independent flesh in the trash can and started living according to the health plan God had for me. The struggles of wanting a diagnosis was over when I submitted wants, thoughts, and actions to God. I asked the Lord for direction towards my illness and finally rested in His hands by waiting upon His will.

My struggles drove me closer to the Lord as I depended on Him. I entered prayer with empty hands, letting Him fill my needs. The sicker I was, the closer I held Jesus hand. I embraced my pain through God's path of sanctification. I was ill but elated simultaneously by a new sense of peace.

My Jehovah-Rapha, lead me to your healing fountain. I am weak, but you are mighty strong. Heal my weakness with your powerful Hands. I leave my stubbornness behind and come to your merciful cross. Amen.

Additional reading: John 15:5, John 9:1-41, Proverbs 3:6, Isaiah 41:13, Psalm 18:2, John 14:16, Jeremiah 17:52.

Self-reflection: As you read 2 Chronicles 16, what do you think King Asa's problem was? Are you depending on God for your life? Are you letting Him take control over your problems? Are you trying to solve everything on your own? Is stubbornness hindering you from having a closer walk with Him?

Comforter

"But the Comforter, which is the Holy Ghost, whom
the Father will send in my name, He shall teach you
all things, and bring all things to your remembrance,
whatsoever I have said unto you." John 14:26

East Coast's summer wiped me out. Heat and high humidity caused
my lung muscles to weaken. I spent many hours by a fan to ease my
shortness of breath since my insurance did not cover a CPAP breathing
machine.

Summer also meant more visits to the emergency room since I
experienced heart abnormalities. I was energy depleted. I used the
energy I had left to stay close to God and grow through my trials. I
never knew if I would die in the middle of the night or wake up the next
morning. My future was in God's hands.

I could only read a few pages of the Bible each day, since my
strength was slowly declining. I wanted to cuddle in God's arms. I
longed to be comforted by Him at all times. I wanted to deepen my
relationship with the Lord with an attitude of absolute trust and faith.

The Holy Spirit, the Comforter, led me to a new insight which
deepened my walk with the Lord. I had no time to waste, no place for
doubt, and no room for fear. I grabbed my white twin size comforter
blanket, a black sharpie pen and began writing powerful Bible promises
on it. The Comforter brought into my remembrance all the tools I
needed in order to stay strong in faith. I wrote on the comforter blanket
about God's daily strength, hope, and power.

If my faith would start slipping into fear, I would read a Bible
promise I wrote on the comforter blanket and was able to keep my faith

strong. During my weakest moment, the writings on my comforter brought me into a deeper strength in the Lord, and fortified me to survive my illness.

The Holy Spirit helped me trust God's promises. His comforting uplifting promises gave me hope in my seamlessly hopeless situation. His words were a divine bounty strengthening my spirit. His promises never failed and I realized, "… nothing is impossible with God." (Luke 1:37) Surviving my illness was not impossible, because He lives and I could face tomorrow.

I was still ill, but I was at peace in the safety of God's embrace. My disability became small potatoes compared to the grace of having a closer relationship with Jesus. My physical pain was traded for spiritual gain. And thorough my spiritual gain, my battle against my physical pain grew stronger.

The Comforter advocated in my behalf as I depended on God for answers. He helped me to stay strong fighting the good fight of faith. He was my helper instructing me in the best road to follow in order to fulfill His divine plan for my life.

My Comforter, you are my Paraclete, who indwells in me. I place my spirit, soul, and body on the altar. May my faith not faulter as I claim your Holy promises. When other helpers fail, you are my comforter helping me during my afflictions. I yield my broken body into your hands. My life is yours. Abide in me. Amen.

Additional reading: Psalm 31:15, 1 Timothy 6:12, Proverbs 16:9, Proverbs 3:5, Romans 8:26, John 14:26, 2 Timothy 1:14, Galatians 5:18, Romans 8:27, Acts 15:8, Jude 1:20, John 14:27, John 15:9-10, John 15:11.

Self-reflection: Have you received the baptism of the Holy Spirit? Is the Holy Spirit your indweller Paraclete? What is the role of the Holy Spirit in your life? What does it mean to have the Holy Spirit as your Comforter, Counselor, and Advocate?

Changing Leaves

"Precious in the sight of the Lord is the death of his faithful servant." Psalm 116:15

Autumn leaves fell from the trees as I sat on my bed looking at the enchanting view from my bedroom window. The different array of colors made me think that humans are similar to autumn leaves. We are constantly going through changes and there's nothing we can do to stop this ongoing process.

The transformation of autumn leaves is like a beautiful song of departure. Different shades of reds and yellows display their final beauty and illustrate their process of life and death. Similarly, we can choose to display a beautiful attitude towards death. After all, we cannot choose how we are going to die but we can choose with Whom we are going to die during death's final voyage.

As with anything else in life, we may choose to spend our trials with God or we may choose to end our days in darkness. But since this is our only life on earth, it makes it the only opportunity to choose God. Once we die, that chance is gone.

Life will always lead you somewhere because life is not a bridge that leads to nowhere. You either cross the bridge dancing towards darkness of the night or cross the bridge dancing towards light of eternal life.

My illness made me realize I've entered my autumn leaves of life. "How long will my autumn be?" God holds my days in His hands. But I sense my leaves are getting red and yellow as I continue through the process of knowing God better. He is perfecting me for my final round. Will my leaves grow green again? Will I have another summer? My leaves flow with God's wind as I entered into His rest. "All is well with my soul" as Philip Bliss' hymn says. I must not lose hope but at the same time I'll be happy with God's lot whatever path He may lead.

I fix my eyes on Jesus. He went through all seasons of His life. His final autumn was agonizing. Yet, He never faulter His trust in God. He chose to spend every second obeying His Father. He did not rebel against God's will. He reverently submitted to God's all-knowing plan.

Lord of Heaven, health or illness, life or ashes, Earth or Heaven, may your will be done as my autumn leaves start to change color one by one. Amen.

Additional reading: Psalm 91:2, Psalm 9:10, Psalm 37:5, Psalm 56:3-4, Psalm 71:5, Isaiah 26:3, 1 Timothy 4:10, Psalm 32:10.

Self-reflection: Are you choosing to have a closer walk with Jesus during the autumn of your life?

Purity Comes From God

"Sanctify them by the truth; your word is truth." John 17:17

I entered into the valley of the shadow of death as my illness took its worst turn. It was difficult to breathe, open my eyes, and even talk. My heart was weak and I could barely walk. I didn't know if I was going to make it another day. Suddenly, I began to panic inside. Fear of death came upon me.

"Are you calling me home Lord?" I asked the Lord as I struggled to stay in my earthly body. At once the Lord reminded me of Abraham's faith. He waited ninety-nine years for God's promise to be fulfilled. He finally was granted a descendent, Isaac. Abraham must have grown extremely attached to his son. Therefore, God commanded Abraham to bind Isaac to the altar as a sacrifice.

Abraham's faith was being tested to show what was occupying his heart. God was testing him on that which he seemed to love the most, Isaac. He was being tested because he was loving Isaac with a tight grip. God was purifying Abraham from his attachment and bringing his face back to Himself. It was a form of curing Abraham's heart because God wanted to make sure his heart was not distracted by loving Isaac more than loving Him.

Abraham bound Isaac to an altar. He submitted what he loved most to God as an act of obedience. Suddenly, the angel of God stopped Abraham by saying "now I know you fear God." (Genesis 22:12) Abraham sacrificed a ram instead of Isaac.

Like Abraham, I was attached to my life, health, and days on earth. I was fighting to stay alive, but once I let go of my attachments to survive, and offered my illness totally to the Lord, I found peace. I realized that God wanted me to stop fearing death, and let Him decide how many days I should live. But, if God would grant me more days, "I would live to tell of what He has done." (Psalm 118:17)

At once I stopped holding onto the desire to live and fears turned into trust. Suddenly, God's presence was my closest companion. The gap from my earthly body to the heavenly gates became closer. I could almost feel my soul departing into the hands of Jesus. All my anxiety of dying transformed into peace. My loneliness, pain, and suffering turned into a graceful abounding love from Jesus. My whole being was being purified by the Lord. He was turning my dying body into something eternally beautiful. I was being purified in the arms of the Lord!

As soon as I bound my life to the altar and completely submitted my attachment to survive this life to the Lord, my illness began to stabilize. I experienced God's pure grace during the most difficult moments of my life. The Holy Spirit produced a gift of peace that I could not have produced on my own.

Obedience caused me to be at peace in the midst of the storm as I was captured by the love of God more than I was captured by anything in the world.

Lord of all grace, thank you for being my greatest companion when I sank into despair. You held my hand during the darkness hours. You restored me into the land of the living. You sanctified and purified me through sufferings. At last, I fully appreciate your pain on the cross. Amen.

Additional Reading: Genesis 17:1-7, 15-16, Hebrews 11:17-19, Genesis 21:12, Psalms 1:1-2, Luke 11:28.

Self-reflection: Do you let any attachment in this world capture your heart more than the Lord? Is anything occupying your heart more than God?

New Year

"The Lord is my rock, my fortress, and my savior; my
God is my rock, in whom I find protection. He is my
shield, the power that saves me, and my place of safety."
Psalm 18:2

I woke up to the New Year reflecting on what God has done during
2010. From a human perspective it seemed like the worst year possible.
I struggled daily with an undiagnosed illness. I've been to emergency
rooms innumerous occasions. Different doctors said the same thing: "I
have no idea what you have!" I experienced life and death crisis more
times than I cared to remember.

My nursing knowledge led to no answers. It seemed impossible to
have a final diagnoses and treatment for my illness.

In 2010, I didn't live life. I survived life in bed with pillows propping
my legs up, a cervical neck collar supporting weak neck muscles, and a
fan blowing close to my face to aid weak respiration. I barely had energy
to walk from my bedroom to the kitchen.

As hard as it was, I realized God showered me with grace because
I was growing to be more like Him during trials. I found refuge in the
Lord who helped depend on Him during suffering. For although my
body was feeble, weakness turned into spiritual strength (see Hebrews
11-34).

Jesus transformed my suffering into something beautiful. The Lord
showed His merciful love during my illness. I could feel His light
surrounding and giving joy during my darkness moments.

The year of 2010 was over and another chapter was about to begin.
I still didn't have a diagnosis. But my heart rested in knowing Jesus had

my life in His hands. He would deliver me on His own time or take me to Heaven. I realized my illness was not an accident or mishap from God. It was a God given burden to polish me into His likeness.

I stopped waiting anxiously by the phone for doctors to deliver good news of a curative treatment. I simply delighted in the Lord knowing He was with me during the good and bad times. My sickness was working together for good because I loved God and was walking according to His will.

Great Physician, I seek refuge in you. You are my helper in times of need. You hear my supplications when I cry in pain and you give peace. I'm sick, but you are with me, and there's no need to fear, for you go ahead of me. Amen.

Additional verses: Romans 8:28, Psalm 62:8, Psalm 46:1, Psalm 46:1-2, Psalm 18:2, Proverbs 30:5.

Self-reflection: Do you find refuge under the wings of the Lord?

Passive Prayer

"And even when you ask, you don't get it because your motives are all wrong—you want only what will give you pleasure." James 4:3

I used to have a refrigerator magnet that said: "Come to God with no agenda." For the longest time I practiced this quote. I came to God with petitions but many times my prayers were not daring for fear of having a hidden selfish motive. I resigned to my illness because I felt it was self-seeking to ask for healing.

Suddenly the Lord met in my inner chamber and showed that my prayers were passive. I resigned my desires instead of being daring in prayers, while all the while, God was the one planting desires in my heart according to His will.

In moments of death's close encounters, I asked the Lord to give me peace if it was time to meet Him in Heaven. I never really dared to pray for healing. I didn't want to be selfish. I prayed for daily strength and depended on Him to carry my cross. God indeed came through with all my prayers, and I learned reverent submission. He aided in my battle and purified me through physical struggles. He gave an extra push during days I needed extra strength. But, God did not heal me for I did not ask Him.

Jesus says in Matthew 7:7: "Keep on asking, and you will receive what you ask for. Keep on seeking, and you will find. Keep on knocking, and the door will be opened to you." Did I feel undeserving of a healing miracle? Did I not want to bother Jesus with big prayers? Did I fear having an agenda? Maybe I just didn't have enough faith in Him at the time. Maybe I didn't have an effective daring prayer. Perhaps all of the above.

I searched deeply into my heart and found out that passive prayer was different than submissive prayer. Jesus wanted me to be daring by asking for healing, but at the same time be open to His better plan.

I began praying for Jesus to heal me and waited for His answer. At the same time I knew that in Heaven all my pain would be gone as Revelations 21:4 says: "He will wipe away every tear from their eyes, and death shall be no more, neither shall there be mourning, nor crying, nor pain anymore, for the former things have passed away."

As I began praying for healing, I realized that healing on earth was not my final destination of happiness and health. An answer to healing in this planet would mean glorifying the Lord even more through the answer of a daring prayer. Heaven would ultimately be my final destination, with no diseases and no sorrows.

My dear Heavenly Healer, sustain and restore me from my bed of illness. Send your healing balm and drive away infirmities and sickness from my body. Turn my weakness into strength and make this suffering an instrument to glorify your name. Amen.

Additional reading: Matthew 21:22, Mark 11:24, John 14:13-14, Mark 9:29, Acts 9:40, James 5:14-16, Ephesians 6:18.

Self-reflection: Do you shy away from asking God for the impossible because of your lack of faith? Are your prayers lined up with God's will?

Pop Quiz

"To answer before listening- that is folly and shame. The human spirit can endure in sickness, but a crushed spirit who can bear? The heart of the discerning acquires knowledge, for the ears of the wise seek it out." Proverbs 18:13-15

One of the first things I learned through disability was to place the Lord before my emotions. But it took panic to learn this lesson. Chronic illness was a new trial and I desperately sought the Lord to empower me to live day to day with victory.

During the onset of the disability I became overwhelmed with fear. I panicked and desperately looked for a way out from my illness. I sought self-preservation. I agonized with the possibility that my body would give out and die.

My mindset led nowhere but to more feelings of despair. I was trying to master problems on my own. I was at the mercy of fickle emotions. My panic lead me astray, but faith led straight into God's promises. Jeremiah 17:9 helped me understand that "The human heart is the most deceitful of all things, and desperately wicked. Who really knows how bad it is?"

God allowed suffering and gave me the ability to endure it little by little, but in the beginning of disability I let my heart take control. I became lost in a forest of fears. But as soon as I understood that God was tailoring every symptom in my body so I could grow in Him, I understood that fears had no use. At last, I received peace during afflictions.

Through time, chronic illness became familiar. Every time I had a negative emotion the Lord empowered me to stay firm in His Word and abide in His grace. Although Satan tried to penetrate through the walls of faith, the Lord was helping seal the negative cracks. He empowered me to fight illness with grace.

In time, I became comfortable in faith as I kept pushing through day to day. Suddenly, I received an unexpected pop quiz on faith. I found out that someone I trusted lied to me. I was caught by surprise and became disappointed and let emotions take over me. I was hurt and angry. I didn't know what to do with my conflicting feelings. I let Satan get through the cracks of faith and play inside me. I became an emotional rollercoaster.

I didn't go to Christ at first. I dwelled in pain and allowed my spirit to get crushed with emotions. Stress caught up and my illness exasperated. Soon, I realized slacking off on faith in any other area of life did not please God. Once again, I turned to Jesus. He showed I wasn't passing His pop quiz. Jesus reminded that prayers should always come before emotions. For prayer is the only antidote for anxiety, as the Bible says in Philippians 4:6: "Do not be anxious about anything, but in every situation, by prayer and petition, with thanksgiving, present your requests to God."

I finally made things straight with the Lord. I forgave the person that lied to me and prayed that she would be convicted of wrongdoing. My prayers were quickly answered; the whole issue was resolved with God's love, intervention, and restoration.

My Reliable God, forgive me for not putting you ahead of every issue. You are the One who can truly solve all troubles in a pure and loving way. Thank you for answering my prayers again. Amen.

Additional reading: Deuteronomy 31:6, 1 Corinthians 10:13, Romans 12:2, Job 23:10, Jeremiah 17:9-10, 1 John 1:9.

Self-reflection: Do you let your insecurities and emotions rule your heart or do you let Jesus be the Ruler of your heart?

Refinery

"He (God) will sit as refiner and purifier of silver, and
He will purify the priests, the sons of Levi, and refine
them like gold and silver, that they may offer to the Lord
offerings in righteousness." Malachi 3:3

I woke up with another episode of breathing problems. My lung muscles
were weak. I had to think before taking another breath. It was an
exhausting effort. The physical exertion to take a breath was almost
more than I could handle. I couldn't get enough air. It felt like an
elephant was sitting on my chest. I wanted to rest my lungs but knew I
would die if I would do so.

It's interesting how humans take it for granted the simple act of
breathing. It's an involuntary automatic response that keeps us alive,
therefore it's not necessary to consciously think of this function. We
don't order our bodies to breathe because it's on auto-pilot. However, the
onset of my illness changed that autonomic act to an act of dependence
on God for respiration and survival. Breathing became the center stage
in my life. My respiratory system became malfunction and I had to
pace myself not to overexert other muscles which would make my lung
muscles even weaker.

James 1:1-3 tells us to be joyful whenever we are enveloped in or
encounter trials because it's through them we are refined. God placed
me in His refinery. I became His gold and silver. He was in the process of
making me into something malleable and ductile. He was transforming
me into something brilliant and polished so I could be of more value
for His Kingdom.

His refinery began transforming me more into His image. He began changing my raw material into something polished. I relied on the Lord to sustain me for every breath I took. By faith, the Lord began to remove the impurities of my soul. My imperfections were being purged out by His process of purification. My sins were being removed by God's tests so I could be perfected into the image of Christ.

Is it surprising? Not in God's economy! "See, I have refined you, though not as silver; I have tested you in the furnace of affliction." (Isaiah 48:10) God has chosen sickness to be my intruder. Not to destroy me, but He knew that only through His furnace flaws could turn into beauty. The Lord heated the furnace of my life hotter than ever before, but His glory shone even brighter.

I shan't dread the heat, but thank Him for choosing me.

My Great Refiner, thank you for purging out sins and refining me into your image. Cleanse me until my heart is free of dross and impurities. May the furnace of afflictions bring me closer to you. Thank you for watching the temperature of the furnace and not testing beyond what I can handle. Amen.

Additional reading: John 16:33, 1 Peter 1:7, Romans 8:28, Psalm 66:10, Zechariah 13:9, 1 Peter 1:7, Isaiah 48:10.

Self-reflection: In what ways is God refining you?

Wheelchair

"A priest descended from Aaron is to accompany the Levites when they receive the tithes, and the Levites are to bring a tenth of the tithes up to the house of our God, to the storerooms of the treasury." Nehemiah 10:38

When I was healthy, I used to take the kids bike riding across a small town in Delaware. My stamina seemed endless from sunup to sundown. But disability engulfed my stamina away. I went from loving my two wheeler bicycle to needing a four wheeler wheelchair. However, I didn't have money to buy one. If I had to go to the market, I would have to use their electric wheelchair.

I prayed God would provide a wheelchair, but due to disability, my empathy for the disable increased. I partner up with "Joni and Friends International Disability Center." Joni's ministry restores and distributes refurbished wheelchairs all over the world to people lacking hope and ability to purchase one. I began donating a small monthly amount to their worthy cause. Even though I didn't get a wheelchair, I was overjoyed because I was able to participate and help those that were going through the same or worst tribulations than I was.

Months after donating to Joni and Friends ministry, I received a letter with a check. It was from Mindy, a missionary living in Brazil which attended the same church as my mom's. I've never met her, but she heard of me through my mom's prayer requests. My cheeks were wet with happy tears. God's hand graciously gave me provision for obedience to tithing. The check provided with money to buy myself a wheelchair.

The Bible is full of stories of reaping what has been sown. Something always comes back as an act of obedience. Jesus said in Luke 6:38: "Give and it will be given to you. A good measure, pressed down, shaken together and running over, will be poured into your lap. For with the measure you use, it will be measured to you."

My Giver, your Spirit falls upon me day and night. Even in my silence, you never forget me! Your surprises light up my day. Amen.

Additional reading: Isaiah 14:3, Isaiah 61:7, Isaiah 65:24, Romans 8:26, Deuteronomy 15:10, Galatians 6:1-10.

Self-reflection: Are you holding back something God is asking you to give? Are you reaping seeds of generosity? How has God blessed you in surprising ways?

The Mystery Of Simple Prayer

"And when you pray, do not heap up empty phrases as the Gentiles do, for they think that they will be heard for their many words. Do not be like them, for your Father knows what you need before you ask Him." Mathew 6:7-8

I went to the market, headed back home and took a long bath. A simple outing was exhausting. It took away my energy and made my muscles stiff. Once again, I immersed in the presence of God.

As I soaked in the bathtub, I tried to pray about many things, but my mind was in a fog. I recalled Mathew 6 and thanked God I didn't have to heap up empty phrases for prayers to be heard. God understood I was physically drained.

I simply repeated the name of Jesus again and again. Then, I remained quiet in the presence of the Holy Spirit. I knew God understood me as Romans 8:26 says: "In the same way, the Spirit helps us in our weakness. We do not know what we ought to pray for, but the Spirit Himself intercedes for us with groans that words cannot express."

It's mind-boggling that God knows what we need before we ask Him. Trusting the Lord's omniscience, I bathed in the tub knowing He understood the longings of my soul. I was certain the Lord knew my needs and of those around me. Soon my emotions entered into God's rest and I became stressed free.

During affliction, my mind couldn't come up with the right words to pray, but God heard the prayers of my heart. In my exhaustion, I was able to feel prayers instead of say prayers.

The prayers of the heart can never go wrong because it's filled with power. It always comes with an answer. Prayers stir us to trust in God more fervently. Prayers make us feel connected with God and bonded by His love. Prayers quiet fears and eliminate anxieties. Prayers change us because we realize God hears our afflicted souls. Prayers heal our agony by His compassion. Prayers are the passport to experience His presence during our darkest days.

"Our Father in heaven, hallowed be your name, your kingdom come, your will be done, on earth as it is in heaven. Give us today our daily bread. And forgive us our debts, as we also have forgiven our debtors. And lead us not into temptation, but deliver us from the evil one." Matthew 6:9-13.

Additional reading: 1 John 5:14-15, Ephesians 6:18, John 14:13-14, Mark 11:24, Matthew 7:7, Mark 9:29.

Self-reflection: Do you pray only when you need God? Or do you pray because you love God and want Him in all areas of your life? When you pray, do you listen to what God has to say to you realizing it's a two way conversation?

Agony

> "So I am willing to endure anything if it will bring
> salvation and eternal glory in Christ Jesus to those God
> has chosen." 2 Timothy 2:10

I had pint-size muscle strength during mornings. It was difficult to
support my head since my neck muscles were limb. I used a cervical
neck brace to support my head. I was cautious not to talk more than I
needed to, or move more than I had to. Every little movement quickly
drained my energy.

Sometimes by mid-day I would feel better but not always. Many
things triggered my illness to flare up. My muscles could suddenly get
stiff and then flaccid. I had difficulty breathing, heart abnormalities,
eye muscle stiffness and more. Once in a while I felt a sense of my old
normal self. Those were blessed days!

There was particular day I felt unusually stronger in the morning.
I took advantage of the sudden spurt of energy and began cleaning
the house. After half an hour, all energy was sucked from under my
feet. I put everything to a halt and took a bath hoping to relax my stiff
muscles. It was difficult to expand my lungs. I began praying but illness
continued to spiral downhill.

I began losing sensation in my legs and arms. I had fasciculation all
over my body. I was not able to swallow. I had to tape my eye lids closed
since I had no energy to keep them shut. I could not handle any kind of
stimulus such as noise, movement, or touch. Any stimuli exasperated
the symptoms. Though I wanted to cry, I knew tears would drain energy
even more. I stayed still as much as possible for I could have died if I

would exert myself even a bit. My mind's only thought was -Jesus! In full-blown agony, I trusted God to nurse me back to health.

By night fall I was still alive. I'd try to doze off to sleep but sudden heat waves would travel through my body causing me to shake. I had a seizure but I finally fell asleep. I woke up surprised that I was still alive and thanked God for pulling me out of agony.

That was not an unusual day. Illness made a nest in my body and fun left life. My past dreams were over. My ballet days were over. Singing in choir was a faraway memory. Instead of being a nurse, I became a patient. Bike riding, hiking, kayaking, and having enjoyment with my children was no longer possible. All my energy was being spent on enduring illness.

As difficult as life was during that time, I knew God allowed illness to occur. He decreed agony to fulfill His purpose in my life. I didn't want to waste away pain, but desired to learn all the lessons the Lord was teaching me through agony. I wanted to honor God and glorify Him by offering sacrifices of praise. Through the thorns of illness, God began molding my soul.

God's Word says that if we suffer with Jesus with a godly attitude we shall also reign with Him. I knew that if I remained faithful and focused, He would see me through struggles. Since I understood He allowed torment, I trusted Him that He would turn every pain for my good and His glory. His promises sheltered me and caused worries to fade away.

God never left me completely depleted of physical energy without replacing what I lost with something greater, which was His grace to see me thorough my weaknesses. I was not suffering for nothing, but for every gift of wisdom He had to offer. Suffering was transforming me into a stronger child of God. Although my path was full of thorns, He was creating in me a blooming rose on top of the stem.

My Jehovah-Rapha, my healer, you are the light quieting my soul. I give you my weakness. You give me your strength. I give you my feeble ill body. You give me the beauty of your majesty. Your grace is my shelter filled with mercy and love. Thank you for opening my eyes to the work of your hands. Amen.

Additional reading: Psalm 72, Hebrews 12:11, Isaiah 41:10, Jeremiah 17:14, 1 Peter 2:24, Isaiah 53:5, Jeremiah 33:6, Isaiah 53:5, Jeremiah 33:6.

Self-reflection: Who do you grab onto when you are ill? Have you surrendered your physical pain to the Lord? Do you let God have His way in your life even to the cost of suffering?

Margins

"My son, give me your heart, and let your eyes observe
my ways." Proverbs 23:26

I wrote a living will during the onset of my physical disability. I wish I could leave behind financial security to my children, but we lived from month to month, so there was little I could leave them materially.

Nevertheless, there were things in life I considered much more important than money. What I wanted the most for my children was for them to have a strong foundation in the Lord. I instructed them in God's way since they were little. I made sure to spend quality time with them on a daily basis. I prayed that God's seed would grow in them after my life on earth would be over.

Every morning since my kids were little, and before the onset of my illness, we sat down together before rushing out of the house. We usually watched a cartoon on television all pile up together on the carpet floor. It was a special time even though it didn't seem like much. It was nothing exuberant, but our daily moments together bonded our love for each other a bit more every day before the kids headed to school.

I remember one such day the alarm clock didn't go off in the morning. We hurried out of our beds. I rushed out the door so I could get the kids on time for school. It was an unusual morning since most of the time, we were on time for our daily routine. That morning we missed spending time together. But the next we're back on track.

The relationship between my kids and I was built in between the *have to do's* of the day. It was during the margins of our daily activities that our bond became stronger and our love grew deeper. During breakfast, lunch, and dinner we shared our thoughts, pains, and laughters at our small dinner table. While driving to school, sitting close to each other, and praying together, we learned to know each other's souls. Without making those simple, yet daily meaningful times together, I'd have probably lost track of who my kids really were and they'd not know me for who I was.

School, work, appointments, and all that entails a family life, could have eaten up the special margins we shared together. Without the special family occasions of the day, we'd have isolated ourselves from each other causing the breakdown of the fiber of our love for each other.

Moments of communion in between us, helped to build a God centered home. Ultimately, my living will for my kids was based on the hope that they'd continue in God's walk throughout their future.

Lord of families, give me wisdom to be the parent you want me to be. Help me to smile at my children every morning as soon as they wake up. May I give them unconditional love as you love me. May my attention be geared into my family's needs. Amen.

Additional reading: Proverbs 22:6, Hebrews 10:24-25, Proverbs 13:20, Psalms 127:3-5, Proverbs 31:28-29.

Self-reflection: How do you prioritize your family life? Do you spend quality time with your loved ones in a daily basis? Do you pray, eat, and laugh together? Do you listen to each other? How do you love each other with action? Do you say "I love you" to your loved ones?

Giving Up Is A Temptation

"For I can do everything through Christ, who gives me strength." Philippians 4:13

I was approaching my death bed during a hot summer day. I had no energy. I barely ate. I hardly talked. My breathing was raggedy, irregular, and labored. I struggled to stay alive. Out of the depths of exhaustion, I called on the name of the Lord, for I was slipping in between two worlds. I was giving up fighting for life.

I thought of my children's life without me. They had no one else in their life to care for them. They needed me to live. My job as a parent was to love and teach them to love one another. Leaving them behind would mean unfinished parental lessons. They already had no father and if I died they would lose their mother. It would be too much for them to bear.

King David said in Psalm 118:17: "I will not die, but I will live and proclaim what the Lord has done." As I dwelled in God's promise, something miraculous happened. My health slowly began to improve. I was able to breathe better. The Lord renewed my physical strength. And, I saw yet another day.

I shared in the communion of Jesus' suffering through my close encounter with death. He purified and refined me a bit more during that long afflicted summer day.

My body said, it's over, but my God said, it's just the beginning! He did not create me to give up on anything. He created me for endurance and perseverance through the power of His blood. God created me to say: I can do all things through Christ who gives me strength (see Philippians 4:13). God gave me divine power to keep on going by saying:

"I will never quit!" And, I didn't quit because God didn't test me without supplies of grace.

Jesus, I invoked your name and here you are! You strengthen and purify me. Let me tell others of your glory and make you famous for you've given me another day. You prove that through you the battles are won. Alleluia Lord! Amen.

Additional reading: Psalm 72:11-14, 2 Chronicles 15:7, Joshua 1:9, Romans 12:11-12, 2 Timothy 4:7, 1 Corinthians 15:58, Matthew 11:28, Mark 10:27, Philippians 4:13.

Self-reflection: Have you felt tempted to give up? How did you deal with the temptation of giving up? What do you do when faced with physical battles? Who do you go to during your battles?

Growing In The Valley

"He (Jesus) went on a little farther and fell to the ground. He prayed that, if it were possible, the awful hour awaiting Him might pass Him by. 'Abba, Father,' He cried out, 'everything is possible for you. Please take this cup of suffering away from me. Yet I want your will to be done, not mine.'" Mark 14:35-36

I often travel in my time machine and revisit good memories. I remember events, textures, smells, colors, emotions, and places I enjoyed the most. Somehow, I'm able to recall images in vivid details such as what a friend of mine ate years ago or how I felt at a particular moment as a ten year old child. I enjoy the stream of good memories because it soothes me during difficult times. However, sandwiched between days which I used to swim by a waterfall and play barefooted in the mud, are painful memories.

I remember suffering for one thing or another since I was a child. I never chose to suffer, yet I went from trial to trial, which brought me closer to the throne of God. It polished me more into His image. Good moments gave me rest from hardships, but it also made me yearn less for God. At some point I understood trials were purposefully planned by God for a good outcome in my spirit.

My Great Physician performed miraculous surgeries in me. He anesthetized me during surgeries. The problems were still there, but at the same time, I received a supernatural peace and joy during His surgeries. At times I felt numb to problems. My life from the outside perspective seemed to be falling apart, but my spirit was quiet in His arms. I was secure and trusting God during trials. The fires of affliction were hot but I was never burned. I was patient in affliction, until the surgeries would be over. Then, God's anesthesia would wear off. Upon waking up, trials were over, and I'd feel refreshed and at the same time transformed into a better me.

God gave me grace to experience joy during happy moments, and remain joyful during difficult times. But His grace is not exclusive to me. It's a gift for all those that follow the Lord.

Trials and tribulations test the faith of believers. It's part of God's path to mature us into His image. God is all-good, all-loving, and all-merciful providing us aid during trials. He supplies us with abundant grace and bountiful favor.

Some people might think that accepting Jesus as Savior gives freedom from pain. But God doesn't relocate us to Disneyland in this world, because this planet is not our final destination. We move to Heaven in the afterlife. A fun filled happy life would not be beneficial or constructive to the life of a Christian. It would not build us up but make us into spoiled complacent lazy children. We grow in Christ during the valleys, when life is hard to bear, and only Jesus can strengthened us with His touching grace.

God sanctioned His son Jesus to go through immeasurable sufferings. Jesus chose to obey His Father and suffer on the cross. If God allowed Jesus to suffer to fulfill a purpose, why wouldn't God allow suffering to fulfill a purpose in our lives as well?

There's a great difference between suffering with Christ and suffering without Christ. Without Christ a sufferer is lost in the obscurity of his pain. A sufferer is lonely and filled with despair. Pain is a negative phenomenon. Trials are unwelcomed because it's an adversary to pleasures.

Suffering with Christ is a positive phenomenon. It is welcomed. It is filled with hope. It is packed with purpose. God allows suffering, gives grace through suffering, and leads us out of suffering. The product of suffering is always a constructive spiritual outcome if we set our faces toward the Lord.

Jesus experienced greater affliction than all of us. He was perfect, yet he suffered for our imperfections. He was deeply troubled and distressed with the coming events of the crucifixion. He was crushed with grief.

He was abused. He was despised and rejected. His appearance was disfigured beyond that of any man (see Isaiah 52:14). He endured trials, torture, and crucifixion for our transgressions. He was crushed for our iniquities, yet He accepted His cup of suffering for our good outcome. Shouldn't we also?

Tester of faith, help me to persevere during trials. My tests are nothing compare to the everlasting bliss waiting in Heaven. Then, light will never fade, brightness will never depart, peace will never be broken, for there I'll be with you in Paradise. Amen.

Additional reading: 1 Corinthians 10:23, James 1:12, 1 Corinthians 10:13, Romans 12:12, James 1:2, 1 Peter 4:12, Romans 8:28, John 16:33, Matthew 5:10-12.

Self-reflection: Why do you suffer? What have you learned from your trials? Why did Jesus suffer?

Christl, My Hero

> "So then, since Christ suffered physical pain, you must
> arm yourselves with the same attitude He had, and be
> ready to suffer, too. For if you have suffered physically
> for Christ, you have finished with sin. You won't spend
> the rest of your lives chasing your own desires, but you
> will be anxious to do the will of God." 1 Peter 4:1-2

A neurologist at Johns Lougheed Hospital asked to describe the physical
symptoms I was experiencing. "Dyspnea, ptosis, dysphasia, lethargy..." I
explained it as if giving him a laundry list. He cut my nursing education
jargon. "I don't want medical terminology. Explain it in lame terms!" he
said insistently. He wanted a subjective description, and not objective
findings. Oddly, I couldn't explain in words the agony I was experiencing
in my body. I was *uggh, yawp, yeow, yowt, yowl,* and *ouch*! It was a pain
words could not describe.

My conversation with the neurologist made me think of Jesus' pain
on the cross. My illness was a pint size of what Jesus went through. I
stop taking Jesus' sufferings on the cross for granted. I recognized the
horror Jesus experienced. Jesus suffered incomprehensible moans and
groans of pain. Jesus endured hours of unlimited agony, successions of
twisting joint cramps, and intermittent asphyxiation.

Jesus bore wide spread affliction. No part of His body was left
untouched by torture. He agreed to be sacrificed on the cross for me!
For you! For everyone! He suffered all, endured all, and submitted all
to the Father. Have you experienced globalized pain in every part of
your body?

Jesus was ridiculed by Roman soldiers. They pressed on His skull a crown of thorns. Jesus' face was completely covered in His own blood. Jesus' nerves sent pulsating and crushing pain throughout His body.

He offered His body to be brutalized and agonized because His love for us was vulnerable and pure. He was completely open to love us and didn't hold any love back. He was willing to be broken because He possessed agape love. He was selfless and benevolent. He offered His life for our salvation. Yet, we malevolently pinned his wrists and feet on the cross. I can't imagine being pinned with a heavy nine inch iron nail, could you?

During Jesus' trial, a soldier beat, blindfolded, mocked, spat, and struck Him on the face. The horror didn't end until Jesus was tortured to death. He was whipped for our sins with leather thongs with two small lead balls at each end. Thongs sliced through Jesus' skin, then to subcutaneous tissue. Jesus went through infinite psychological and spiritual sufferings as He atoned for the sins of fallen men. He paid for my lies, selfishness, and every sin. He took my place. Not only mine, but yours. Did anyone else ever love you as intensively and unconditionally as Jesus?

In Gethsemane, Jesus arteries constricted causing His blood vessels to rupture and mix with sweat. His love for us meant suppression of human self-preservation to survive. He didn't run from pain. He didn't walk away from crucifixion by denying God's will for His life. Heroic Jesus faced the cross! Did you ever run from pain because every part of you trembled in fear? God asked Jesus to be crucified. How would you feel if God asked you to be crucified for a serial killer? Or for a baby? Or any human being?

Fatigued and abused, Jesus carried the instrument of His torture. Jesus dragged His cross to Calvary. His skin and muscles were lacerated. He was weak due to blood loss. He fell and tried to rise. Simon of Cyrene was ordered to carry the cross. Dehydrated Jesus followed Simon.

Upon arriving at the place of execution, Jesus' slow and horrific death continued. Jesus was bruised, battered, and exhausted. Stripped of clothing, Jesus hands were tied to a post above His head. With His arms outstretched, legionnaires nailed his wrists, and raised the platibulum. Feet hammered. Body sagged down. The torture lingered on and on.

As Jesus hung on the cross, His body slowly sagged down. He pushed upward several times as His pectoral muscles were stretched to the maximum causing shortness of breath. Inhaling became harder as He was too weak to push His body up. Jesus' diaphragm went into spasms. His oxygen demand was not being met. His heart began to fail. He uttered several last short breaths and loved us by praying: "Father forgive them for they know not what they do…It is finished… Father, into your hands I commit my spirit." (see Luke 23) Jesus' lungs collapsed. His heart ruptured. Literally broken hearted, Jesus suffocated to death- for us!

Jesus' path of pain was exemplary. How do we deal with pain? We complain, want a way out, get mad at doctors, and get mad at God! Jesus didn't curse the ones that tortured Him. He didn't curse God. He didn't focus on His pain. He didn't get mad at the world. He didn't get disgusted with humans. Wouldn't you get disgusted with humans if they would torture you?

Jesus focus was on obeying God's will. His focus was on loving us unconditionally. God's purpose of salvation was fulfilled (see John 19:30). "… He was wounded for our transgressions; He was bruised for our iniquities: the chastisement of our peace was upon Him; and with His stripes we are healed." (Isaiah 53:5)

Have you ever given someone love and received stones in return? Christ gave His perfect sacrificial love for our sins, and received boulders in return! Christ fought boulders of violence by retaliating with forgiveness and love. Shall we love and follow Heroic Jesus Christ?

Heroic Christ, you had an option to run from pain or be crucified. You're brave and bold. You took the path of agony for my sins. Oh matchless courage! Oh incomparable love! Your sacrifice was unsurpassed. May I grasp "how wide and long and high and deep" (Ephesians 3:18) is your love for me. Help me follow your example of courage all days of my life. Amen.

Additional reading: Ephesians 5:1, Matthew 27:46, Isaiah 53:9, Psalms 22:1-3, John 3:16, John 1:14, John 1:1, Isaiah 53;12, Isaiah 7:14, Psalms 110:1, Acts 17:11.

Self-reflection: Have you accepted Jesus sacrificial love? "… if you confess with your mouth the Lord Jesus and believe in your heart that God has raised Him from the dead, you will be saved." (Romans 10:9)

Virgin Mary's Faith And Trials

"Jesus parents were amazed at what was being said about Him. Then Simeon blessed them, and he said to Mary, the baby's mother, 'This child is destined to cause many in Israel to fall, but He will be a joy to many others. He has been sent as a sign from God, but many will oppose Him. As a result, the deepest thoughts of many hearts will be revealed. And a sword will pierce your very soul.'" Luke 2:33-35

My children are a grand heritage from the Lord. A great blessing because they walk in God's truth. We say innumerous "I love you" a day for no apparent reason. We feel sudden blasts of love that can only be released if verbalized. I say to them smiling: "I knitted in my womb my best friends forever." God blessed me but at the same time, He reminded not to squeeze blessings too tight, for my comings and goings belong to God. One day I live, the next I will die. I will either leave someone I love, or I'll be left behind.

Three mothers in my family were left behind. Their children died suddenly. One aunt lost her two teenage sons. A drunk semi-truck driver slammed their vehicle. The kids were instantly decapitated. The other aunt also lost her son due to an auto accident. The third aunt's son died in a motorcycle accident. My aunts coped grievously with the loss of their precious blessings. They were shocked, confused, and unprepared. One of my aunts was grief-stricken for the rest of her life, and ended up with a hard heart towards God, and died due to alcohol intoxication.

Virgin Mary was also a mother who lost her Son. Her heart was pierced with sorrow. God knitted Jesus in Mary's womb. He was wonderfully made, yet on the cross, "His face was so disfigured He seemed hardly human, and from His appearance, one would scarcely know He was a man." (Isaiah 52:14)

Mary did not rebel against God's will. She didn't go through denial, anger, bargaining, and depression. She did not end up angry and bitter for the rest of her life. On the contrary, she reverently submitted her will to God. She stood by Jesus as He atoned for our sins. She didn't squeeze unto her blessings too tight, but opened her hands towards God's better plan.

Mary's obedience to God did not warrant her life to be free of pain. It did not exclude her from afflictions. "And a sword will pierce your (Mary's) own soul too - so that the secret thoughts of many may be laid bare." (Luke 2:33-35)

Mary's pain was not a result of her sins. It was part of God's design for her life and the salvation of mankind. Mary adjusted to the loss of her Son because she loved the All-Knowing God.

Virgin Mary gained virtues through tears. God filled her with grace. She remained pure, prudent, humble, faithful, devout, obedient, patient, and merciful through sorrows.

Mary taught us to focus on the Blessor more than on the blessings. Mary focused on God and was blessed to bear the Messiah to the world, but with that came the sacrificial pain of losing her beloved son Jesus.

Every blessing God bestows upon us is contingent to the fact that it comes with a purpose to fulfill a grander plan. Blessings mold us into Jesus' image. Jesus was a supernatural blessing in Mary's life. Jesus was and is a supernatural blessing to all mankind because He came to transform the lives of all those who accept Him as Savior.

When the Blessor removes a blessing, He remains present to guide us to the next blessing. We must trust Him during the transition. He always has a reason for everything He allows in our lives. As Mary taught us, our attachments should always be greater towards the Blessor, than to the blessings.

My Blessor, there are times hardships seem unceasing. Help me remain faithful to you during pain. Shine your light in my darkness. Hold my hand when I lose the ones I love. Help me to trust you that temporary pain on earth means everlasting joy in your eternal Reign. Amen.

Additional reading: 3 John 1:4, Psalm 127:3-5, Psalm 139:13-16, Job 1:21, Luke 1:38, Isaiah 7:14, Galatians 4:4, Luke 2:19.

Self-reflection: How do you react when the Lord removes a blessing from your life? How do you deal with unexpected suffering? Are you more attached to the Blessor or the blessings?

Stress

"Pay attention to this, Job. Stop and consider the wonderful miracles of God! Do you know how God controls the storm and causes the lightning to flash from His clouds? Do you understand how He moves the clouds with wonderful perfection and skill? When you are sweltering in your clothes and the south wind dies down and everything is still, He makes the skies reflect the heat like a bronze mirror. Can you do that?"
Job 37:14-18

Our modern world causes us to engage in a flight-or-fight response daily. However, not like our ancestors, because we don't run from wild grizzly bears or hunt bisons. Our sympathetic nervous system seems to be constantly ready for some kind of battle because we get stress out about work, school, stock market, health, jobs... The struggles to survive our days are endless.

Our stomachs are constantly tied up in knots. More than ever before, people seem overwhelmed by the pressures of daily life. On top of it all, new technologies and new information created an overload in our brains, causing us not to be able to handle our priorities appropriately. The worst symptom of the technological world is that families are sandwiched between the cracks of our days. Even conversations are squeezed between text messages. Worst yet, people don't have God centered in their lives and don't follow His guidance.

Not too long ago I was also living the fast pace life, even though I was centered on the Lord and family. I'd rush throughout the daily routine and tasks just like a robot. But after the onset my illness, I was faced with no other choice but to put a halt on life. Activities of the world ran clockwise, but I sat on my bed and lived time slowly. However, in my new sense of stillness, I was able to consider God's wonders. I began gazing outside the window and admiring God's beautiful nature.

My new found quietness helped me appreciate God's miracles…

It was twilight during the tail end of winter. The sun set slowly holding all the tints, shades, and hues down to the next cold day. The red sky turned into an orange yellowish shade. The color of space hid behind residues of maple trees saying farewell to the freezing frosty day. The geese vocalized to each other goodnight songs. They were getting ready for another night full of stars illuminating their way.

My illness led me to prioritize little moments more than when I had a fast paced life. God's nature became my companion during pain. Gazing at the stars, lake, trees, and deer made stress melt away. It offered an inward peace and a closer walk with the Lord.

God provides everything that is beautiful yet humans tend to be overwhelmed with stress and anxiety because they don't stop to smell His flowers. Jesus said, "Therefore I tell you, do not be anxious about your life, what you will eat or what you will drink, nor about your body, what you will put on. Is not life more than food and the body more than clothing? And which of you by being anxious can add a single hour to his span of life?" (Matthew 6:25, 27)

EL-SHADDAI, Almighty God of the mountains and lakes, thank you for slowing down my life. I consider your great wonders and your nature melts every anxiety away. Thank you for your wondrous creations. Amen.

Additional reading: John 14:1, Psalms 34:4, Philippians 4:6-7, Psalm 55:22, John 14:27, Job 12:7-9, Matthew 6:26, Matthew 6:28-29.

Self-reflection: Are you missing out on the sceneries of your life? Would you invite the Lord to slow down your fast pace life?

Man Sitting On The Porch

"So God created the great creatures of the sea and every living thing with which the water teems and that moves about in it, according to their kinds, and every winged bird according to its kind. And God saw that it was good." Genesis 1:21

Years ago, while I was still married, Tom and I hiked on the mountains of Catawagua, in the West Coast. We were eager to have the day cramped with fun activities. On the drive up to the regional park, we spotted an old rustic house on the side of the road. The place was isolated and surrounded by trees. An old man sat on the porch. It seemed like he was the only human being for miles. He was watching birds, trees, and occasional cars passing by on the road. He looked satisfied with a simple life as the minutes of the day passed right before his eyes.

While the old man sat on his porch, Tom and I finished our long hike. Hours later we drove down again through the isolated road and sure enough, we spotted the little rustic old house again. The old man still sat on the porch soaking the last minutes of daylight.

That old man never left my mind. He seemed satisfied with simplicity. Tom and I were the opposite. The more things we did, the more we thought we conquered. We hardly ever rested. We used to always get ready to live life to its fullest but we never really stopped to smell the flowers. We had much to do and so much to take care of, that there was little time to "sit on our porch of life" and contemplate on the minutes of the day going by.

As much as illness caused me sufferings, I can't help but thank God for the lesson He'd taught me. I learned to "sit on my porch" of life. My memories of the old days taught me even more to have a new sense of appreciation for things I couldn't hear before, such as the honking of migrating flocks of geese flopping their wings on my backyard. There was a new sense of peace and appreciation for every small detail God placed under the sun.

I realized slowing down makes life more enjoyable. I had lost appreciation for small things by letting life pass right before my eyes. I learned to find more pleasure in every aspect of existence. At last, I became fully present and enjoyed the moments God bestowed upon me, even during the trials of illness.

Great Creator, help me to pause, think, and reflect on the greatness of your creation. Give me new insights so I may understand the beauty of your phenomenal work. Amen.

Additional reading: Psalm 19:1-4, Psalm 119:18, Deuteronomy 3:24, Psalm 40:5, Psalm 77:1.

Self-reflection: When was the last time you paused and reflected on God's handiwork?

Discernment

"For God is not the author of confusion but of peace, as in all the churches of the saints."
1 Corinthians 14:33 (KJV)

A seemingly meaningless moment in my life stayed with me for several years. I was riding in Tom's pick-up truck while gazing at the hills. Suddenly I had a vision from God. He placed in my heart the realization my life would be filled with His special favors. God showed me I would be living for His glory for a specific reason. However, at that particular moment, it seemed the furthest thing from my mind because I was married, raising children, and taking care of farm animals. My days consisted of changing diapers, feeding sheep, chickens, and ducks. Nevertheless, I've heard God's calling. I trusted Him and it was undeniable.

Another seemingly meaningless moment stayed with me. When I turned eighteen, I sensed that my life would end in the year of 2010. I didn't object much to that idea because I was still young and full of life. However, time went by fast, and the end of 2009 was near.

The onset of my illness was in 2008. My health deteriorated, and I felt anxious about the vision of death-day. My thoughts of dying during 2010 were hunting me, and I'd wondered if my vision was clear.

One month before the year of 2010, Laura and I talked about my death arraignments, since there was a great indication that disease would end my life at any moment. Somehow, on the spur of the moment, I told Laura about the vision I had of death-day. Surprisingly, she said: "Mama, since I was a little girl, I also thought you would die once I reached my adulthood."

Laura and I held hands and prayed. Suddenly peace began to flow. We realized our visions were based on fear and confusion. We read 1 Corinthians 14:33(KJV): "For God is not the author of confusion but of peace, as in all the churches of the saints."

We realized fear never comes from the Lord. It comes from Satan who tries to stop God from advancing His plans in our lives. He is a liar and a thief misleading God's people. We overcame confusion through the Word of God. Laura and I stood in faith and God's peace returned to our hearts. We acknowledged confusion and peace could not mutually co-exist.

Dying in 2010 was a false vision because "For God has not given us a spirit of fear and timidity, but of power, love, and self-discipline." (2 Timothy 1:7)

The beautiful vision I received while riding in Tom's pick-up truck came to pass because my brokenness and bruises were restored by Christ into more of His beauty. He took all of my sorrows and crushed pains into praise to His name, making my life of service to Him.

Visions from God are confirmed by peace He instills in our hearts. Visions are a blessing from the Lord. He gives visions through sudden mind pictures instead of words. The Bible affirms our visions. Time reveals if it's from our own imagination, Satan, or if it's a vision that the Lord is revealing to us. If the vision is from God, it will come to pass. He will make it happen and guide us to it. If it is not from God, then He will take it away.

Heavenly Father, give me a spirit of discernment to know what comes from you. Help me see your path clearly. You are a peaceful lamp guiding my footsteps. Amen.

Additional reading: John 8:44, 1 John 3:8, Luke 4:35, 2 Corinthians 10:3-5, Amos 3:7, 1 John 4:1, Philippians 1:9-10, 1 Thessalonians 5:21.

Self-reflection: Do you have any hidden confusion in your heart? Are your visions being backed up by the Word of God? Are your choices congruent with God's will for your life?

Hearing From God

"Then, after doing all those things, I will pour out my Spirit upon all people. Your sons and daughters will prophesy. Your old men will dream dreams, and your young men will see visions." Jonas 2:28

My life has been paved with different visions. I remember one particular time I had a conviction but wanted it to come to pass on my own timing instead of God's timing. I'd try to fall asleep but couldn't quiet my thoughts. I was restless with "what ifs." I was concerned about the future.

God gave me a vision, and instead of leaving the course of events unfold according to His will, I let assumptions fog my mind. I thought of worst possible scenarios and negativity was killing my hopes. I wondered if the vision was a fabrication of my mind, and pessimism led me to think that nothing good was ever going to happen.

Suddenly, I was tired of entertaining stinking negative thoughts. God reminded me He was in control of everything. Instead of worrying about problems, I decided to respond to the tests according to God's will. He assured I could rest my days in His hands. I trusted He was going to make all things right according to His wise Hands. God helped me to be content where I was while I waited on the vision to come to pass.

Has God given you a conviction, vision, or dream? At times God gives His children visions of events to come. Faith makes the visions a definable target, but instead of letting faith takes us to the target, we want to meddle with God's plans. We try to do something about it by exercising our own plans. We run ahead of God's timing and attempt to control the visions by speeding up the process. The reason for that is because we want to relieve our anxiety of the unknown.

If the convictions of visions don't become real on our time frame, we try to avoid, fight, or escape from it. We don't like living in the "unknown" zone. It's hard to tolerate it, so we try to transform it to something known and comfortable.

We analyze and calculate visions and situations in life and always come up short. Facts and figures don't add up. We dwell in negative thoughts because we see the impossible. That's when we should stop doing the math. We should stop thinking of how small our hands are, and consider how mighty our Lord is! Every time our thoughts go to "what ifs," we should substitute the thoughts to my God is!

God's convictions, dreams, and visions require us to have faith. Faith moves mountains and believes that which cannot be seen. Faith waits for the fruits of what it has believed.

Many people abandon faith in God just because they can't wait on God. However, I'm convinced that God has placed visions, desires and dreams in us in order to humble, mold, and test us to see what's hidden in our hearts. Trusting God for the impossible is a good pointer whether or not we will follow Him or wander away.

Faithful Father, you know me from the inside out. You know every thought and every doubt. Help me keep my eyes on you when hesitation reaches my heart. I try to meddle with your plan but I end up tearing down the better works of your Hand. Forgive me for trying to run ahead of you. Restore my schemes back into your plans. Amen.

Additional reading: Habakkuk 2:2, Jonas 2:28, Genesis 40:8, Job 33:15, Jonas 2:28, Genesis 46:2, Numbers 12:6, Proverbs 29:18.

Self-reflection: Do you take God's plan into your own hands?

Trenton

"The thought of my suffering and homelessness is bitter beyond words. I will never forget this awful time, as I grieve over my loss. Yet I still dare to hope when I remember this: the faithful love of the Lord never ends! His mercies never cease." Lamentations 3:19-22

"Mama, I'm pregnant!" Laura said with happy tears in her eyes. Mark and Laura were trying to conceive since they joined in marriage. When it finally happened, the excitement was heightened by the good news. It was a moment in Laura's life which she thought nothing could go wrong.

Laura soon developed a connection with her fetus. She often massaged her belly as a prelude to rocking her baby. She sang and talked to the developing fetus in the womb. She imagined how her baby would look like. She sparkled daily with a special pregnancy glow. Her face shined as she embraced her pregnant tummy. Mark and Laura picked a name for the baby right from the first trimester. Baby Trenton!

During the second trimester of pre-natal care, Laura went to the routine fetal ultrasound check. Her smile turned upside down when the obstetrician informed that Trenton had gastroschisis. He referred her to a neonatologist at Delaware University Medical Center, who coordinated care with a neonatal surgeon who was going to operate on Trenton as soon as he was to be born. The doctor said the surgery was safe and successful. Trenton's congenital abdominal protrusion would be closed. The care team assured Trenton's problem was manageable and carried a low mortality rate.

The following months were packed with doctors' appointments at Delaware University Medical Center. Things were going as expected.

Trenton's breathing, heart rate, and growth seemed healthy other than his congenital defect.

On the other hand, Laura was not well. She was losing weight. She was getting weaker by the day. Her energy level was low. I took her to the obstetrician, but he didn't know what to make of it. He told her to rest and that she didn't have anything to worry about.

I drove Laura to the hospital every week for fetal monitoring. She loved hearing Trenton's heartbeat. "It's the most beautiful sound!" she'd say every time with love overflowing from her eyes.

At her thirty eight weeks of pregnancy, we headed again to the hospital. The nurse strapped the monitor belt around her petit pregnant belly. The sweet and talkative nurse suddenly became quiet. She kept moving the belt around Laura's belly. She left the room to call the attending obstetrician. The physician moved the Doppler device around her belly and conducted an ultrasound. "I'm so sorry, there's no heart sound," the obstetrician said. I looked at Laura's face. It took a second for grief to swallow her whole.

We left the hospital and I drove Laura to a beautiful green meadow. We sat down by the light of the sun and dedicated a life that never was- back to the Lord. Her hands embraced dead baby Trenton still in her womb. Tears flowed down her face. The door for Laura's pain and sadness suddenly opened wide.

Laura carried dead baby Trenton for one week in her womb until she was admitted in the labor and delivery room to birth her limb baby. Her face spun into expressions of disarray. Her eyes lost its shine. The obstetrician began to induce her labor with Pitocin to expel the fetus.

Trenton was born- dead. He had strawberry blond hair, button nose, delicate fingers and toes. He looked beautiful but was a limb bundle of aches, who longed to rest back into God's embrace. I passed baby Trenton into Laura's arms to hold and love one more time. Her fingertips caressed his lifeless body with tender love and care. Laura's spirit was crushed as if dark death swallowed her whole.

Laura's broken heart enveloped her life. The empty aching feeling of not having Trenton would not depart her soul. She searched for other little boys that would be Trenton's age and imagined how her son would be like. She went into deep depression conjoined with sadness beyond console.

I wanted to comfort her. "Trenton is in Heaven, God knows best!" She didn't want to hear that. She wanted Trenton alive in her arms. She didn't care to hear "time will heal." She was in the middle of a storm not knowing how to get out.

At some point in time, Laura couldn't hold all the pain inside anymore and gave her brokenness to Jesus. God's light broke the darkness that invaded her soul. She simple said: "I have gone through a horrible thing, but God knows what He is doing. This darkness will not take Jesus from me! That will never change."

Why would a God of love allow more suffering in Laura's life? Pain moved in her life and became her companion. Suffering wore her a thousand guises. Yet, in her fear of doom, she began to hold onto the thousands of "fear nots" the Bible promises.

Laura's pain lingered on a few years past Trenton's death, but she accepted her pain and hoped in Jesus. She learned to stop grasping everything on earth with tyranny. She learned that the Lord gives, and He takes away according to His purposes (see Job 1:21). God drew Laura closer to Him through pain. She spent much time asking God to cure her of the daily hardship, until she considered that the very hardship was curing her from earthly attachments. Through pain, she achieved greater spiritual gain and a closer walk with the Lord.

Trenton was a treasure on earth. However, every treasure on earth is vulnerable. Everything can go away and be destroyed in a minute. The only treasure that is protected, firm and assured is our treasure in Heaven (see Matthew 6:19-21).

Lord God, you are the Hope for my hopelessness. Your mighty hand eases my sufferings. During sleepless nights of trials, you hear my desperate pleas by setting my broken heart free. The aching of my sorrows makes your mercies near, revealing your great love for me. Amen.

Additional reading: 1 Corinthians 2:9, 2 Peter 3:13, Revelation 22:1-5, Hebrews 11:10, Hebrews 13:14, 2 Chronicles 31:18, Hebrews 11:16.

Self-reflection: Have you asked God to cure your hardships, just to realize your hardships were curing you? Is God your ultimate source of hope? How do you react when tragedy strikes your life? Do you grow bitter or better? Is Jesus the answer to all your pain?

Caterpillar

"Do not conform to the pattern of this world, but be transformed by the renewing of your mind. Then you will be able to test and approve what God's will is- his good, pleasing and perfect will." Romans 12:2

My youngest daughter Anna didn't fit in with her peers during junior high school. She fell alone in a room full of other kids. She thought some kids her own age were making bad choices and decided to be with the out crowd. She wanted to be with others but not to the cost of peer pressure.

One day Anna said with a sweet sparkling smile she wanted to serve God and be all that He wanted her to be. God heard her prayer and that very same week began working in her life. She didn't want to conform to the world, so God began transforming her into Jesus' image as little Max became rambunctious.

Anna expected Max to be sweet and kind towards her, but he became defiant and difficult. Anna noticed love was more than just a feeling. She had to pray for God to give her patience and understanding towards Max.

In the midst of Anna's struggle, she realized her burden was God's answer to prayers. Jesus was perfecting her love walk. She became more patient and loving. As a result Max felt loved and wanted.

Anna was like God's caterpillar. He began creating metamorphosis from her sinful nature to a sanctified Christ like nature. She was going through a process of sanctification, which was causing her to be purified, and perfected by separating herself from the world with an unveil face before Christ (2 Corinthians 3:18).

Anna was not an exception. We are all God's caterpillars. We go through many stages from the pupa to a butterfly. Each state may take anywhere from a minute to a whole life of transformations from brokenness to holiness.

My Transformer Jesus, create in me a clean heart renewed by your Spirit. Purify me so I may have your Spirit of love, joy, peace, patience, kindness, goodness, faithfulness, gentleness, and self-control. Amen.

Additional reading: 2 Corinthians 5:17, 2 Corinthians 3:18, Galatians 2:20, Romans 5:1-21, 1 John 3:2-3, Psalm 51:10-122, Timothy 2:15, Philippians 1:6, Galatians 5:19-26.

Self-reflection: Are you allowing God to transform your life? Do you see changes from your past brokenness to a new holiness in Christ?

Apple-Computer

"The woman was convinced. She saw that the tree was beautiful and its fruit looked delicious, and she wanted the wisdom it would give her. So she took some of the fruit and ate it. Then she gave some to her husband, who was with her, and he ate it, too. At that moment their eyes were opened, and they suddenly felt shame at their nakedness. So they sewed fig leaves together to cover themselves." Genesis 3:6-7

I gave Mike an apple-computer once he turned fifteen years old. I prayed about giving him a laptop because I knew it could lead him to wholesomeness or naughtiness. The laptop exposed him instantly to a new world apart from our harmless G-rated lifestyle. I entrusted him to exercise self-control due to many pros and cons of the internet. I knew he could easily damage himself if he would choose to navigate into suggestive sites.

In a way, computers reminded me of the Garden of Eden. God placed Adam and Eve in a beautiful place and gave them a wonderful life. God permitted them to eat anything from the garden except from the tree of knowledge of good and evil. Nevertheless, a serpent tempted Eve to eat the forbidden fruit. Eve manipulated Adam to taste the no-no fruit. They chose to fall into temptation and disobeyed God.

Consequently, God banished them from their beautiful garden. Their disobedience opened the door of suffering for all of us. They risked everything they had for the sake of curiosity. They had everything going for them, but they made an awful and irreparable choice. They sinned and experienced spiritual and physical consequences. Before they've decided to disobey God, there was no death. After they sinned, death was launched into the world.

Adam and Eve lost their innocent G-rated world by disobeying God. On top of that, they tried to cover their sin by not acknowledging their fault. They tried to pin the blame on each other. Adam even blamed God by saying: "I didn't ask for this woman. You made her."

When I gave Mike the laptop computer, I said he could use it in every possible way, but warned him to stay away from pornography: "You may freely eat the fruit of every tree in the garden, except the tree of the knowledge of good and evil…" (Genesis 2:15-16) I cautioned to follow God's guidance, assuring that choices lead to consequences, which he would have to live with, just like Adam and Eve.

Adam and Eve's choices had deadly consequences. Likewise, our choices always have physical and spiritual consequences. Sinning causes to reap the consequences of sin, but Jesus came to give us a soft landing to our sins because He brought forgiveness to mankind, so we don't have to pay for the fullness of our transgressions.

Just as Adam was perfect in body, mind, and spirit, the last Adam was created by God, perfect in every way- our Lord Jesus Christ. Adam brought death to us due to the original sin, but Jesus came to redeem the acquired sin and opened the gates of Heaven to all of us who claim His name as Savior.

Jesus came to restore that which Adam and Eve broke. They brought death to us all, but Jesus brought life by doing us a favor which we actually don't deserve. He took our place of punishment, bore our shame, and set us free. His grace paid for us. Now we have a ticket to Heaven if we choose to know Christ and have a heart of repentance.

Christ's grace saves us from getting what we truly deserve. We get "a free ride many times" because Jesus doesn't treat us as our sins merit. He has mercy beyond our comprehension when we have a heart of contrition. Do we always reap the consequences of our sins? No, thanks to Jesus!

The Lord makes it possible for us to receive grace from our sins. He realizes that we cannot meet the standards of holiness by our own efforts. He realizes the door of sin has been opened by Adam and Eve. And the more we know of God's law, the more obvious it is that we can't obey it (Romans 3:20). The Christian life is a gift of "abundant poverty," for we get everything for our nothingness.

Abba Father, your Son has paid it all for my sins. You give me everything while I deserve naught. You understand my inadequacies and give me ability to stay strong by your grace. I pray my soul for more of you and less of me. Amen.

Additional reading: 1 Peter 1:3-5, Titus 3:5, Ephesians 2:1-10, Romans 6:14, Titus 2:11-14, Matthew 5:7, Acts 13:38-39, Romans 4:1-8, Hebrews 10:1-14.

Self-reflection: Do you see yourself as not being able to follow the law? Do you see yourself as not being treated as your sins deserve to be treated? Have you received God's forgiveness and grace?

Growth Spurt

"When I was a child, I spoke and thought and reasoned as a child. But when I grew up, I put away childish things." 1 Corinthians 13:11

Mike acted childish at eighteen. He watched cartoons and enjoyed hanging out with his sisters and Max. He always made good choices. He never went through the wild teenage phase. It seemed nothing would ever change.

Out of the blue, Mike went from acting like a little boy to acting like a man. I was flabbergasted he changed almost overnight. Most boys reach adulthood gradually. Not Mike! He changed abruptly upon his acceptance at a university. He decided to put childish things behind. He said goodbye to his old self and looked ahead onto the future. He discussed career goals and wanting a family of his own someday.

I was pleased to witness the progress on Mike's behavior. As a parent I knew he reached the point in which he had to put away childish things and grow up to be an independent and reliable man in society.

Mike's change in behavior made me ponder about the difference between aging and maturing. In our society paying bills, owning a car, and having a career are equivalent to self-sufficiency and self-actualization. That is aging, not necessarily maturing.

In God's economy, maturity and aging means something different. Once we accept Jesus into our lives, we begin to mature in Him. As we first walk with Christ, we consume milk just like babies. As we continue to follow Jesus' guidance and teachings, we stop drinking milk and begin eating solid food. Maturity in Christ means working our salvation.

God's solid food contains nutrients for our souls. It enriches us with wisdom and understanding. It strengthen us with spiritual gifts such love, joy, peace, longsuffering, gentleness, goodness, and faith (see Galatians 5:22-23).

God's nutritional solid food satisfies the soul. The more we mature through His spiritual food, the less worldly junk food we crave.

Maturing in Christ means praying, reading the Bible, gathering with other believers for worship and fellowship. Most importantly, maturing is taking Christ's example as a model and asking Him to transform us into His likeness.

My Jehovah-Maccaddeshem, you are my Lord who sanctifies me through the process of salvation. Knowing you is the goal of my life. Let me attain full maturity so I may be all that you wish me to be. I am captured by your beauty and excellent ways. Amen.

Additional reading: Colossians 1:9-10, 1 Peter 2:1-25, Philippians 4:13, Psalms 1:1-3, Ephesians 4:10-16, Hebrews 5:12-13, 1 Corinthians 14:20, Hebrews 6:1, Hebrews 10:25, Exodus 31:13.

Self-reflection: Are you drinking milk or eating solid food? Is there anything in your life hindering your walk with God? How do you view aging, social maturity, and spiritual maturity? Have you had a spiritual growth spurt lately?

Suicide Bridge

"Don't you realize that your body is the temple of the
Holy Spirit, who lives in you and was given to you by
God? You do not belong to yourself, for God bought
you with a high price. So you must honor God with your
body." 1 Corinthians 6:19-20

Occasionally I'd drive the Chesapeake Bay Bridge to reach the West side
of Maryland. The giant bridge has a dual-span suspension, is nearly five
miles long, and is one hundred and eighty six feet high. It was originally
built in 1952, and the parallel span was added in 1973. Since then, the
state has repaired the bridge many times. Today, it looks like a quilt that
has been patched up innumerous times.

I think driving on the Chesapeake Bay Bridge is like going through
a drive of faith or despair. Due to the frequent violent storms, bad
visibility, and intimidating heights, drivers such as me, resort to praying
for five miles in order to get from one shore to the next. However, for
some, it's a bridge of total despair. Every year you read reports of people
jumping off the bridge.

A few years back I read about a man who took his shoes off and
plunged off the bridge. His shoes marked his departure. Why did he take
his shoes off before jumping? No one really knows. Maybe to let others
know he gave up on hope. Perhaps he didn't want to die, but wanted the
confusion, frustration, pain, and feelings of emptiness to go away. The
shoes left behind were his final mark in this world.

Possibly the man took his shoes off symbolically, hoping to enter the
afterlife. No one will ever know because he gave up on this life due to
hopelessness. He didn't know how to live anymore, so he tried the dusk

of death. Maybe he cried out for help and no one heard him. Regardless of the reason, one thing is for sure, he felt the only way out of despair was to quit life by taking the plunge. His body was washed ashore as a reminder we couldn't help him.

From time to time, Christians also feel despair and desire to take control of their lives by contemplating suicide. That's a pointer they are being led by their emotions instead of the Holy Spirit. But like anything else, that is a temptation that through Christ needs to be resisted. The Holy Spirit dwells within us, therefore suicidal idealizations never comes from God. As a matter of fact, if we set our eyes on Christ during our tribulations, despair turns into repair and confusion turns into understanding. Jesus died to give hope to the hopeless. He can bring us up from the lowest pit if we depend, trust, and rely on Him.

Moses, Hannah, Saul, David, Elijah, and Job from the Bible suffered stages of hopelessness and depression. Hopelessness came after they have gone through some kind of defeat. God didn't punish them because they were downhearted. He loved them by given them strength to keep on going (see 1 Samuel 30:6). They didn't take their shoes off to take the plunge. Despair hit them, yet they kept their eyes fixed on God.

I feel your presence my Jehovah-Shammah. My pain is hard to bear and it seems no one really cares. I want to spread my wings and plunge into the waters of death. Instead, your Spirit opens my wings and I fly higher to the hope of your joy. Quiet my tormented soul Lord. Lead me to the hope of the cross. Amen.

Additional reading: Jeremiah 29:11-12, John 14:16, Matthew 28:20, 2 Corinthians 5:7, Deuteronomy 31:8, Joshua 1:9, Psalm 34:18, Ezekiel 48:35.

Self-reflection: Are you in despair? Do you want to give up on living? Have you tried fixing your eyes on Jesus and putting your hope in Him? He holds your hands and says: "… do not fear, for I am with you; do not be dismayed, for I am your God. I will strengthen you and help you; I will uphold you with my righteous right hand." (Isaiah 41:10 NIV)

Body Of Christ

"But our bodies have many parts, and God has put each part just where he wants it. How strange a body would be if it had only one part! Yes, there are many parts, but only one body. The eye can never say to the hand, 'I don't need you.' The head can't say to the feet, 'I don't need you.'" Corinthians 12:18-21

Years ago my family and I travelled to the Amazon region, in Brazil. We walked deep inside the jungles. We set up camp by the Rio Negro, which is the largest black water river in the world. It allocates one of the most notorious fish, the piranha. I marveled at the vast evergreen and coniferous forests. The large tree leaves roofed the ground like a giant canopy. I gazed at macaws, toucans, and parrots. Their colors were as bright as a rainbow. Their loud screeches awaken the forest from its sleep.

I canoed on the black water river in a marupa dugout canoe. Civilization felt inexistent. I was close to God and His encompassing nature.

I decided to leave the security of the canoe and swim in the Rio Negro River. It was a surreal experience. I became part of the water, piranhas, and trees. I became interlaced and hugged by His creation. I was nature and nature was me. Interwoven but still unique. I was touched by God's majestic world. Everything worked in a harmonious synchrony.

The rainforest reminded me of the body of Christ. God desires us to be interwoven with one another in a harmonious synchrony. At the same time He makes us unique. We are intricately connected with each other, but retaining individual gifts. "God has given each of you a gift from His great variety of spiritual gifts. Use them well to serve one another." (1 Peter 4:10)

The body of Christ is a unit, joined together in Christ's salvation. We partake of His death and resurrection. We follow God and represent His righteousness in the world. The body of Christ is God's family. We fellowship, seek God's guidance, and pray together. We love, encourage, and practice forgiveness. Our souls are nourished with each other by hearing the Word and worshiping in unison.

God canopies the body of Christ through His love, power, and grace. His church awakens the world by spreading the Good News and by reflecting Jesus' attributes of goodness and wholesomeness. We are called to be His church. We are God's ambassadors fulfilling His plan for the world.

Our Cornerstone, we love your Sanctuary. You reign in your house and hearts. We break bread and drink in your name. We are united with each other in your Holy name. We share our trials and smiles; you heal us. We are called to go out and share the good news of your salvation, for you were willing to pay the price for us all. Amen.

Additional Reading: 1 Corinthians 10:17, 1 Corinthians 12:27, Ephesians 4:12, Hebrews 13:3, Ephesians 5:23, Colossians 1:24, Matthew 18:19, James 5:16, Galatians 4:19.

Self-reflection: Are you part of a body of Christ? What drives you to a church? How have you been blessed by belonging to a group of Christians sharing the same faith as you do?

Bungee Cord

"Let me say first that I thank my God through Jesus Christ for all of you, because your faith in Him is being talked about all over the world." Romans 1:8

My mom's friends, Mindy and Jonas, have the kind of faith that is talked about all over the world. I've heard of their faith in Jesus eight thousand flight miles away.

Some people talk about faith, others, like Mindy and Jonas exercise faith that moves mountains. They are missionaries in Brazil, raising their three children. They serve at their church, but God has called them to an even higher mission.

They are working on adopting four Brazilian siblings which were found abandoned on the streets. They were considered feral since they were severely neglected. They lived in heartless conditions. Their father died and their mother tried to kill the young siblings. They were isolated from human contact, care, and love. The local orphanage took them in and now Mindy and Jonas wait for the finalization of the adoption papers.

Although some in Mindy and Jonas' community discouraged the adoption of all four siblings, they stood firm in the conviction that the Lord called them to rescue and love the abandoned orphans.

Mindy and Jonas' ears were attuned to Jesus' voice, just as Noah's ears were attuned to God's voice. Everyone thought Noah was crazy for building an ark in a place where rain was non-existence. But Noah simply trusted and obeyed. As a consequence, God's will was fulfilled and blessings were dispersed. Similarly, the couple trusted and obeyed the Lord's guidance during adversity. Friends in their circle discouraged them because of the potential heartbreak and probable difficulties in dealing with orphan children with serious behavioral problems. Others discouraged them because the children were older and traumatized. But Mindy and Jonas fixed their eyes on God, who brings promises to fruition.

The couple bungee cord their souls and spirits into God's adventurous skies. Since Mindy and Jonas' security was based on God's faithfulness, His elastic rubber cord sustained them and never broke.

Is God asking you to trust Him with something grandiose while others are trying to snap the vision away from you? God never lies, but the enemy will try to distract your faith by putting doubt in your heart. If so, stand in faith and know that if God gives you a mission, He will also equip you to fulfill the task. Do not be discouraged. Stand strong in faith!

God validates His visions with signs and wonders. Turn off negative voices of the world and follow His lamp which guides your feet. God will make you prosper with whatever mission He entrusts in your heart. God will lead you by His peace and the doors will open supernaturally.

The most challenging times in life require you to bungee cord in God's arms. Fly in God's skies through faith. He will sustain you. After faith, come blessings. And blessings are the aroma of precious times.

My Sustainer, you've given me a grandiose vision. It seems impossible to realize it. I can't do it on my own. I follow you. I depend on you. You have miracles at hand! Doors open one by one. I marvel at your plan. Thank you for penciling my life. Amen.

Additional reading: Psalm 17:4, Mark 16:20, Psalm 119:105, Isaiah 55:11-12, Deuteronomy 1:30-33, 2 Samuel 7:28, Psalm 9:10, Psalm 13:5, Psalm 20:7.

Self-reflection: Is God calling you to do something extraordinary? Are you depending on Him to accomplish His will for your life? Are others trying to discourage you from fulfilling your calling?

To Facebook Or Not Facebook

My social experiment

"Those who live in the shelter of the Most High will find rest in the shadow of the Almighty. This I declare about the Lord: He alone is my refuge, my place of safety; He is my God, and I trust Him. The Lord says, "I will rescue those who love me I will protect those who trust in my name. When they call on me, I will answer; I will be with them in trouble. I will rescue and honor them." Psalm 91:1-2, 14-15

I spent hours on the social network site, Facebook. I opened the account as a tool to minister to others through Christ's love. As time went on, my motives became smudged. I felt a need to belong to a group of people that expressed love and acceptance towards me. However, my needs were rarely met because people can't satisfy completely, for only God can embrace that which is lacking.

I chatted often with friends, but noticed that during chats, I emptied all thoughts which were weighing in my mind. I was often self-seeking, and I hardly returned to silence without having less of God's grace. At times I emptied concerns on someone's shoulder while Jesus' chat line was on green. I chatted with Facebook friends before chatting with Jesus.

At some point in time, I noticed Facebook was hurting more than satisfying my needs to belong. I decided to deactivate the account for twenty days. I called it FF: Facebook-Fasting. I submerged completely in God's Word and was consumed by Him.

I had dreams with Facebook during my first few nights of FF detox. My dreams were with my favorite chatters. I missed my friend's posts, selfies, jokes, articles, and long chats. I began wondering what posts and photos I was missing.

I prayed to resist temptation to reactivate Facebook. Days went by, and my focus remained with God. I enjoyed my present moment and appreciated the people in my life outside Facebook more than ever.

Once my FF ended, I reactivated Facebook. My mind was clearer. I reconnected with friends but was free from trying to be fulfilled by Facebook.

Deactivating Facebook helped realize my need to belong to a group could not be satisfied by a social-network. Satisfaction could only come through God's love because His embrace lacks nothing.

Leviticus 20:26 says: "You must be holy because I, the Lord, am holy. I have set you apart from all other people to be my very own." I acknowledged the privilege of being set apart for God. He is my complete fulfillment. There's no substitute for the Lord. No one could ever fill my deepest need of belonging because God created me to belong to Him.

Jehovah-Shammah, you are always present in my life. You've chosen me to be yours. You accept me entirely without any excitation. You don't look at me as humans do. You look at my heart. You never let me down. I choose to embrace you. Amen.

Additional reading: 1 Peter 2:9, Psalms 139:13-16, Jeremiah 29:11, Ephesians 1:4-5, 1 Samuel 16:7, Psalm 25:16-17, Psalm 121:1-2, John 14:1.

Self-reflection: Who are you in Christ? To whom do you belong? Does a social network fulfill your desires to be loved and accepted? Do you come to Christ's open chat rooms to empty all your thoughts?

Prayer Via Satellite

"Before daybreak the next morning, Jesus got up and went out to an isolated place to pray." Mark 1:35

During my twenties I isolated from all distraction in order to spend time alone with the Lord. I soaked in God's presence by gazing at a peaceful meadow or a majestic mountain. Nature always brought me closer to Him. I carried one book with me, the Holy Bible. I brought my best friend, Jesus.

Today, my prayer and Bible reading time are often different than my past days. I'm mostly indoors with a laptop computer. I pray a little. I surf Christian web sites some. I don't pray outdoors as much as I used to. Something has been lost in the transition from God's nature to the high tech world. Now, I'm always sitting in front of my computer or closing my eyes to pray in the comfort of my home.

It's peculiar that some Christians went from a close personal prayer group to a web prayer group. Some went from fellowshipping with God up on the hilltop, to praying and gathering with other Christians on Facebook and Skype. Some of us even stop attending church all together and adopted the online church services.

Imagine Jesus today. Would He adhere to technology? Would he carry an iPad to connect to His followers? I can't imagine Him going to the wilderness to pray with an iPhone, so His prayers would reach El Shaddai via satellite.

Jesus withdrew to nature to pray in solitude (see Luke 5:16). He removed himself from every distraction in order to be completely connected to God. He didn't need technology. Once Jesus returns He will not need a Smartphone to get closer to God.

Jesus connected to God on the mountaintop. We should also elevate ourselves to the highest point of intimacy with our Shepherd. Our connection with the Savior fills our emptiness, cures our loneliness and satisfies our starved souls by receiving spiritual nourishment.

Sometimes we wonder why we don't hear from our Shepherd anymore. He is calling us at all times, asking us to seek Him. But all the while, our ears are being soaked with sounds from headphones and bombarded by internet multimedia. Meanwhile our Bibles keep collecting dust on our bookshelves.

Our Shepherd wants us to have a relationship with Him through prayers and devotions. Prayers bring blessings and light out of darkness. Prayers restore our peace. Prayers transform our souls from our mundane world to God's higher world. Prayers bring us back to God and it's our link to finding His bountiful mercy.

As much as I pray the Lord will use high-tech to forward His Kingdom, I have a feeling that sometimes high-tech gadgets are all too much. As we adhere to the present we should not forget our past ways in connecting with the Lord on the mountaintop.

My shepherd, I hear your voice. I see you, and I want to follow you. I put away my high-tech gadgets and seek you at the mountain top. I feel your love. I sense your grace. I receive your miracles. I embrace your comfort. I hear your guidance. I sense your calling. I experience your peace. Most of all, I receive your unconditional love. Amen.

Additional Reading: John 10:27, Ephesians 6:18, Mark 1:35, Luke 5:16, John 17:11, Luke 10:21, Luke 22:44.

Self-reflection: Would you like to hear from the Shepherd? Don't text. Pray! Would you like to see your Shepherd? Don't Facebook. Pray!

Βιβλία

"Let the message of Christ dwell among you richly as you teach and admonish one another with all wisdom through psalms, hymns, and songs from the Spirit, singing to God with gratitude in your hearts." Ephesians 5:19

I was majoring in music while in college. My favorite course was chorus. Sopranos, altos, tenors, baritones, and bases sang with gust. Our conductor, Fertelli, was a charismatic Italian man. His class was packed with laughter, drama, and conundrums. But when it came to music notes, he was no laughing matter. He was able to single out a slight pitch error from any given student.

I remember a time when he stopped the chorus abruptly because he detected I was off pitch. I tensed up in fear. He stared straight into my eyes. Then he sternly told me to sing the same note over and over again until I got it right. If I was slightly above pitch he would yell; if it was slightly below pitch he would scream. I had to sing in perfect pitch or else he would threaten to shun me from chorus.

Fertelli wanted his music to be as beautiful and perfect as possible. He trained us day after day for perfect performances. We had to read and interpret music as well as be led by his baton. Thanks to his hard work and our determination to follow his instructions, we had loud applauses, bravos, and encores. Fertelli entertained, petrified, and worked us to the bones, but it paid off in the end.

I see the Bible in a similar light. In order for choral music to be beautiful, all singers need to sing on pitch and accord. Likewise, for Christians to be what God wants us to be, we need to follow His instructional Book and be on pitch with His Biblical instructions. We should also live in accord with His commands by the grace He instills in us. If we accept just part of the Bible as being divine and others as being not important, we end up being undeveloped Christians, rejecting the truths of the Word. If that happens, others cannot see the light of Christ in us.

As choral singers work on their music repeatedly, we also need to work incessantly to mirror Christ by reading the Word of God. The Bible should be interpreted by the guidance of the Holy Spirit, just as diligently as singers interpret sheet music. We must remain alert at all times and monitor our walk with the Lord, as singers are completely alert to every note and movement of the baton.

God's Word is the foundation of Christian living. You can't use bits and pieces that fit a life style and leave the inconvenient pieces out. That would be singing out of tune and changing a whole song and making it your own. It would be like distorting an opera, and making it into a pop song. Rejecting a Biblical truth here and there is equal to rejecting the entire faith.

The Bible contains spiritual nourishment. It corrects, instructs, and reproofs us into righteousness. It's a light to our paths. It is our handbook to wisdom. Understanding the Bible means God is the maestro with a baton conducting us to Holy insights.

My Holy Maestro, please help me to have perfect pitch, timbre, and dynamics as I follow you. Conduct my life. Mold me into a fine tune so I may shine brighter for you. Let your Word be like music sheet, alive and vigorous dwelling in my heart. Let me sing of your mercies with many bravos for your glory. Amen.

Additional reading: Hebrews 4:12, 2 Timothy 3:16-17, 2 Timothy 3:16, Jeremiah 23:29, Psalms 119:105, Ephesians 6:17, John 17:17.

Self-reflection: In what ways do you appreciate the Bible? Do you believe parts of the Bible and reject other parts that don't fit your lifestyle? How does God reveal His wisdom through His Word? How does the Bible help you cement your walk with God? Is your walk with God in tune with the Bible?

Build Your House On A Rock

"Everyone then who hears these words of mine and does them will be like a wise man who built his house on the rock. And the rain fell, and the floods came, and the winds blew and beat on that house, but it did not fall, because it had been founded on the rock. And everyone who hears these words of mine and does not do them will be like a foolish man who built his house on the sand. And the rain fell, and the floods came, and the winds blew and beat against that house, and it fell, and great was the fall of it." Mathew 7:24-27

As a commercial airline pilot, my father used to fly from Los Angeles to Tokyo every month for a period of two years. He used to tell us about Tokyo's unsettling earthquakes. He didn't enjoy being there because Japan had one small earthquake every five minutes.

Japan is well prepared for natural disasters. They've engineered buildings to outstand major earthquakes. They also have loud sirens for Tsunamis, and their population is well trained in case of a massive problem.

Regardless of how well prepared Japan is for natural disasters, on March 11, 2011 an 8.9 magnitude earthquake hit their land. It also triggered a massive Tsunami which swept away people, cars, homes, and everything on its path. The death toll reached several thousands. Streets were filled with debris and hopeless faces.

Japanese placed their hope in the government's national disaster prevention. They placed their security through the knowledge that yesterday would be pretty much like today and today like tomorrow.

They depended on houses with running water, electricity, and food. They didn't realize the government would not be able to protect them from a mega earthquake.

Japan had to deal with the aftermath of a major natural disaster. Japanese's security was removed by the earthquake and the Tsunami. They lost the foundation of their lives in which they depended upon for safety.

Whether we go through a natural disaster or not, humans tend to rely on what's tangible. We think that's what gives us security. Reality is, lives can change in the blink of an eye. Our foundation is only truly safe when we depend on God. That sets us free from fear of tomorrow.

As my father mentioned, the ground in Japan is never still, but no ground in this planet is ever reliable and tranquil. That should be a clue we shouldn't place our dependence on men nor country nor nature. The only foundation that is trustworthy and dependable is God, because whatever He befalls upon us was first prescribed by Him. God gives us the confidence that every problem He allows comes with a divine solution. Earthquakes, Tsunamis, hurricanes, or tornados may come and take homes away, but the peace of God remains through every situation when trusting in God remains.

Eternal Jesus, you are the rock of my salvation. Although the earth might shake from underneath, I can remain steadfast in your arms. You are my chief cornerstone that remains indestructible forever. I rest my confidence in you. I dwell in your safety. Amen.

Additional reading: Deuteronomy 33:27, Psalms 16:8, Palms. 23:4, 2 Timothy 2:19-21, Matthew5:38-48, 1 Corinthians 3: 10, 11, 16-23.

Self-reflection: Are you building your house on the solid rock of Christ? Are you resting your confidence in the Lord?

Gossip

"The reason of our love of talking is that we seek by interchange of speech to be console by one another and long to relieve ourselves of all the various thoughts which weigh upon our minds... If it is lawful and good to talk. Let us talk on edifying topics." -Thomas a Kempis

One of the professors in nursing school taught us about Client Privacy and Confidentiality: "Medical practice is no place for gossip. It's the patient's right to tell his/her own story. It's not your story to tell!"

Clients' privacy encourages open communication with care providers and safeguards their information. Nurses need to be vigilant not to gossip because it's considered an unprofessional conduct.

Confidentiality practice should not be limited to the medical field, but should be applied in our Christian walk as well. We have ownership to our own stories yet gossip runs rampant everywhere. People constantly fall under the temptation of spreading misinformation in order to carry a scandal. Even churches deal with idle chats and rumors of personal trivial nature.

In some twisted way we feel better about ourselves by putting others down. It reveals our tendencies to passive aggressiveness by isolating and harming others. It spreads strife by revealing secrets that don't belong to us.

There was one such week in a small town of North Caroline, where gossip was spreading like wildfire. The town's hot topic was about a couple who had a brawl in the middle of the street. After the strife, the couple decided to go their separate ways for a few days. Preposterous rumors began escalating from one neighbor to the next. Those who were on the husband's side gossiped against the wife. Those who were on the wife's side, gossiped against the husband. People's eyes sparkled as they whispered delicious morsels of gossip. No one really knows what fueled the rumors. All hearsay turned out to be bogus causing erosion of trust and morale towards everyone. In the end of the day, the couple was emotionally victimized by the town's folks.

Jesus taught us in Matthew 18 about conflict resolution in regards to disputes at churches. Gossip is considered a sin because it always causes harm to others. We should always speak truthfully to one another without any corrupt conversation (see Proverbs 20:19).

God is not pleased with us when we lie and hurt innocent people by fabricating wicked gossips. It causes discord among Christians. He desires us to have a courteous and gentle spirit leading to truth and accord. The Bible teaches us the Golden Rule in Luke 6:31, which says that we should treat others as we would like others to treat us.

When we see pain, our first response should be to pray. When we're tempted to gossip, we should ask for forgiveness. If we gossip, we should realize the harm we cause others. Like my nursing professor used to say: "It's not your story to tell!"

My God of all truth, I realize I often sin and fall short of your glory. I wish to dwell in your Holy Hill. Guide my footsteps so I may be blameless and do what is right. Let my tongue be tamed with self-control so I might find myself pure, lovely, and commendable in your sight. Amen.

Additional reading: Ephesians 4:25-29, Proverbs 16:28, Proverbs 11:13, Proverbs 20:19, Proverbs 6:16-19, Titus 3:2, Exodus 23:1, Psalm 34:1, James 4:11, Ephesians 4:32, Exodus 20:16, James 3:7-8, Romans 12:2, Proverbs 18:8, Proverbs 26:22.

Self-reflection: Do you find yourself gossiping? Do you discuss edifying topics with one another or do you put others down? How often are you tempted to gossip? What is your first response to the temptation?

Sin Is Sin

"And when He comes, He will convict the world of its sin, and of God's righteousness, and of the coming judgment." John 16:8

A friend walked away from God and began making poor choices. The situation weighed heavy in my heart. I wanted to approach her with the hopes of steering her back into the hands of the Lord. I didn't want to be judgmental but wished she would make better choices.

I prayed God would direct my words when speaking to her. Suddenly the right moment came and I approached her. The Lord answered my prayers and our meeting was productive. She was able to acknowledge her poor choices and returned into God's arms.

I headed back home after our meeting and noticed I became puffed up. I couldn't help but glow after my successful encounter. I thought I've done a great job helping my friend by saying the right words. I wanted to pat myself on the back, but I had a feeling in my heart that something wasn't right. Immediately the Holy Spirit poked my shoulder, "wait a minute, you asked for God to intervene, why are you patting your own back and giving yourself credit?" The Holy Spirit cut right through my prideful nonsense.

I approached my friend with her sin and in returned I sinned myself. I became proud. After all, sin is sin, big or small. But praise be to Jesus that He convicted me of sin and forgave my transgression.

Lord of Forgiveness, thank you for convicting me of sin. Big or small, you wiped it all on the cross. Your compassion and love lifts the heavy burden of guilt from my soul. Amen.

Additional verses: 2 Timothy 3:16, Hebrews 10:22, 1 Samuel 2:3, Proverbs 8:13, Proverbs 11:2, Obadiah 1:3.

Self-reflection: Have you been ignoring a burden of guilt in your heart? Are you ready to ask Jesus to forgive you?

Immovable Faith

"So be truly glad. There is wonderful joy ahead, even
though you have to endure many trials for a little while.
These trials will show that your faith is genuine. It is
being tested as fire tests and purifies gold—though your
faith is far more precious than mere gold. So when your
faith remains strong through many trials, it will bring
you much praise and glory and honor on the day when
Jesus Christ is revealed to the whole world." 1 Peter
1:6-7

I was delighting myself in the Lord and enjoying the day. My faith in
Him was strong like the noonday sun. I was filled with faith because
everything was fine. I was not being tested by the Lord at that particular
moment. My faith was not going through fire, but savoring still waters.

"Ring, ring," to my surprise a phone call transformed my trust in
God into fear and panic. My friend delivered bad news which shook the
stability of my faith. A new problem caused me lose inner peace. My
faith spun up and down like a yo-yo.

My first response to the problem was to leave God out of the
equation. I panicked and my brain enveloped itself in bitter possible
scenarios. Moreover, I realized overthinking was not based on God's
truths and promises.

God was polishing my faith in view of another problem. He was
teaching me to remain steadfast and deeply rooted in Him no matter
what new storm would come my way.

Faith was like a muscle. In order for it to be strong and implanted in God's Word, it needed to be worked against resistance. Faith could only be enhanced by endurance during trials just like weight training.

God was operating in the principle of overload by increasing the weight of trials so I could grow stronger in faith and dependence on Him.

Apostle Paul described strong faith as an act of remaining faithful to the point of death. Our ancestors worked their strong faith muscles as they remained steadfast in God, while they were stoned, flogged, murdered, destituted, swayed in two, mistreated, persecuted, hid in caves, and while they wandered in deserts and mountains.

As I read Psalm 37, I committed new trials into God's hands. As my faith grew in steadfastness, I became stronger in Christ and found peace and answers to prayers.

Faith Tester, in the midst of suffering, I see that faith in you works. Faith quiets my soul and gives me rest. I ascribe to you all troubles, for I want you to reign in all parts of my life. I call on you and you answer my prayers. Amen.

Additional reading: Psalm 1:1-3, Hebrews 4:1, Colossians 2:6-7, 1 Corinthians 15:58, 1 Corinthians 15:58.

Self-reflection: Are you growing in your faith from trial to trial? What is your first reaction when you encounter a sudden problem?

Community Property

> "So dispute broke out between the herdsmen of Abram and Lot...Abram said to Lot: "Let's not allow this conflict to come between us...take your choice of any section of the land you want, and we will separate. If you want the land to the left, then I'll take the land on the right." Genesis 13:7-9

A few years ago a friend called me because his life turned upside down. He and his wife had a bad argument. Torrent emotions splashed in every direction. He stormed out of the house because he couldn't deal with his wife's temper. Meanwhile, the wife became infuriated because he left her in the middle of an argument. Then, she decided to pack all of their community property and leave the house. Turbulent emotions were high and impulsive actions took its course.

After my friend cooled down, he returned home. He was shocked to find out his wife left him and the house was empty. Everything was removed from the living room. A few items remained in the bedroom. The refrigerator was almost totally empty. I stood next to my friend watching as he went from room to room with a surprised facial expression. Bewildered, he lifted his arms and said: "*Grrrrr*, she only left me one roll of toilet paper!"

I began praying for a peaceful reconciliation for both of them. Minutes later his emotions settled down. He said he would leave all material possessions to his wife and give her alimony if she wished for a divorce.

In the beginning of times, Abram and Lot also had a dispute over property. Abram came up with a resolution over the fight. He showed great wisdom by opening his hands to Lot by asking him to choose the piece of land he wanted. His solution was to give him a choice. Lot didn't consider what was best for Abram and covetously took Sodom, a fertile and well watered land.

Even though it seemed like Abram was the bigger loser during the dispute, God was pleased with how he handled the situation. Consequently, God rewarded him with a land that stretched north and south, east and west. Abram build an altar to the Lord because he recognized God's mercy and kindness towards him.

Lot, on the other hand, who seemed to get the best real state, was captured by invaders in Sodom, a place where people lived evil and wicked lives.

My friend reminded me of Abram's wisdom. He seemed like the bigger loser for opening his hands to their community property. Yet, his kind decision toward his wife spoke volumes of wisdom which echoed in God's ears and those around him. A day later, his wife brought all their community property back to their home. They hugged, kissed, and were back together again. They are still together to this day.

Merciful Lord, you forgive and restore the brokenness I created. Thank you for showing me the same path of wisdom you have shown Abram. Amen.

Additional reading: Psalm 25:9, Proverbs 3:5-6, Proverbs 2:6-9, Psalm 25:12, James 1:5, Jeremiah 29:11, Proverbs 16:9, Matthew 6:14, 1 Corinthians 13:4-7.

Self-reflection: Are your choices based on God's wisdom or are you making choices out of self-preservation and fear? How do you act when the person you love the most offends you? Are you quick to forgive or do you hold a grudge?

Call On His Name Always

"The highest form of worship is the worship of unselfish Christian service." -Billy Graham

"I have an ear ache! Can you come over and check my ear?" My neighbor phoned one evening. That evening was like many others. If she had a stomach ache or any other ailment, she'd call me. She wanted my help due to my nursing education. Her help requests went on and on. If she had marital problems, she and I would go out for coffee to discuss her situation. If she needed to borrow cash, she'd ask me.

If my friend was not going through a crisis, I'd go weeks without hearing from her. She didn't share good news, just the bad ones. She'd forget me during good times. She considered me a 911 friend. I was a shoulder to cry on. I was the ears to hear her sorrows. I was happy to be her emergency crisis contact, but I couldn't help feeling used at times.

I'd have liked her to call and ask how I was doing once in a while. My relationship with her was not like the table game Ping-Pong. I "Ping" her, but she never "Pong" me back. The ball of our conversation never bounced back on my side of the table. However, I was no different than my friend when it came to my best friend, Jesus.

When I was ill, I called on the name of the Lord! When my family was not well, I called on the name of the Lord! When I experienced financial instability, I called on the name of the Lord! When I'd get my breakthroughs, I'd forget the name of the Lord.

Jesus wanted to hear details of happy days, not only sobbing ones. He wanted me to call on Him for everything, good or bad! I tended to ignore Jesus when I was cheerful and I'd slack off on my prayer life.

"Jesus, I'm ok now. I can handle fun on my own," is not something the Lord wanted to hear from me.

Christians should love God for who He is and not only for what He can give us. God wants us to love Him because He is worthy to be loved. He is wonderful, compassionate, kind, and forgiving. He truly satisfies our needs when we diligently draw near Him in all areas of our lives, not only during the hard times, but the good times as well.

Worthy Lord, I confess slacking off when it comes to worship during good times. Forgive my selfishness. You created all things including me. You never reject or ignore me. You always bring me peace. You are the source of all true wisdom. You never leave, forsake, or mislead me. You never overlook or forget me. You are my unsubstitutable best friend Jesus. Amen.

Additional reading: James 4:8, Philippians 2:9-11, James 4:8, Revelation 5:9, Revelation 4:11, Exodus 33:9-10, Psalms 100:4, Romans 12:1-2, Psalms 59:16, Psalms 63:3-4, Psalms 66:4, Psalms 150.

Self-reflection: Do you love God, Jesus, and the Holy Spirit? Do you take a vacation from God during easy times? In what ways do you worship Him? How do you define God's love? Is Jesus your best friend?

Whiny Prayers

"And even when you ask, you don't get it because your motives are all wrong—you want only what will give you pleasure." James 4:3

At five years old, Mike knew how to wear me down until I capitulated to his desires. Many times when we hiked as a family, Mike would refuse to walk. He would throw himself on the dirty trail and have a temper tantrum: "I can't walk, carry me, carry me! *Wah, wah, wah!"* I'd stand in the middle of the trail and encourage him: "Mike get up! Keep walking! You can do it!" But the more I encouraged him the more discouraged he would become.

Carrying Mike was no easy task, especially going up a steep hill. He was dead weight. He didn't wrap his arms tightly around my neck, so his weight was hard to bear because of the absent of effort on his part. Even thought I'd refuse to carry him by saying "no," he'd whine twice as much. My patience would wear thin until I'd lose the battle of wills. He'd have the victory to his heart's content.

I would then hike uphill carrying Mike while having back pain and sore muscles. My mistake was to say "yes," while I should have stuck to my "noes."

In the back of my mind I knew I should have made him walk because of the benefits of hiking. It'd have provided him a hands-on experience with nature. He'd have played with rocks, plants, and learn about the outside world by using his imagination. His muscles would have been stronger and he'd have learned not to quit.

Interestingly enough, adults are not that different than Mike at five years old. When we ask God for something, we tend to whine our prayers to our Heavenly Father. We have a tendency to think that if we repeat our prayers over and over again or if we ask a vast amount of people to pray for what we desire, God will answer our prayers. We think we can wear God down with the quantity and repetition of whining prayers until He capitulates and says "yes" just like I did to Mike. But God is a much better parent to us than I was to Mike. He sticks to what is best for us because He doesn't get exhausted when we relentlessly pressure Him. God doesn't erode and say: "Yes, whatever, I'll give you what you want if you just stop whining!" God's defenses are never down because He is firm and only gives us what is best.

God doesn't give us what we want, because at times our prayers would not create a good outcome in our lives or in the lives of others. Also, sometimes we pray with wrong motives. God realizes our prayers are contaminated with our sinful nature. We pray for more happiness, not more holiness. We pray for more health, not more humility. We ask for more success, not more service. We ask to be more loved, not to love more.

God wants to give happiness, health, and success but it comes with a contingency to bring us consecration and not desecration. He grants our hearts' desire as long as it doesn't cause us to distance ourselves from Him. Our prayers should be according to His will: "This is the confidence we have in approaching God: that if we ask anything according to His will, He hears us. And if we know that He hears us—whatever we ask—we know that we have what we asked of Him." (1 John 5:14-15)

We can't conceal from God the true motives of our hearts when we pray. God knows that due to Adam and Eve's sin, selfishness became a successful human characteristic, while unselfishness became a virtue given by the Holy Spirit. We tend to pray with an attitude of "me-only-myopia" due to self-preservation, while God is more interested in answering saintly selfless prayers which enrich us spiritually.

God doesn't want our empty void to be filled with selfish desires. He wants our empty void to be filled by Him because He knows that our selfish petitions cannot fill the void. He knows how to say "no" to whiny prayers because if He would give everything we want, it would degenerate our walk towards holiness. God only answers prayers which will cause a divine nearness to Him.

And, a divine nearness to God is what Daniel from the Old Testament, experienced during prayer. King Darius signed a law strictly forbidding everyone to pray for thirty days or they would be thrown in the den of lions. "But when Daniel learned that the law had been signed, he went home and knelt down as usual in his upstairs room, with its windows open toward Jerusalem. He prayed three times a day, just as he had always done, giving thanks to his God." (Daniel 6:10) God miraculously saved Daniel from the power of the lions because he served Him faithfully. Daniels' prayers had right motives.

What if our president would decree a law stipulating we couldn't pray for thirty days or we would be thrown in prison? Would we give up prayer all together? Would our loyalty be towards God or country? Do we pray because God is the reason for our living? Do we pray whining prayers to get what we desire?

I couldn't give up prayer for a day, much less thirty days. At times, I have a tendency to whine some of my prayers, but I'm quick to understand when God says "no," He has something better for me. Not praying for thirty days would cause a demolition in the fabric of my being because I depend on prayer for guidance. I would be a sheep without a shepherd. I would be lost and in despair. It would be like losing communication with a parent, best friend, provider, teacher, guider, and place of safety all at once because God is my all. It would be utter loneliness and loss of hope. My life would lose purpose. I would run in circles without a compass.

Prayer is vital for it's the only way I can have a connection with God. Prayer is my link to intimacy with Him. I am completely transparent and vulnerable through prayerful self-disclosure because I trust God's unconditional love.

A prayerless life would cause me to be alone in the vast universe, for without God I am no one. Without God I have no meaning. Without God my soul is irrelevant and empty. Without God life has no purpose.

A prayerless life would be the end to the only way to have a complete alignment with God.

Lord Jesus, you entice me to your Holy presence. I immerse myself into your arms. I wish to lose myself in you. I'm consumed by your company because I love you and I'm hungry for your righteousness. Conversing with you is my life. I have unbroken union with you because you hear my prayers. You answer me by giving me fresh supplies of grace. Amen.

Additional verses: 1 John 5:14-15, Philippians 4:6 -7, James 5:16, Ephesians 6:18, James 4:3.

Self-reflection: Do you whine your prayers? Do you have a personal relationship with God through prayer? Why do you pray?

Cup Of Suffering

"'Teacher,' they said, 'We want you to do us a favor. When you sit on your glorious throne, we want to sit in places of honor next to you, one on your right and the other on your left.' But Jesus said to them, 'You don't know what you are asking! Are you able to drink from the bitter cup of suffering I am about to drink? Are you able to be baptized with the baptism of suffering I must be baptized with?'" Mark 10:35-38

We begin life's journey with our first cry to survive the oxygen rich planet. We are evicted from the protective womb where we first develop. The trauma of labor expels us out of the warm uterine cozy environment to a detached neonatal hospital crib. Afterwards, we sleep several hours to recover from our first traumatic experience. It confirms C.S. Lewis statement: "We were promised sufferings. They were part of the program. We were even told, 'Blessed are they that mourn.'" We begin life gasping for air; we depart life gasping for air! Birth is suffering, living is suffering, and dying is suffering! Why then, are we so surprised when suffering knocks on our door?

Like birds, we attempt to break out of our painful cages, seeking after every kind of pleasure to avoid the stings of suffering. We seek our desires. If we love money, we work hard to achieve fortunes. If we love success, we work hard to be successful. Our minds are fixated in pleasing sensations. Our energy is placed on fulfilling carnalities. Once achieved what we sought after, we come back dissatisfied by wanting more. Then, we attempt to find happiness in something else. We struggle to build a pain free life, but utterly fail in our conquest for utopia on earth.

When things don't go our way we blame our parents: "I didn't ask to be born!" We blame God for misfortunes when we get old: "Why was I born?" But, if we were born to experience happiness only, then why are we born in pain and die in pain? Why do we suffer?

Though we seek happiness, our days on earth are filled with sorrows and difficulties. We avoid pain and embrace pleasure for that's a fundamental human longing. We seek things which produce a good bodily sensation and fear any kind of displeasure.

Even Jesus wanted to avoid the pain of crucifixion. "He withdrew about a stone's throw and prayed, 'Father, if you are willing, take this cup from me; yet not my will, but yours be done.'" (Luke 22:41-42) However, Jesus didn't shrink from His commitment to die for our sins. He understood the benefits of His suffering on the cross. Instead of saying no to emotional and physical pain, He submitted to God's cup of suffering, and was crucified for us.

The answer to suffering is acceptance that God allows pain for a greater good. Trials produce an ultimate benefit to our souls, just like having a fever. A high temperature causes us to take over the counter drugs to bring the fever down in order to alleviate uncomfortable symptoms. But our bodies don't require over the counter drugs for fever. God designed human bodies to develop fever because it's the immune system's way to fight off infections. Fever medications merely mask the symptoms of the actual illness, and prolong the illness rather than resolve it. Fever, therefore, is the way God designed our bodies to cure infections. Likewise, if we mask problems with pleasures or addictions by not facing the full extent of pain, we only prolong the problems. We don't grow from it, but stunt our souls from developing in Christ. God allows pain to cure us from our sinful nature. The cure for pain, therefore, is to face trials with God's grace by allowing Him to cure our inner lives.

God is not interested in over the counter pain medications to resolve problems. He is only interested in cleansing our souls from impurities. Suffering is His cleansing mechanism to bring about what's hidden in our souls. Suffering is the sandpaper that purifies, transforms, and heals our brokenness.

Suffering stretches our faith in Christ. It deepens our prayer life. It solidifies our love for the Creator. During sorrow, longing for Christ is satisfied because our lives become more abundant as we receive God's beauty.

The key to suffering is meeting pain in God's terms by learning from it. The balm for suffering is leaning on Christ, who bore our sufferings to a path of healing. Through His wounds we are healed and receive a passport to Heaven!

"Have Thine own way, Lord have Thine own way. Thou art the potter, I am the clay. Mold me and make me after Thy will. While I am waiting, yielded and still."-Crystal Lewis

Additional reading: Psalm 22:14-18, 2 Corinthians 5:21, Philippians 1:6, Psalms 105:16-19, Isaiah 53:4-5, Mark 10:32-34, Romans 8:18.

Self-reflection: Are you learning the lessons Jesus teaches you or are you running from pain? Are you ready to take your cross and follow Him? Is your suffering going to waste?

Numb To Pain

"You keep track of all my sorrows. You have collected all my tears in your bottle. You have recorded each one in your book." Psalm 56:8

It was a beautiful hot summer day and my health was still intact. I watched the kids splash and wade in the pool water. I was happy to see them playing with each other. It was a perfect day! Or so I thought...

We headed back home. At night, the routine went on. The kids showered and got ready for bed. I called my parents to check on them. My mom and I talked endlessly as usual. Everything was fine my way; everything was fine their way.

It was my turn to shower. "Ring," Anna handed me the phone. It was my mom again. *"Emilia, daaaddy died,"* my mom sobbed trying to get her words out. Emotionally paralyzed, I felt numb. I shut down my feelings and consoled her. As time went by, I continued to shut down my grief.

I couldn't cry or feel pain. I couldn't grasp the reality that my father died. I heard my mom's words, but I was too stunned to comprehend it. The fact that my father was dead was too much to take in. I dissociated from the reality of his death as numbness took over.

I didn't talk about my disassociation to anyone. I didn't grieve properly, even though I felt devastated. My tears were plugged deep inside my soul. I was not able to lament so I stayed stuck in disbelief. I thought I had to be strong for my kids and mom, so I let feelings engorge through time.

I lost several pounds months after my father's passing. I didn't know what to do with the reality that my father was no longer alive. So, I veiled suffering from everyone and myself. I didn't know how to let it out. I didn't find a shoulder to cry on.

Time went by and numbness began to recede as pain began to swell. Two years after my father's passing, my soul couldn't contain the sadness anymore. I went in the shower and my eyes went from sniffles to sobs. I was finally able to kneeled down on the shower and feel God's embrace. I found God's healing shoulders. God washed my anguish down the drain. The Lord collected all my tears, embraced the pain, and fixed my broken hearted spirit.

Three years after I found God's healing shoulders, I still remembered my mother's tone of voice on the phone: "Emilia, daddy died." I still remembered her sadness and panic. In the first three years after my father's death, I used to think of him almost daily. Suddenly, I began to think of him on occasions. It seemed his life and death was slowly vanishing from my mind. Even if I wanted to hold on to all the memories, my life went on. Or did it?

One day, out of the blue, I thought of dad again. I was angry at myself because his memories were fading from my mind. I was letting go of him as if he was a balloon ascending to the sky. The higher he rose the less I could see him and the farther I sensed him. It was painful but then I thought: "my dad took a piece of me to Heaven!" Suddenly, my eyes were wet with an outburst of emotions. I understood I was just waiting for the glorious day I will see dad again. I will hug him for he is waiting for me in Heaven! God has provided a place of Heavenly family reunion, where laughter will prevail and tears will be no more. As Revelations 21:4 says: "He will wipe every tear from their eyes, and there will be no more death or sorrow or crying or pain. All these things are gone forever."

Part of me is already in Heaven because I'm piece of my dad. But the biggest piece of me in Heaven is Jesus. Although I have not seen Jesus face to face on earth, I'll finally see Him face to face in Heaven. I will see the One who transforms and beautifies my life daily. The One who never disappoints and who is and will always be my best friend!

My Heavenly Homeland waits for me. I will have no more pain, no more sorrow, and no more death. Amen.

Additional reading: Isaiah 25:8, Revelations 21:4, Psalm 9:9, Psalm 18:2, Psalm 22:24, 2 Corinthians 5:8, Philippians 1:21-23.

Self-reflection: Are you longing to hug someone in Heaven? How do you picture your eternal Home?

Ready For Departure

"Very soon your life here will be at an end: look then at the state of your soul. Man is here today and tomorrow he is dead; and when he is out of sight, he is also quickly out of mind. Oh! The blindness and stupidity of a man who thinks only of the present, and forgets to provide for the future. You ought to be as careful in every word and deed as if you were to die that very moment. If you had a good conscience you would not dread death very much. It is better to guard against sin than to try to escape death. If you are not ready today, how will you be ready tomorrow? Tomorrow is an uncertain day. How can you tell whether you will have tomorrow?" -Thomas à Kempis

A person's identity is soon lost upon death. It becomes a "body," hardly retaining a name. People say, "Jack expired" as if Jack was a milk cartoon. Funeral homes plan the arrangement for the "body," such as dressing, casketing, and cosmetizing. Then someone says: "Lower the body into the grave." Then Jack is out of sight, and out of our earthly minds. Jack's corpse becomes null and void. His soul meets the Lord's throne, who judges earthly decisions.

Like everyone else, my earthly identity will also be lost. I'll be a body being lowered into a grave. My tomorrow is a mystery, but if I continue to live as Emilia En L'air, I will live for Christ. When I die, my body will be null and void, but my soul will enter the Heavenly Gates. I no longer fear death, for I know I'll be united with the Lord because God has been the center stage of my life since childhood.

My father, however, was not concerned with Godly things while he was alive. He lived to fulfill worldly desires. He sought things in this world other than seeking God, which led him to constant despair, guilt, and regret.

My father went about life accomplishing his career goals and ambitions. He didn't stop to take account of his soul. He piled up debris of pain and remorse. He catered to his flesh and was careless in regards to having a good conscience before the Lord.

My father's death process was lengthy and agonizing. Every day he thought it would be his last. However, God kept stretching his life of pain in order to soften his heart towards Him. He couldn't breathe well. He exerted every breath with crackling sounds and crunching pain. He suffered much as he approached the end of his life. Nevertheless, God had a purpose to bring dad into His Heavenly Kingdom, and his sufferings ultimately led him to the Lord (see James 1:1-13).

Three years before dad passed away, the Lord squeezed his conscious and shook the pride out of his soul. Out of the blue, he called me at five in the morning: "I'm very sorry, I'm very sorry, forgive me, please forgive me!" he begged me repeatedly while sobbing uncontrollably. My heart also grew soft towards him. I forgave him for the abuse he inflicted on me during childhood. Dad carried guilt for innumerous years. I was quick to forgive dad, for Jesus had already washed his sins.

It has been a blessing to have God in my heart since childhood. I wish it'd been the same for my dad.

Our choices towards God remind me of college deadlines. The teacher assigns a project. Some of us finish the project way ahead of time. Some of us finish on time. Some of us finish a few days later, and some of us give up and flunk the course.

I was fortunate to finish my project way ahead of time by inviting Jesus into my life at a young age. Some people leave it for the last minute. They pile debris of sins, guilt, and regrets which need to be resolve before death come knocking at the door. They repent and Jesus welcomes them into His Kingdom during their last days. Others give up on themselves and rebel against God. They die without Jesus washing their sins away.

Life is temporal. Our days fly by. Why leave the health of our souls for the last minute? Why not provide for our souls with all that God has to offer right now? Why risk dying without God's embrace?

Our earthly life with Jesus is but a rehearsal for our eternal Heavenly Homeland. Our earthly life without Jesus is a waste of pain and suffering, seeking and not finding. Death for these is painful, for they received an invitation from God, but never take time to respond. Will you invite Jesus into your life?

Dear Lord, thank you for preparing a place for me at your Heavenly Homeland. Guide me to your counsel. Lead me to your glorious destiny. Let your Heaven fill my earthly thoughts with longings to be with you. Amen.

Additional reading: Romans 14:10-12, Ephesians 2:8-9, Psalm 13:5, Palm 23:6, Revelations 21:4, Psalm 73:24-26, Colossians 3:1-2.

Self-reflection: When you die, will people talk about your resume or your eulogy? What is the state of your soul? Are you a citizen of Heaven?

Peaceful Departure

"Since you have been raised to new life with Christ, set your sights on the realities of Heaven, where Christ sits in the place of honor at God's right hand. Think about the things of Heaven, not the things of earth." Colossians 3:1-2

"Why would you like to become a nurse?" My nursing instructor, Ms. Karina, asked before assigning me to a patient during hospital clinical. "I'd like to nurture others by combining nursing practice and God's love," I answered enthusiastically. She immediately placed me with the most challenged patient, Helen, who was in the "dying room."

Helen was a Christian elderly patient in palliative care. Her room was set aside from other patients since she embarked in the process of dying. Her eyes were glassy, her blood pressure was dropping, her pulse was either high or low, and her skin color was pasty. Dying was her last experience on earth and she brought uniqueness to her departure.

She was separating slowly from her physical body. She withdrew from the world. She had one foot on earth, and the other in Heaven.

It would seem like a gloomy experience but every time I entered the "death room," I was enveloped in a cloud of Heavenly peace. Jesus had stepped in the scene and angels were flying around her. Helen's venture towards death brought a sublime contagious beauty. I could tell she'd walked with Jesus all her life. She was not shaken or afraid. Her body was resting in God's safety. She was ready to receive her Heavenly inheritance.

Helen's family gathered around her. There was a sense of love and admiration about every aspect of her life. They didn't seem to be mourning. It looked like they were rejoicing because she was going to see Jesus in Heaven.

Helen was an example of peace and strength during dying moments. She portrayed death as a welcome visitor. Finally, she inhaled one last long breath, and her soul departed into the arms of Jesus.

Helen's journey to the afterlife was beautiful because her soul was ready and purified to join the Lord. It seemed by her families' stories and calmness that she dedicated her days to meet the Lord. However, most people are not ready for death, even though it is the most certain thing that will happen in life. People die every second, yet they take life as a never ending story.

Many people are only concerned about the securities of this planet. Each passing day becomes a relentless quest to fulfill voids that exists in their lives. Some seek financial security and everything this planet is able to provide. Others stumbled on different things as they voyage throughout life by worshiping their physical appearance, pleasures, and status. They are too busy or too proud to seek God. Some think He doesn't exist.

On their quest for fulfillment, people unavoidably get broken and seek alternatives to get fixed in order to obtain a happy existence in this world. They don't try to get fixed for the next life. They think they are home, but this planet is not home! It's just a passing place.

People don't realize every brokenness they go through is intended for the sole purpose to bring them to the arms of God. Everything in this existence is about polishing souls to see Christ. God has a reason for everything because He is not interested in emptiness. No event escapes His hands. Neither the smiles, nor the tears. Neither the pains, nor the delights.

People's blind irresolution towards God causes their mind to think the eternal home is a non-existent matter. Some say: "Life is not supposed to be a preparation for death. It's morbid to spend life preparing for death." They take refuge in earthly desires. But eventually terror invades their souls when death comes to meet the Maker. Then they ask: "Is it going to be painful? I'm afraid of the unknown! Is there an afterlife? I'm afraid of being punished. I fear loss of control when I die." Death for them is a formidable enemy. But God placed us in this world to live and to die as well. Why not invite Jesus to be the indweller of our souls?

Like Helen, I have been preparing for my eternal home since I was a teenager. Death will be a welcome visitor. Jesus will carry me in His arms toward the light of Heaven. He will pour His most unconditional pure love on me. I'll be immersed in His complete embrace. His light will fill my soul with His presence.

My Eternal Father, thank you because this world is a rehearsal for Paradise. You point my desires towards Heaven. My future home fills my thoughts. Amen.

Additional reading: Revelation 21:1-4, Colossians 3:1-2, Philippians 3:20-21, John 14:6, John 3:16, John 3:36, Acts 4:12, Psalm 10:3-4.

Self-reflection: Are you ready to die right now if God summons you? Have you invited Jesus into your life? Has this life increased your desire to move into your Heavenly homeland?

Doll Face Is Now In Heaven

"If we endure hardship, we will reign with Him..." 2 Timothy 2:12

During my late teens, mom had a friend named Guina. Her husband, nicked named her Boneca, which means doll in Portuguese, because she looked sweet and delicate. Boneca had given her life to Christ and attended our small church in Los Angeles.

Boneca began losing weight. She felt fatigue and had stomach pain. She didn't seek medical attention at first, thinking her ailment was indigestion. Months later she made an appointment at a clinic. Endoscopy and CT scan revealed the frightening and overwhelming diagnosis of stage III adenocarcinoma.

Boneca's life changed once she heard the doctor's "bad news," by saying the word "cancer." She cried and began to shake. At that moment, a path of arduous hardships entered her life. She experienced problems related to pain due to cancer as well as chemotherapy and radiation.

Boneca lost her beautiful glow, hair, and doll face. She no longer recognized her reflection in the mirror. Her body was transformed into a deformed image of what it used to be. As a consequence, she lost the support and love of her husband who sought other women while she lay in a hospital bed. Her children were busy with friends. Everyone seemed to leave Boneca during her darkness moments. But God and my mom remained.

Mom and I visited Boneca at the hospital almost every day. She was fighting her last fight. Cancer was winning over Boneca's body and claiming her life slowly. We prayed for healing, but Jesus didn't remove the cancer. However, He gave her strength to go through suffering. She knew that by enduring cancer, she would receive the crown of glory in Heaven. Her family slowly abandoned her but Jesus upheld her. Suffering was her path to Heaven. Guina traded her doll face for Jesus embrace.

On a sunny Sunday we visited Boneca once again at the hospital after church service. That day, she seemed to be more energized. She was having a good day and we thought she'd have more days ahead of her. We returned home. I went to bed and fell into a deep stage of sleep. It was during such moment that Boneca visited me during a beautiful lucid dream. She said goodbye to me because she was going to Heaven. Her presence was so overwhelming in my dream, that once I woke up, I asked mom to call the hospital to see how she was doing. "Guina passed away last night, I'm very sorry," the nurse said to my mom on the phone.

Guina had gone to see the Father. Her earthly body was left behind. Her damaged skin, weight and hair loss did not go to Heaven. She waved cancer goodbye. She received an improved model of her old sick body. God gave her a brand new doll Boneca face.

"Do you believe?" That is what Jesus asked Martha in the Bible. "Jesus told her, 'Your brother will rise again.' 'Yes,' Martha said, 'he will rise when everyone else rises, at the last day.' Jesus told her, 'I am the resurrection and the life. Anyone who believes in me will live, even after dying. Everyone who lives in me and believes in me will never ever die. Do you believe this, Martha?'" (John 11:23-26)

Do you believe you will rise like Martha's brother and Boneca? Do you believe Jesus is the resurrection and the life? Our pain and suffering prepare us to meet Jesus face to face. In Heaven we will have a first class body immune from suffering. It will be a place with no more pain, just gain. Our weak mortal bodies will change into a glorious body like Jesus (see Philippians 3:20-21).

Heaven is a mystery, but the Lord promises that, "No eye has seen, no ear has heard, and no mind has imagined what God has prepared for those who love him." (1 Corinthians 2:9) It's going to be a wonderful surprise! We will be with Jesus! We'll see those we long to see. We'll have improved bodies. We'll be eternally at peace. All our hungers will be satisfied. It will be our ultimate everlasting reality. Do you long for Heaven?

Resurrected Jesus, your resurrection is real and my only hope. To live is gain, and to die is gain as long as I'm with you and you are with me. Let my life on earth be a path to a life in Heaven! Halleluiah, I worship you, Christ, my King. Amen!

Additional reading: 1 Corinthians 15:52-53, Mathew 13:43, John 11:25, 1 Thessalonian 4:14, John 6:40, Acts 24:15.

Self-reflection: Would you make Heaven your future home?

The Kingdom Of Shades

"A time to cry and a time to laugh. A time to grieve and a time to dance." Ecclesiastes 3:4

I danced classical ballet for several years wrapped in my bubble world. The more I danced, the closer I felt to God's embrace. But the pressure towards technical precision was a road of sweet sorrows. In order to continue to exist in the dance world, I devoted hours of daily training to have graceful and precise movements. I became movement; I became the character in the ballet. Dance demanded emotional sacrifices. Training was a challenge of inner tenacity to achieve what's humanly impossible- perfection.

Ballet was my sacred magical world. Dancing toe shoes brought fantasies alive of an ethereal world. All inner emotions were relieved by light, music, and movement. Dance colored my soul with purity. Every musical note penetrated in me as I danced ballet fairy tales of love and loss, desire and death. It was a way to express my story of pain in its deepest core and feel close to God at the same time.

My days were filled with pointe work, turn-outs, and high extensions. Dance was my body's song: sacred and celestial. Performing masked pain with beauty by communicating what was deep inside me. During teenage years, dance consumed my every hour.

La Bayadere was my favorite ballet. A story of eternal love set in the past Royal India. The second act is called the "Kingdom of the Shades." Nikiya, a temple dancer, choses death over life without her beloved Solor. She dances as a spirit, in a nirvana on the peaks of the Himalayas. On top of the mountains, she reconciles with Solor, her beloved, and they are reunited and spirited off towards heaven. I was enchanted by the story. There was a part of me that wanted to be Nikiya and experience a heavenly world without pain. I wanted to dance towards Heaven, for I thought the world outside my bubble was corrupt and sad.

I never danced the role of Nikiya, for I had to stop dancing ballet during my early twenties. I felt a loss of identity and was devastated for having my dream collapse. Never again people stop to ask, "Are you a ballerina?" I bid God to help me be a prima ballerina. I wanted to be the best dancer and live the role of Swan Lake, with its blissful movements. I wanted to be Aurora, living the magical myth and fairy tale. I expected God to fulfill my wishes for ballet perfection. But He closed the door of dance without fulfilling my desires. Yes, my desires!

"God give me what I want!" I cried out to Him. I was chasing my desire to be a principal dancer, and wanted God to bless it. Determination and sweat had a pitfall. I lived in a state of anxiety. I couldn't maintain a balance. I couldn't be happy unless I had what I wanted. I wanted future happiness and dismissed enjoying my present moment. I thought I would only find joy once at the top of the dance career. It was an *ad infinitum*. A never ending chase for the completion of my desires.

I grew to realize my desire for perfection in dance was like being dehydrated from God's desires for me. It was running after a fata morgana, the mirage of an oasis in the desert. The chase to fulfill cravings ran my life. God's will took a back seat. I was living in the agony of my wishes and wanted God to bless it.

I read in Psalms 37:4, "Take delight in the Lord, and He will give you your heart's desires." I delighted myself in Him, and expected God to be the genie in the lamp by granting my wishes. But, He didn't grant my wishes and I was devastated. Dance was slashed and cut out of my life. I spent months in self-pity. I didn't want to watch or hear anything related to Ballet anymore. I got rid of everything that reminded me of it. I wanted all or nothing. And, I got nothing!

My understanding of Psalm 37:4 changed once I understood Psalm 145:19 (GNT): "He supplies the needs of those who honor Him; He hears their cries and saves them." I realized my wishes were cut and slashed because I wasn't glorifying or honoring God through dance. Instead, I was glorifying self-centeredness. Taking delight in the Lord was a way to use the gifts He gave me to honor His name, not my name. God wanted me to be attached to Him and not the gift of dancing. He didn't want me to worship my talents. He wanted me to worship Him through my talents.

Did I waste my time practicing, rehearsing, and performing ballet? Absolutely not! God allowed everything to bring me closer to Him. Nothing was wasted. Every good thing, every hardship, was a given opportunity to be closer to the throne of God. "Every good and perfect gift is from above, coming down from the Father of the heavenly lights, who does not change like shifting shadows." (James 1:17)

I learned to see things through the eyes of God. I had set my mind in being a principal dancer because I thought it would be my ultimate happiness and refused to open my eyes to God's better plan. I learned that happiness is not found in dancing, work, or having fun. Happiness is found in being in the center of God's will. Today I only dance in my heart, but I know that one day, I'll dance in Heaven, not as Nikiya, but Emilia En L'air. Then, I will be forever with God in His Kingdom of Shades.

Your Kingdom of Shades offers the key to complete happiness. It's a shelter for all those who love you! It's a home of eternal bliss and absence of every sorrow. It's the culmination of all dreams! Thank you for giving me a future home full of hope. Amen.

Additional reading: 1 Corinthians 15:19, 2 Corinthians 4:16-18, Psalm 27:4-5, John 4:13-14, Hebrews 11:1.

Self-reflection: Do you have hopes for this life only, or do you have hopes for life after death? Do you lose heart when you lose your dreams? How do you cope with it?

Ephemeral Life

"For you have been born again, but not to a life that will quickly end. Your new life will last forever because it comes from the eternal, living word of God. As the Scripture say, 'People are like grass; their beauty is like a flower in the field. The grass withers and the flower fades. But the word of the Lord remains forever.'" 1 Peter 1:23-25

Have you noticed anything puzzling about time? Time puzzles me. When I was a child, time went by slowly. I was on turtle time! I was in a hurry to grow up and be independent. A day seemed like a week. A month seemed like an eternity. School would never end. It was torture! I used to check my watch dozens of times. The seasons seemed to be on paralyses.

Nowadays my time is no longer paralyzed. My turtle time became turbo time. A day seems like half a day. A month goes by in a blink of an eye. I wake up and it's already time to go to sleep. It's obvious I was born to a mortal life that will quickly end.

Life quickly ends because humans are like flowers, as written in 1 Peter 1:25. It reminds me of beautiful Japanese cherry blossoms, called Sakura. Their blossoms symbolize life as ephemeral. The flowers of the trees have a short-lived nature. They quickly blossom to an intense beauty and quickly wither away. Their nature illustrates mortality.

In the East Coast, I observed Sakura trees for seven seasons. It was the scenery on the other side of my window. Every year they opened the curtain to spring. Their light flickered with each little white pedal. They blossomed like white snowflakes. Temperature and humidity harmonized their wake. Blossoms scattered their pollen to pollinators. Suddenly, the ocean wind would shake and twist the Sakura branches. Almost at once, pedals would die, falling onto graveyards under naked Sakura trees.

The pedals of Sakura trees have a short time to pollinate. The blossoms waste no time because earth depends on its pollen. Why do we think we are any different than cherry blossoms? Why do we think we have time to waste? We are born and then our lives quickly fade away. We tend to misuse time thinking we will never turn gray. We place every desire ahead of God's. We seek perishable things, and put our hearts on temporary things. We fulfill the longings of the flesh. We don't realize our lives pass swiftly like blossoms.

Why are we born? For self-seeking pleasures? For living paycheck to paycheck? Are we not like flowers that will wither away? What if we were born for more than shelter, food, and sexual intimacy? What if we were born to have a purposeful life that will never end?

Scripture says we were born to a short lived life. The better life is the one that will never end if we make Jesus the Lord of our lives. This mortal life is just a preparation for what lies ahead. The best is yet to come!

We can choose to live for the now, by making this our only life. Or we can make choices to live for the future and eternal life.

I don't want to waste my time with perishable things that first bring pleasure and then grievous remorse. I wish to be a pure white blossom pedal for Christ's sake. I want to pollinate God's Word and echo His love to others. I don't wish to wither away in a graveyard of grey regrets under the graveyard of my own Sakura tree. I want to live for Christ in this life and be eternally with Him in the next.

Eternal Lord of life, I do not fear death for it will be a perfect white blossom. I offer my fleeing existence on earth to you. Mold me into your likeness. You give meaning to my fragile life. Make me a pure white pedal because I love you and wish to be in your company forevermore. Amen.

Additional reading: Deuteronomy 30:19-20, Proverbs 14:27, Proverbs 18:21, Romans 5:10, John 3:16, John 3:36, Romans 6:23, Matthew 10:28, Revelations 14:11.

Self-reflection: Your sufferings on Earth are like a splatter of eternal damnation, like a sample size of eternal torture. Can you imagine having torment for eternity? Would you make Jesus your refuge and have eternal life with Him?

Emergency Landing

> "Then, when our dying bodies have been transformed
> into bodies that will never die, this Scripture will be
> fulfilled: 'Death is swallowed up in victory. O death,
> where is your victory? O death, where is your sting?'"
> 1 Corinthians 15:54-55

The commercial jumbo jet took off from Rio de Janeiro to Paris. My
mom, brother, and I sat together in the aircraft. My father was the captain
of the airplane. Flight attendants demonstrated safety and emergency
procedures. The airplane was gaining altitude as it climbed up to a
twenty two degree angle. We were strapped in and reaching a probable
ten thousand feet altitude.

Suddenly the airplane shook and made loud noises. I noticed the
plane stopped gaining altitude. I asked my mom nervously, "Why is
the airplane not going up anymore? Why is it shaking so much?" My
father informed the passengers we were heading back to Rio de Janeiro
for an emergency landing. The door had a malfunction which caused
depressurization.

I was terrified of dying as the emergency descent began. My mom
said that everything was going to be fine. But I knew she was just trying
to calm me down. I looked at the passengers' faces. They had widened
eyes filled with terror.

In my panic, I closed my eyes and drew close to God. I waited for
His peace. I've noticed I wasn't afraid of dying, but how it was going
to happen. "Were we going to explode? Were we going to catch on
fire? Was it going to happen in midair or during landing?" I began

overthinking because I was afraid of having physical pain more than death itself.

I knew God had prepared a place in Heaven for me and my family (see John 14:12). I began letting Jesus calm down all my fears and soothe my thoughts. Gradually, He replaced panic with a calm assurance that He was in control of the emergency.

During the scary landing, my soul was lined up with God's will. Fear of death and physical pain was relieved by submission to God's plans. If I'd died it would have been fine, as long as I was with Christ.

"Ready for landing," my father informed the passengers from the cockpit. I closed my eyes and a blast of inner bliss from the Lord rushed inside me. I received such vast inner peace that made me crave for that terrorizing moment to last forever. God gave me a foretaste of eternal peace. He answered prayers and calmed my fears through a heavenly mist of special grace.

The passengers clapped as the pilots landed the plane safely. My young life, my families', and everyone's in the airplane continued that day. Yet, I changed. The events of that flight will always live with me. Not because of the drama of the airplanes' depressurization, but because of the glimpse of perfect Heavenly peace I received during my time of trouble and fear.

Peaceful Jesus, your presence lives in me during my deepest darkness moments. You transform fear into peace. Death never stings with you by my side. Thank you for bringing victory to trials, for I tested your promises in the Bible. I believe it. I experienced it. I count on it. Amen.

Additional reading: Isaiah 26:3-4, Romans 8:6, Psalm 29:11, Colossians 3:15, Philippians 4:6-7, John 16:33, John 14:27.

Self-reflection: Have you experienced Jesus' peace during the darkest moments of your life? God holds your hands during your scariest moments. Have you invited His hands upon your hands?

Game Over

"The day of death is better than the day of birth."
Ecclesiastes 7:1

Life is like a video game. In order to advance to the next level of spiritual growth, you need to play a quest. Advancement is only achieved once the quest is completed. There are many quests, and to win a game all levels need to be concluded. The game is won after successful completion of all levels. The end of the game is a successful achievement for gamers, as the end of the "spiritual game" is a fruitful eternal achievement for Christians.

The video game of my life began at time of conception. Every birthday mom tells me the story of my birth: "I had to go through excruciating pain. The labor lasted for ten hours. You were finally born, but the doctor had to use forceps!" My first cry expanded my lungs and I began life outside the womb.

Obviously, I don't remember the birth, but I know my life's first test was passing through mom's small pelvic with a pair of tongs maneuvering my skull in order to be born into our oxygen rich planet.

The next level of my life's game was at age three. The tip of one of my fingers got chopped. I was having a temper tantrum and lashed out by opening and closing the front door of the house. I slammed the door as hard as possible until suddenly the tip of my finger got caught and slashed out. Blood gushed all over. It was the first time I felt broken hearted because my grandmother laughed at my misfortune. My three year old mind had to make a choice to either continue to love and accept her or despise and reject her. It was a difficult level for my young life because she disappointed me. And, a test that eventually I had to pass in order to keep growing spiritually.

My life's tribulations are not a virtual game which comes with bows and arrows, lances and physical strength behind a computer screen. My trials are spiritual life games which come with many tests. My life's spiritual weapons consists of wearing the full armor of God, so I can stand ground against life's adversaries and stand firm. It consists of wearing a belt of truth and a breastplate of righteousness with shoes fitted to promote God's peace. It consists of wearing the helmet of salvation and the Spirit's sword, which is the Gospel. All my life's trials are seasoned with submission to God's will. All my life's trials began at the foot of the cross and will end with my eternal inheritance with Jesus (see 1 Timothy 6:12).

The "game over" of my life will occur once I depart to my Heavenly Homeland. By faith, I know that my death day will be better than my birthday, because my game of life has been fought with God's weapons. I'll enter Heaven with no more games, just gain.

My death day will be my eternal birthday!

EL-OLAM, you are my Everlasting God. I surrender the game of my life to you. Help me to fight the good fight of faith and pass the tests you have set before me. May I be pleasing to you. I praise you for giving me life. My story will end on earth and will begin again in Paradise. Amen.

Additional reading: Ephesians 6:10-17, Isaiah 64:8, Psalm 66:8-12, 1 Corinthians 10:13, Job 23:10, Romans 10:9, James 4:7.

Self-reflection: Are the negative events of your life keeping you from putting on the helmet of salvation? How does Ephesians 6:10-17 translate to your everyday life?

Lethal Injection, Electrocution, Or Hanging

"Two others, both criminals, were led out to be executed with Him (Jesus). When they came to a place called The Skull, they nailed Him to the cross. And the criminals were also crucified—one on His right and one on His left. Jesus said, 'Father, forgive them, for they don't know what they are doing.'... One of the criminals hanging beside Him scoffed, 'So you're the Messiah, are you? Prove it by saving yourself—and us, too, while you're at it!' But the other criminal protested, 'Don't you fear God even when you have been sentenced to die? We deserve to die for our crimes, but this man hasn't done anything wrong.' Then he said, 'Jesus, remember me when you come into your Kingdom.' And Jesus replied, 'I assure you, today you will be with me in paradise.'"
Luke 23:32-34, 39-43

I wrote a college essay regarding the pros and cons of death penalty in the United States. My research was based on political, ethical, and economical issues. It was tough to conclude if it was right or wrong to execute criminals based on National Polls and studies. My lack of conclusion was due to our society's constant flux of viewpoints. Taboos are constantly changing and our world has no fixed moral standards.

This week capital punishment was brought up by the media, which made me ponder if Christians should fight to abolish death penalty.

Should we rally outside City Halls and prisons in order to put a stop to cruel and unusual punishments? What is our role regarding executions?

Jesus instructions are solid and constant: "Love your enemies!" Jesus has practical peaceful answers to death penalty. His followers should act with compassion. Christians should ask the State to spare someone's life. But first, as representatives of Jesus, Christians should reach out to their souls, and then fight for the survival of those being executed. Finally, we should pray for the hearts of those who are condoning executions so they can learn to practice love towards enemies.

Jesus doctrine is to love our neighbor as we love ourselves (see Mark 12:28-31). That makes serial killers on the death row -our neighbors! Jesus loves them just as much as He loves new born babies. Jesus loves without preferential treatment. And He calls us to love one another without preferential treatment.

Jesus is also clear regarding forgiving others as He forgives us (see Colossians 3:13). Jesus offers forgiveness to death row inmates; therefore, we should forgive them just the same, instead of advocating for the legalization of the lethal injection, electrocution, or hanging. Forgiveness gives freedom to the worst kinds of chains: the chains of the soul, which are confined by anger and hatred. Forgiveness is a healing balm to the hearts' wounds. Forgiveness reaches Heaven's gates!

Jesus would not send an inmate to death row because He loved His enemies, and didn't come to punish criminals by cruel inhumane deaths. But at the same time He didn't get involved with the Mosaic Law. That's because His priority was to save souls, not so much save physical bodies. Since Jesus was a pacifist, His work was to prepare people for eternal life.

At times, instead of imitating Jesus, we tend to get entangled with social standards and neglect to follow Jesus' practices. We make excuses and sway into society's standards instead of Jesus' teachings. We should follow Christ's teachings even when there's no comfortable way to love our enemies. We need to get out of our comfort zone, because we are call to do it, and can't ignore Jesus' preaching. We can't neglect to love people that need us the most.

When Jesus was sentence to death penalty, a place called The Skull, He gave His life to our lost sinful souls. Jesus crucifixion also atoned for the sins of the worst of criminals.

God sent Jesus as a template for us to imitate His footsteps. His actions on the cross in relation to the two criminals demonstrated how to rally regarding death penalty. Jesus expressed love and forgiveness towards them. However, He didn't set them free from death penalty. Jesus changed water into wine, healed the sick, raised the dead, fed five thousand people, walked on water, and more. However, Jesus' miracles excluded sending the two criminals back to their cells. They were both executed. Jesus did not fight against the State, even though He was against violence. At that moment, during the crucifixion, He fought for the soul of the criminal next to Him. Jesus was pro-soul, by saving others from eternal damnation. Jesus fought for love, forgiveness, and giving us a place in paradise.

As imitators of Christ, our biggest concern should be to visit inmates on death row, and act as Jesus acted. We should present the Gospel of eternal life. If we're able to rally against capital punishment, then let it be so. Nevertheless, our greatest concern in the end shouldn't be to rally against how they die, but with Whom they die.

Today, our State prisons are the place of The Skull, our Golgotha. We don't find skulls lying around after hangings, such as during Jesus' time. Yet unnecessary cruelty still goes on. This leaves Christians with the job of advocating and praying for the souls of death row inmates.

Everything in the life of a Christian should be based on Jesus and not societies' rules. Jesus made statements of love by how He lived, which was against everything that was going on during His time. He showed love in a violent world. He showed forgiveness in a vengeful world. Now, we are His footsteps.

Forgiving Jesus, before I rally, before I make a statement, I ask you, what would you do? Let my thoughts be your thoughts; let my footsteps be your footsteps. Let me be in the center of your will so I may rally for what is worth rallying. Let me waste no time in cultural values. For your values are my values. Let your time, be my time. Amen.

Additional readings: Matthew 5:18-19, Luke 16:17, Mathew 5:38-39, Matthew 26:51-52, Romans 13:1-5, Acts 6:8, Mark 14:62.

Self-reflection: John 8:3-8:11 describe an adulteress scheduled for stoning. Jesus told the executioners, "He that is without sin among you, let him first cast a stone at her." These verses illustrate Jesus' opposition towards death penalty. Matthew 5:21-22 describes Jesus opposing killing. However, He doesn't seem to oppose the Mosaic Law. How do you respond to capital punishment?

Sister Wives

"Then the word of the Lord came to Isaiah: "Go and tell
Hezekiah, 'this is what the Lord, the God of your father
David, says: I have heard your prayer and seen your
tears; I will add fifteen years to your life' 'You restored
me to health and let me live. Surely it was for my benefit
that I suffered such anguish.'" Isaiah 38:4-5, 16-17 NIV

My children and I visited a church in Delaware. We attended the service
and hoped to be welcomed in the house of God. At the end of the service
the pastor came to greet us. "Where's the children's father?" he asked
me inquisitively. "*Hum, umm*, he is out of the picture," I said nervously.
"Are you divorced?" he looked at me with a condemning expression.
He immediately started preaching to me that divorce was not part of
God's plan.

I grabbed my children's hands and with a distressed heart, headed
back home. The pastor barely knew my name. He didn't know anything
about the story of my divorce, but he decided in his heart that I was
an unwelcomed sinful guest. I wished the church had a poster outside
written, "Single struggling moms, keep out!" then my children wouldn't
have to experience the sting of rejection. I was not accepted. My kids
were discarded. Case closed.

After that bitter experience, church for a while, was in our home
with just my kids and me, where I knew God loved us with open arms.

Nevertheless, not all churches react rashly towards divorcees. Some
churches open their hearts to everyone, others seem to lose step with
the love teachings of Jesus. The fact is that every single mother has a
unique story. My story is unique, but so was Diana's.

Diana was left behind by her husband, who suddenly disappeared leaving his two daughters behind. She became a single parent, left to fulfill the role of being mom and dad. The husband found another woman, in another town, in another state, and started his love life from scratch, pretending his past never happened. This new woman was- my mother.

My father kept his first marriage a secret. When mom found out about my father's past in regards to Diana's existence, she forgave him. She was also able to soften his hard heart in order to bring Diana and his daughters back in the picture of our lives.

I was seven years old when I found out I had two half-sisters. I was shocked and confused. One was already a teenager, with long beautiful hair. The other was permanently handicapped. A year after my half-sisters visited our home, my parents took my brother and me to a faraway place where his first family lived. I met Diana. She was a simple woman, with a kindred heart.

Four years went by, and our lives took a sudden change. "I trust you like a sister, Linde! My oncologist done everything he could. There're no more treatments in my hometown. My doctor gave me six more months... I need your help!" Diana said to my mom on the phone. "It can't be the end, and I won't give up on you," my mom encouraged her. Following that phone call, mom found the best oncologist near our home. One week later, Diana packed her suitcases and either stayed at our home, or in the hospital for surgical and chemotherapy procedures.

Diana groaned in pain at my parents' guest room. "Let her rest, Emilia," mom told me with concerned eyes as she nursed Diana's recovery from chemotherapy. I was observant of everything that went on in our home. My small ten year old feet walked quietly not to disturb our guest. I knew the circumstances of our family were extraordinary in comparison to the usual household. I was trying to understand the new dynamic of our family.

Mom called us for dinner. My father and mother sat at opposite ends of the table. On the right of dad, sat my brother and one half-sister. I sat on the left of dad, with the oldest half-sister. On the right of mom, sat Diana. And, for a few months, we were a peculiar household, not by ties of marital certificates, but by ties of love and compassion.

Diana lived four more years much thanks to mom's persistent caregiving. I was blessed to witness the interaction between my father's first wife and mom. The usual dynamic of a new wife could have been to remove the ex-wife from the family dynamic by passive aggressiveness, but mom was able to foster love for the sake of Diana's health condition. My mom built a healthier life for the entire family including my father. It was nothing short from extraordinary to see love flourishing from painful beginnings.

Diana used to be my father's discarded wife. He got tired of her and wanted to begin his life anew. But once mom found out about the conditions in which she was left behind, she brought her into our lives not as a cast away left to die, but a guest of honor, who was offered support, dignity, and a kindred heart.

Mom's devotion to Diana brought to mind the Biblical interaction between Hagar, mother of Ishmael, and Sarah, mother of Isaac. Sarah couldn't bear children due to her advance age and used her maid Hagar to be impregnated by Abraham. After Sarah was able to conceive Isaac, Hagar became an inconvenient competitor for Sarah. Consequently, Sarah decided to get rid of her. Sarah and Abraham sent Hagar away into the desert with her son Ishmael. It seems that Hagar would be bitter against life, but God assured her that He had a special plan for Ismael. We know through history that God fulfilled His promise because the Arab nations are descendants of Ishmael. Meanwhile, Isaac became the descendant of Israel. Up to this day we experience the consequences of the contention between Sarah and the slave Hagar. It seems to be one of the original reasons for the Arab-Israeli conflict.

Sarah's decision still affects our world today. Sarah was not able to display a mature role and function as a team with Abraham, Hagar, and the children to further the health of the family's dynamic. Sarah felt threatened by Hagar. Sarah's inability to solve the emotional discord led the descendants of Isaac and descendants of Ismael to be antagonistic towards each other.

Diana and mom became like a sister wife, and a sister ex-wife, not by sharing a husband, but by prioritizing love over discord. What if Sarah and Hagar had opted to become peaceful allies? Would Arab-Israeli conflict have fewer tensions?

JEHOVAH-SHALOM, you are the Lord of peace. You instituted the covenant of marriage, but when divorce befalls, help us to be joined by your blood. May blended families love each other through your wisdom. May separate homes be rebuilt by a warm new haven of safety where you are the center piece. Amen.

Additional reading: Genesis 11:27-31, Genesis 17:15-19, Hebrews 11:11-12, Genesis 16:15, Genesis 21:10, Genesis 21:14, Genesis 41:14, Judges 6:24.

Self-reflection: Sarah was a woman of great faith because she trusted God to give her a child against the fact that she was already advance in age. But at the same time, do you see Sarah going ahead of God's will by finding an alternative solution to give Abraham an heir by proxy? How do you express your love towards blended families, single-parents, and divorcees?

Vision

"Faith is the confidence that what we hope for will actually happen; it gives us assurance about things we cannot see." Hebrews 11:1

I traveled many times since I was a child. It came with the package of having a father who was an international airline pilot. I was six years old when I first flew with him. He was the captain flying from Rio de Janeiro to Los Angeles, stopping in Anchorage, with final stop in Tokyo.

My father called me to the cockpit right before the plane began to approach Ted Stevens International Airport in Anchorage. I sat at the third occupant seat of the cockpit, and gazed my young eyes at the glacier icy waters of the Gulf of Alaska. On the other side of the cockpit's window, the tidewater glaciers were breathtaking. Inexplicably, in a split of a second, I knew Alaska was my future home. God gave me a subtle vision of events that were to come in the future. God touched me with an "aha" moment. That little second never left my mind, even though it seemed like a preposterous thought, because I was a six year old child living in Brazil, knowing little about geography and life.

Since that "aha" moment, I moved twenty-eight times. I encompassed the globe. God led me to other places, but I knew Alaska was still my "aha home." It was a place I had to take my family, and knew God had a reason for it.

God's vision remained in the time capsule of my heart, even though everything pointed out I was going to die while I lived in the East Coast. Was I ever sure if I would survive my illness or wake up the next day? Not at all! My strength was sucked by illness. Moving from the bedroom to the living room was great effort. Moving to Alaska seemed like an outrageous preposterous thought due to my poor health. On top of the health problem, I lived from month to month. I had just enough money to cover daily needs. I had no back up financial plan. Moving six feet under seemed the most plausible real state relocation at the time.

Alaska was a faraway place from where I was living. A distance of four thousand miles was definitely a lot greater than moving to an adjacent neighborhood. I had neither family nor friends in Alaska. My life seemed to be ending but God's vision was still ringing in my ears, which deepened my faith in Him. I began to rely on God's miracles. Only God could make the impossible, possible. I needed only one ingredient- faith!

I realized I'd to let go of my physical security such as home, finances, medical care, and jump on God's wings to Alaska. I started to let go of my attachments in the East Coast and placed my faith in a new future in Alaska. I had to make a choice to either trust God or trust my basic commodities where I was living. I couldn't have both, for that would have been faith with a backup plan. I had to trust God by having confidence on that which I could not see.

God stretched my confidence to consider His vision something concrete and reliable. I knew He would work through the impossibilities by fulfilling that which He planted in my soul. I hoped in spite of my hopeless situation, because I didn't consider how bad circumstances were, I considered that God was bigger than my circumstances.

The outward appearances of my life made it seem impossible that anything good could ever happen again. It seemed my life was about to end, but by faith I believed it was going to begin again. It was improbable I would ever be able to move to Alaska, but God's vision told me otherwise. By faith I knew what He whispered in my ears, He would bring to pass (see Psalm 37:5).

Designer of my life, I'm absolutely convinced you deliver what you promised. You are aware of earthly impossibilities, but you are bountiful and generous, whispering secrets in my ears. You resurrect my broken bones into a future home by your miraculous hands. Amen.

Emilia En L'air

Additional Reading: Romans 5:14, 2 Corinthians 2:14, Romans 4:18-21, 2 Timothy 3:16-17, Proverbs 3:5, Ephesians 2:8, 2 Corinthians 5:7, Hebrews 11:6, Philippians 4:13.

Self-reflection: When God whispers in your ears, do you have faith that He is speaking to you? Do you trust in Him or do you lean on your own understanding? Do you believe God wants to perform miracles in your life?

Don't Wait For All Circumstances To Be Right

"One day Terah took his son Abram, his daughter-in-law Sarai, and his grandson Lot and moved away from Ur of the Chaldeans. He was headed for the land Canaan, but they stopped at Haran and settled there. Terah lived for 205 years and died while still in Haran." Genesis 11:31-32

I was seen by a geneticist at Johns Lougheed outpatient center. The doctor was attentive to my health needs and took many notes in order to find a correct diagnosis. He said he'd send a sample of my muscle biopsy to a laboratory in Texas for a mitochondrial evaluation, and would call me within two weeks with the test results.

I left the consultation hopeful, thinking my mystery diagnosis would be revealed. I had barely made it alive through last summer and anticipated that within days I would have a treatment at hand which would improve my health.

Weeks went by and I didn't hear from the doctor. I waited patiently with hopes up, but the doctor didn't call back with the results. Finally, I decided to call him but the medical assistant said he was busy. Then I waited two more weeks for him to return my call. "Your muscle tissue was not sent to the lab yet, but we will send it next week," he said it as if I was a number in a butcher's shop. All my hopes sunk. I knew the doctor didn't care if I lived or died. He had also told me cases like mine were difficult to diagnose. I felt he gave up on me without even helping me.

Meanwhile, my medical chart collected dust as my health deteriorated. I'd lay awake at night resenting the geneticists' incompetence and lack of empathy. I noticed my thoughts were being wasted in anger. I had to forgive the doctor and place my trust in the Great Physician Jesus.

I was placing my hope on doctors, tests results, and treatments, in order to move to Alaska feeling healthier. However, God showed me the focal point of my hope was misplaced. My hope needed to be focus solely on the mercy of God, the deliverer of distress and sorrow.

The Lord spoke to me as I read Genesis 11. Just as Terah, Abram's father, settled and died in Haran, I would die if I settled in the East Coast. God gave me a vision of Alaska as my promised home, just as He gave Terah a vision of Canaan as the promised home. But Terah decided to settle in Haran and never reached the promised home of Canaan. Terah's son, Abram, was the one who reached Canaan and therefore was able to see God's promise to fruition.

I had to make a decision to move to Alaska by faith, or settle in the East Coast and die. And, I decided to crawl, roll, or move at a snail's pace. I was not going to settle for anything less than what God had promised me. Giving up was not an option. I armed myself with God's courage and disposed of fears.

Placing faith on doctors was like navigating in worldly hopeless waters, but I found a new divine hope in the Lord. I gathered my children: "Guess what? We are moving to Alaska in six months!" I don't know why I told them six months, but my word became a declaration that something was going to be done. They had a smile from ear to ear. Anna said: "Can we start packing today?"

It was April of 2011. Powered by faith, God began guiding us to our new hope, in a new unforeseen land. Meanwhile, the last piece of muscle tissue was still frozen in liquid nitrogen at Johns Lougheed Hospital. I never heard from the geneticists again. My medical chart grew mold. "But I received the grace of faith, which was seeing the invisible, believing the unbelievable, and waiting to receive the impossible." -Corrie Ten Boom

Awakener of emotional convictions, thank you for helping me take the first step of faith. You are my path opener. I am convinced that you can do all things beyond the reach of human proof. Amen.

Additional reading: Acts 20:32, Romans 15:4, Psalm 119:105, 2 Peter 1:21, Jeremiah 29:11, Luke 12:32, Psalms 36:5, Psalms 89:8.

Self-reflection: Are you settled in a place in your life because it seems convenient, while all the while, God is convicting you that He wants you to move to a new horizon?

Follow The Lord's Road Sign

"So the Lord must wait for you to come to Him so he can show you His love and compassion…For the Lord is a faithful God. Blessed are those who wait for His help…Right behind you a voice will say, 'This is the way you should go, whether to the right or to the left.'"
Isaiah 30-18, 21

I searched online for places to rent in Alaska. There were many options, which made me confused and lost. Nothing led me to God's peace. I finally put a halt on the search and asked God to lead me to the right place of residence in Alaska: "God I lack strength and health to look for places to rent. Show me whether to go to the right or to the left. Let me hear your voice behind my ears. Amen."

Immediately my web search ended up at Kachemak Glacier Housing. It was the end of the confusion and the beginning of peace. Their business offered opportunities available to individuals who fell within a low income guideline. God just pointed to the right direction! I filled out an online application and the rental business placed me on a long waiting list.

Five months went by and Kachemak Glacier Housing did not respond to my application. I told my children five months prior that we'd be moving to Alaska in six months, but there was a standstill in the air. God was silent. My circumstances were in a state of inertia.

By faith, I placed a notice to vacate my apartment in the East Coast without having a future residence anywhere on the planet. I was banking our lives solely on the vision God gave me when I was six years old.

Assumptions I could be wrong about my vision began to fill me with doubt. "Did God really speak to me about moving to Alaska? Did God really lead me to Kachemak Glacier Housing? Why is it Kachemak Glacier Housing didn't answer my request for housing? Maybe I'm wrong about everything!" I thought.

My restlessness led me to another senseless web search. I stopped trusting God and tried to find a vacant apartment in Alaska without His guidance. I wasted several hours but the results were the same as before. I became lost and confused again. I was drained and feeling ill. Then, I clearly heard God saying: "Stop!" I finally put everything to a halt. God whispered behind my ears, "You are not following my sign posts. You either trust me blindly or you are on your own!"

My lack of faith wanted to control God's leading instead of being guided by Him. My anxiety paralyzed me to a point I couldn't tell what was coming from God and what was coming from my personal desires.

I logged off the computer and abandoned the ship of disbelief. I went back to confident trust and continued to follow God's sign posts even though I wasn't seeing breakthroughs ahead. Behind my ears, the Lord whispered, "Wait upon me, I am always on time."

I ceased looking at my circumstances horizontally and became determined to set my eyes vertically to the throne of the All-knowing God. At once, the stormy anxiety turned into a tranquil sunshine day.

Noah's ark came to mind. Noah didn't have a naval architectural background. God was the One who whispered in Noah's ears the ark's design. God gave Noah precise step by step instructions on how to build a safe vessel. Noah simply trusted and obeyed God and stuck exactly to what God wanted him to do. The design included one window in the roof of the ark- a skylight.

The ark's skylight reminded me of Noah's relationship with God. Noah looked up to the skies. He had a vertical relationship with the Creator. If Noah would have had a horizontal relationship with God, then he would have been confused and anxious. He would have listen to his friends instead of God. He would have calculated negative circumstances instead of building the ark. Many people thought Noah was crazy, and considered him a "nutcase." However, Noah's ears were tuned off to horizontal whispers. Noah's ears were tuned into a vertical relationship with God, causing him to obey even if nothing was making sense in the natural. The result of Noah's vertical focus was the flood and the fruition of God's promises.

I'm confident that God whispers, God gives visions, God delivers, and God blesses a vertical relationship with Him when I wait, listen, and obey His step by step instructions.

In stillness, I continued to gaze at my vertical skylight.

Refiner of my faith, may uncertainty turn into certainty. May my faith be polish, so I may follow the whispers of your voice without the dubious voices of the world. Amen.

Additional verses: Genesis 6:14-16, Psalms 119:105, Proverbs 4:18, Psalms 16:11, Proverbs 2:9, 2 Samuel 22:37, Proverbs 4:12.

Self-reflection: The story of Noah found in Genesis 6:1-9:17-21 describe him as righteous and blameless. Noah found favor because he obeyed God wholeheartedly. Do you follow God vertically like Noah, or are you negatively influenced by the people around you, thereby following the world horizontally?

All Is Well With My Soul

"But I know that the king of Egypt will not let you go unless a mighty hand forces him. So I will raise my hand and strike the Egyptians, performing all kinds of miracles among them. Then at last he will let you go. And I will *cause* the Egyptians to look favorably on you." Exodus 3:19-21

Anxiety to move to Alaska vanished as God gave me peace. I received grace to wait upon His direction. Meanwhile, I continued my routine in the East Coast.

All was well with my soul. I followed Jesus' compass and was open to whatever road He'd lead me. If He wanted me to move to Alaska, then all the doors would open naturally. The impossible would be made possible because God is omnipotent.

God's omnipotence brought Moses into mind. The Egyptians discriminated against the Hebrews, yet God *caused* them to look favorably at Moses in order to fulfill His plan, which was to free His people of slavery and lead them to a land of milk and honey.

The word *cause* according to the Merriam-Webster dictionary means to make something happen. God is the one who makes things happen. He is in control of everything. I became aware that nothing was a coincidence. Life was not a game of chance. God was the one who would *cause* all events in my life to take place. God was constantly watching over my comings and goings. He always knew where I was. Nothing was out of His *causative* control. God's ability to be present in everything gave me immeasurable security.

I opened myself up to all possible divine plans the Lord had. I was in complete agreement with God. I didn't want to meddle with His design. If I touched anything by my desires, I knew I could spoil His work. My hands were down, and His Hands were at work. "His way, not my way," I thought. Whatever route He would lead, I knew it would be a prosperous one, leading to hope and a godly future. I realized God could *cause* me to stay in the East Coast, thereby closing Alaska's doors. If so, then peace would come through that path, because God doesn't lead His loved ones into a direction of unrest.

My new found security in Jesus increased my love for Him. I began loving God more than ever for whom He is and not just for what I could get from Him. I loved God's kind Spirit evermore. I loved God's constant listening and caring abilities. If I was sad, He embraced me; if I'd fall, He'd lift me up. Though tomorrow was unknown, He went ahead of me. I longed for Him day and night. He was engraved in my heart.

God *caused* my soul to be satisfied whether I stayed in the East Coast, or moved to Alaska. God *caused* me to be satisfied in the parameters of His good will. God *caused* me to be satisfied with my daily bread. God *caused* all to be well with my soul.

My eyes are always on you Lord. You are mighty, just, forgiving, and everlasting. You are All-Seeing and All-Perceiving. You're the convictor and the corrector of my transgressions. You are the Leader; I'm the follower of your path. You are the fulfiller of all my prayers. Your will be done, on earth as it is in Heaven. Amen.

Additional reading: Psalm 121:8, Isaiah 37:28, Jeremiah 29:11, Matthew 6:9-13, Psalm 25:10-15, Matthew 11:28-30, John 14:27, John 16:33, Philippians 4:6-7.

Self-reflection: What are the events God is *causing* to take place in your life?

Looking Back And Looking Ahead

"And he (Moses) said, 'O Lord, if it is true that I have found favor with you, then please travel with us...' The Lord replied, 'Listen, I am making a covenant with you in the presence of all your people. I will perform miracles that have never been performed anywhere in all the earth or in any nation. And all the people around you will see the power of the Lord—the awesome power I will display for you.'" Exodus 34:9-10

Slowly, peacefully, and miraculously, God *caused* all pieces to fall into place. My children and I were ten days from leaving the East Coast to a new life in Alaska. God provided financial support through the kindness of those that were sharing our faith in the Lord. I booked our flight and made reservation for a one month stay in an extended hotel in Alaska.

We emptied our apartment in the East Coast. We packed eight suitcases to move to our new life. God was traveling with us! He was performing consecutive miracles, and making it possible what seemed impossible.

I was living in a magical miraculous Godly bubble world. The greatest part of my circumstances were not so much the blessings, but experiencing the awesome display of God's power. He was opening doors only He could open. The Lord was the one navigating my ill body and impoverished pocket to the Arctic. The vision I experienced when I was six years old, while in the cockpit of an airplane with my father was becoming real.

Like Moses, I was confident in God's whispers and wonders. My job was to follow God's illuminated lanterns on the road leading to the

Arctic. But before proceeding, I was alert to God's "stop signs," as well as "proceed signs."

At a "stop sign," I reminisced on the seven years I lived in the East Coast. The Lord paved my road with blessings during times of storms. Every year I experienced a new challenge, yet God was my strength during stress. He led me into His wisdom, pointing out solutions for every problem.

My home was my family's safe haven because God dwelled within us. We were poor, but never homeless. We were poor, but never hungry. We were poor, but never without clothes to wear. I've been ill, but never without God's strength.

Our physical address in the East Coast was gone. We had a one month stay in an Alaskan hotel. We had no permanent housing in the Arctic. Our lives were not stable, but I realized that security was not on my physical address, or the state or country in which I lived in. Security was in knowing I was where God wanted me to be. God was my physical address and hiding place. He led me in the right path and made His direction easy to follow.

My road Guider, all the roads lead to you. Take me with you across the lands. I dwell in the secret place of your shadow. You are my refuge and fortress. I have no fear of the future because I am with you. I trust you. Amen.

Additional Reading: Psalm 91:1-16, Psalm 17:8, Psalm 27:5, Psalm 31:20, Psalm 32:7, Psalm 90:1, Psalm 119:114, Psalm 5:8, Psalm 32:7, Psalm 121:5, Isaiah 25:4.

Self-reflection: Is the Lord guiding your way? How do you see His miraculous hands in your life?

I Want Chocolate Flavored Manna

"…and they began to speak against God and Moses. 'Why have you brought us out of Egypt to die here in the wilderness?' they complained. 'There is nothing to eat here and nothing to drink. And we hate this horrible manna!'" Numbers 21:5

"Ready for landing," pilot from Alaska Airlines announced from cockpit. I looked through the airplanes' window and gazed at the breathtaking glacier icy waters of the Gulf of Alaska. Looking down, I saw our new home city. I was no longer six years old, but someone who understood God's visions were authentic, tangible, and genuine. It was nothing short of a miracle. God's vision became a reality!

Mike, Anna, and Max picked up the suitcases at the carousel. Laura and husband were schedule to move to Alaska at a later date. A collection of taxidermy black bears, Kodiak brown bears, polar bears, and musk ox were the welcome décor at Ted Steven International Airport. Subsequently we knew we're moving into wild country!

Within one week after moving from the East Coast to Alaska, God blessed us in many ways. I booked an extended stay hotel which gave us one month to find a permanent home. I purchased a car, and began transferring documentations to Alaska. My health improved, which helped me move around more than while living in the East Coast. I was able to get things done.

Although God provided our needs and fulfilled my vision, everyone in my family, including myself woke up on the eighth day after our moving, on the wrong side of the bed. My son complained about Max, my daughter complained about my son, and I complained about all of them. The eighth day was our first Alaska day of moanings and groanings.

It was at that moment God brought to my attention the time when the Israelites were brought out of Egypt. They were freed from slavery because of Moses' obedience to God. They journeyed towards their Promised Land. The Lord provided manna from the sky, which was a white like coriander seed. It tasted like honey wafers. The Israelites would have gone hungry without God's miraculous manna, but somewhere along the line, they became cranky and bored. They started to complain about the manna. They wanted meat, fish, and melons. They became bored with God's provision. Their bright vision of the Promised Land turned dim by their negative and ungrateful attitude.

Likewise, my kids and I were infected by the complaining virus just like the Israelites. God provided us with many miracles. It was like our manna. But somewhere along the line, we started to complain and want "chocolate" flavored manna. It was a display of ingratitude towards God. We acted like spoiled children wanting to receive more than we were getting.

God convicted us of unappreciative behavior. We sinned by complaining. We should have been counting our blessings! We misused our tongues and turned something positive into something negative. We grumbled against each other, while we should have been doing everything without complaining or disputing. We were getting on each other's nerves instead of bearing with one another in love in order to keep the unity found in the Holy Spirit.

My Convictor, forgive me for murmuring. I've been ungrateful. You miraculously changed my life when all seemed forever lost. You showed me your love by casting your grace on my soul. My dark path seemed endless, but you rekindled me and renewed my life. I praise you for your miracles. Amen.

Additional reading: Philippians 2:14, Numbers 11:1-4, 1 Corinthians 10:10, Exodus 16:8, Psalms 106:25, Philippians 4:11-12, Exodus 16:30-32, Number 11, James 5:9, Philippians 2:14-15, Ephesians 4:1-3.

Self-reflection: Are you murmuring? Have you asked God what you have in your life to be thankful for? Would you name the different "mannas" God provides you in a daily basis?

Inupiat-Yupik Hit And Run

"Never be lazy, but work hard and serve the Lord enthusiastically." Romans 12:11

I cruised around the city strip with the kids six days after moving to Alaska. Our new city sits in a bowl close to an ocean inlet and is surrounded by the snow covered Chugach Mountains. While driving we spotted a moose roaming around a parking lot. Some people stopped their cars to take photos. It was extraordinary to drive in the city and see a large animal calmly eating from a birch tree. However, the dendritic antlers said: "Stay away. I kick and strike!"

As I drove back to the hotel, we saw a native Inupiat-Yupik lady sitting down in the middle of an intersection. Her facial expression revealed extreme pain. Her brow was lowered and her eyes were tightly shut. Cars were driving around her but no one stopped to her aid.

My nineteen year old son Mike immediately asked me to stop our vehicle to help her. I parked the car around the street corner and waited for Mike to assist her. Mike helped the Inupiat-Yupik lady walk to the sidewalk because she'd been run over by a car. He dialed 911 and soon police and ambulance were on the scene. She was taken to the hospital after the hit and run.

The Inupiat–Yupik lady siting down in the middle of the intersection reminded me of the parable of the Good Samaritan. According to the Gospel of Luke, a Jewish traveler was attacked, stripped of his clothes, and left for dead. A fellow Jewish priest and a Levite avoided him, even though they were the same lineage. However, a Good Samaritan stopped to help the Jewish traveler. He did everything he could to help him even though Jewish and Samaritans despised each other fiercely during Jesus' days. The Good Samaritan didn't show any prejudice against the Jewish traveler. He showed love and empathy towards his enemy.

Their seemed to be a lack of Good Samaritans for the Inupiat–Yupik lady that day since we're the only ones that stopped to aid her. I later found out there's a marginalization towards Alaskan Natives.

It was interesting to notice during our city cruising, cars didn't stop to help her, but cars stopped to take photos of a moose. Discrimination against her ethnicity left her alone and in pain. This specific incident revealed that racism is embedded in Alaska. If the victim of the accident would have been a white blond female, she'd have been most likely helped right away. But since the lady was native, she was left hopeless and powerless until Mike aided her.

God calls Christians to be Good Samaritans to all races, genders, and ethnicities. God created us all equal, in His image, and likeness. No race is superior to the other. God does not show favoritism or partiality, and neither should we.

Jesus instructs us to love and serve one another. We're not supposed to be apathetic bystanders by ignoring the needy. God calls us to offer all possible means of help to victims. We should be alert to emergencies and willing to participate in all forms of direct assistance.

We should imitate Christ when it comes to ethnic animosity and divisions. Jesus was Jewish, yet He treated Samaritans with equality. Jesus chose a Samaritan to teach about loving your neighbor (see Luke 10), approached a Samaritan woman at the well (see John 4), healed a Samaritan man (see Luke17), and chose to share the Gospel and welcome the Samaritans into the church (see Acts 8).

Jesus made someone else's problem- His problem. Jesus didn't overlook other's suffering. He was able to recognize pain and heal suffering by His power.

Our Creator, forgive us for the plague of racism. We are all brothers and sisters in you Lord. May your grace be poured on the victims of racism, discrimination, and prejudice. May love be active in our hearts towards one another. Amen.

Additional Reading: Genesis 1:26-27, John 3:16, Deuteronomy 10:17, Acts 10:34, Romans 2:11, Ephesians 6:9, James 2:4, James 2:8, Ephesians 2:14, John 13:34, Ephesians 4:32, Galatians 3:28, Luke 10:25-37.

Self-reflection: Do you judge others by God's equality or by social standards? Do you ignore people's problems?

Conflict Resolution

"Indeed, we all make many mistakes. For if we could control our tongues, we would be perfect and could also control ourselves in every other way. We can make a large horse go wherever we want by means of a small bit in its mouth. And a small rudder makes a huge ship turn wherever the pilot chooses to go, even though the winds are strong. In the same way, the tongue is a small thing that makes grand speeches. But a tiny spark can set a great forest on fire. And the tongue is a flame of fire. It is a whole world of wickedness, corrupting your entire body. It can set your whole life on fire, for it is set on fire by hell itself." James 3:2-10

Alaska's summer sky was filled with the sun's brilliant cascades. It was our first week in our new city and I found a playground for Max to play.

The playground was a quaint downtown park called Elderberry. Anna and I sat on the bench and enjoyed the view of the Cook Inlet bay, while Mike and Max rolled downhill on the grass. We spotted a tunnel where people were bike riding. The tunnel led to a trail on the Coastal area of the Knik Arm. However, being new to the area, I didn't realize the trail was eleven miles long. There were also warning signs advising tourist to stay off mudflats.

Mike wanted to walk on the trail to watch the view of the Knik Arm. Due to my disability, I was not able to walk very far, so I told him to take Max to see the scenery just past the tunnel nearby. I asked him to be back in ten minutes. Anna and I sat on the bench waiting for the boys, and gazed our eyes at the Alaska Range and Mount Susitna, also called the Sleeping Lady.

Ten minutes went by. Mike and Max were not back. The hands of the watch did not stop turning, and an hour went by without the boys return. Anna and I fixed our eyes at the tunnel, but they didn't head back to Elderberry Park.

I didn't have physical strength to go after them. I didn't know anyone in Alaska that could come to our rescue. I prayed but began imagining the worst. I visualized Mike and Max running towards the treacherous mudflats of the Cook Inlet. "Did they walk on it despite the warnings not to?" I thought to myself. I was terrified they were stranded, stuck, or dead in the glacial mud composed of glacial silt. It would have been like walking on quicksand.

I drove around the trail to see if Anna and I could spot them from the car. We headed back to Elderberry park with my two boys lost somewhere in our new State. Terrified, I dialed 911. A police officer found them three hours later and eight miles away from Elderberry Park. They were both intact but oblivious of how concerned they made Anna and I feel.

I praised God for having my family intact and like Shakespeare's play title says, "All's Well That Ends Well." But there was a part of me that wanted to yell at Mike for not being attentive when I told him to get back in ten minutes. The conflict gave me an ill feeling, like an itch I wanted to scratch. I was stressed and angry but didn't want the conflict to manage my emotions. I wanted God to manage the conflict. I kept my mouth tamed because harsh words would only stir up more anger. It was not a Godly way to resolve conflict.

God gave me grace to approach Mike softly. Before voicing my opinion, I asked him questions to understand the reason he was gone for so long. I listened to what Mike had to say. He apologized. I asked him to be more attentive next time. He agreed and words brought healing to the situation.

Jesus responded to conflict in a wise and merciful way. Jesus resolved a conflict and saved a woman from being stoned by saying: "Let he who is without sin throw the first stone." (John 8:3-11) He reacted to evil occurrences in a positive way and overcame evil with good. Jesus was gentle and courteous towards all people. He spoke words of wisdom to retaliate the unwise. He demonstrated there was a time to be silent and a time to speak. Jesus walked in the Spirit and was not led by emotions. Jesus' words were used to build up, instruct, and love others.

My perfectly wise Jesus, let my mouth speak of blessings and not of curses. May my lips be prudent to speak of your wonders. When I stumble, guide me back into your wisdom. May my household be filled with gentleness and be quarrel free. Guard my tongue, so I may not sin with my words. Amen.

Additional reading: Proverbs 21:23, Ephesians 4:29, Proverbs 12:18, Proverbs 15:1, Psalm 34:13, James 3:10, Matthew 15:11, Psalm 37:30, Psalm 39:1, 1 Peter 2:1-25, Psalm 51:6.

Self-reflection: How do you deal with conflict resolution in your household?

Fifteen Days From Being Homeless In Alaska

"Trust in the Lord with all your heart; do not depend on your own understanding. Seek His will in all you do, and He will show you which path to take." Proverbs 3:5, 6

We had fifteen more days left at the extended stay hotel in Alaska, but still didn't have a permanent residence.

While I lived in the East Coast, I searched online for places to rent in Alaska. There were many options but none that gave me God's peace. I prayed God would lead me to the right place of residence, "God I lack strength and health to look for places to rent. Show me whether to go to the right or to the left. Let me hear your voice behind my ears. Amen." Immediately my web search ended up at Kachemak Glacier Housing Corporation. Their business offered opportunities available to individuals who fell within a low income guideline. God pointed to the right direction! I filled out an application and the rental business placed me on a waiting list. Time went by and they never called back, so I entrusted the matter into God's hand. We moved to Alaska and waited on God for a new home.

Days after our arrival in Alaska, I drove by some of the rental units belonging to Kachemak Glacier Housing Corporation. Their rental units were adorable and I visualized living in one of them. Later, I stopped by their business office. They bumped me up on the waiting list because I was staying at a hotel with no real residence. However, they couldn't guarantee a vacancy within fifteen days. We needed a giant miracle!

Meanwhile, I was running low on money, and if I didn't have a residence in fifteen days, we would be literally homeless and alone in Alaska.

The Lord provided all our needs to that point in time. However, my mind began to wonder again towards doubt and unbelief. "Will God really provide us with a home in fifteen days? Will we be homeless?" My disbelief led me to a one day desperate pursuit for a rental apartment outside the Kachemak Glacier Corporation umbrella. I searched in the internet and newspapers. There were many places for rent but none gave me peace. I finally stop nursing my fears. I was searching in vain because God was not in my search. I placed everything to a halt. Once again I trusted the Lord and waited on Him.

I began counting the blessings we've received in the past two months. I went from being almost completely bed bound to being able to move across United States. As the moving date approached, the Lord caused me to slowly get better. I was able to pack, have a pleasant flight, and our suitcases and boxes arrived in Alaska incident free. The Lord provided a car and a one month hotel stay. But the biggest blessing of all was seeing the smiles on my children's faces.

Peace returned to my heart as my mind reminisced on God's wondrous blessings. He really took care of every little detail. Just as He provided before, I trusted that He would continue to provide for the needs of my family.

Many times people see God's hand in the big picture. They talk about big stories and big miracles. But God is in the little things as well as in the big things. Through little things, God constructs big things! God cares about our daily needs and provides for our daily bread. Our daily bread might be in the form of food, clothes, a car, or a house. Or it may well be a new school, healing, or the fulfillment of our heart's desires.

God cares about every tiny little detail in our lives even though we are so small compared to the vast Universe. Situations that seem insignificant such as buying a car or buying a new outfit, matters to God. He values and gives meaning to our lives. He goes before us and places His hands of blessings upon us.

Our job in God's economy is to trust and obey. The moment we substitute trust for doubt, we lose God's path. All obstacles can be overcome with the Lord. He guides us to victory little by little. The Lord is faithful and aware of all our circumstances. He sees everything ahead of us. Trust, perseverance, patience, and obedience are the ingredients to receiving everything God has for our lives. However, God does not operate miracles in our time. It's always on His time. Therefore, we should never forget that God is never late!

My Giver of tranquility, you provide me with peace in a restless world. I cast all cares on you, because you care for me. You save me from disaster. You carry me to safety. You fix my brokenness. You put me back together. You never leave me because you are my loyal Jesus! Amen.

Additional readings: Psalm 139:5-6, Deuteronomy 7:22, Jeremiah 1:5, 1 Peter 5:7, Psalms 127:1, Job 38:41, Psalms 46:1.

Self-reflection: Does God become real to you when you see your prayers being answered? Do you go ahead of God when your prayers are not being answered?

Ten Days From Being Homeless In Alaska

"Yet I am confident I will see the Lord's goodness while
I am here in the land of the living." Psalm 27:13

Once again, I cruised around the city with the kids. We saw rental signs throughout town, but I didn't stop to inquire on any of the apartments. Mike became nervous because I drove by vacancies without stopping for information. "Mom, we are going to be homeless in ten days! We need to find a place to live!" he said with a pronounced gesture of anxiety. "Wait, wait! Don't touch! That's what God is whispering in my ears Mike! We will wait on God's green light. Now, we will enjoy our day!" I answered my son indicating everything was under God's control.

Even though everything pointed out we'd be sleeping on the streets of Alaska, God told me otherwise. I stayed calm and collected because God gave me grace to trust He had a miracle in His magic hat. Every time Mike would panic, I'd let him know God wanted me to wait on Him by not messing up with His grandeur plan. God wanted us to have the best, while my own path would lead us to second best.

We were on a waiting list at Kachemak Glacier Housing Corporation for a place God pointed out since we lived in the East Coast. I waited for the right timing, instead of checking every place available, because I didn't want to disobey God again by going ahead of Him. Obedience meant being patience for God's plan, and direction.

Nevertheless, it was a temptation to meddle with God's work. When I felt weak and wanted to go ahead of God, my daughter Anna helped me get back to my resolute faith. "God will come through for us, mama,

He always has!" she'd say sweetly. Through love, we encouraged each other in the Lord.

My instincts were opposite to faith. It'd have been easier to dig for solutions without God by renting the first place available in the market, but faith went ahead of instincts. I suppressed instincts in order to obey God's guidance. My faith said: wait! Instincts said: grab what's needed! Faith said: act through peace because God is a mighty planner. Faith won!

God's heavenly Spirit guided me through every step. My hands had another Hand operating through me. It was invisible to the world but visible to me. I felt His mighty love. The Lord caused my earthly body to understand the guidance of His path. I waited in stillness, until He caused the pieces to fall into place.

"Ring," I picked up the phone at the hotel room. "Emilia? Are you able to stop by the office today to sign some papers? We might have a rental unit for you." It was Kachemak Glacier Housing Corporation. God's miraculous magic hat was at work!

Path Guider, I seek, hear, and follow your small lamp in the dark world. Little by little you light up the path, showing the step ahead. Amen.

Additional Reading: Proverbs 3:5, Philippians 1:6, Matthew 11:29, 2 Corinthians 9:8, Psalm 28:7, Isaiah 26:4, Psalm 37:3, Jeremiah 17:7, Psalm 62:8, Psalm 25:1.

Self-reflection: Are you following your instincts or God's voice?

Four Days From Being
Homeless In Alaska

"And we are confident that He hears us whenever we ask
for anything that pleases Him. And since we know He
hears us when we make our requests, we also know that
He will give us what we ask for." 1 John 5:14:15

"Ring," I picked up the phone at the hotel room. "Emilia? Are you able
to stop by the office today to sign some papers? We might have a rental
unit for you." It was Kachemak Glacier Housing Corporation.

I went to their office and signed another application for income
qualifications. The landlord had two units available in which four
families applied for. One of the units was a two bedroom apartment.
The other was a three bedroom house. I had no idea how the units looked
like, or if we would be accepted since our income was lower than the
other potential applicants. We were either going to live in an apartment,
a house, or on the streets. We could be homeless in four days, but God
was in control.

I returned to the hotel. We prayed and waited for another phone call
from Kachemak Glacier Housing Corporation in regards to the lease
status. If we were to be accepted, Kachemak Glacier Housing would
choose the kind of housing we would live in accordance to my past
history and income.

When I first applied for Kachemak Glacier Housing while living in
the East Coast, I prayed boldly to the Lord: "God, I lack strength and
health to look for places to rent. Show me whether to go to the right
or to the left. Let me hear your voice behind my ears. Amen." God led

me to apply with their Corporation. They placed me in a long waiting list. But my prayers didn't stop there. I also dared to pray for a house with abundant sunlight coming through the windows. I asked God for a washer and drier, because I was physically exhausted from taking everyone's clothes to Laundromats, especially after the onset of my muscle disease, which made washing clothes difficult. I petitioned God for wood floors, a two story home with a garage, and with a mountain view.

Living in a house seemed impossible due to our financial situation. My reality was that I wouldn't get more than scraps according to my income status. Maybe we'd live in an old apartment, smelling like mildew, carpet stains, and sharing a washer and drier with many other tenants. It'd still be a blessed Alaskan home. But I had a vision God would provide more than scraps. I trusted Him for the best of the crop.

It had been thirteen years since we lived in a house. Once the kids and I heard of the possibility of getting accepted for a house unit, we were elated. But the landlord warned to keep my hopes down because the financial personnel of Kachemak Glacier Housing would have to approve of my lease. The possibilities were miniscule and we were back to God praying that He would make the impossible, possible!

We began to dream of a house. Suddenly, my trust in the Lord was replaced for an overwhelming feeling of wanting to have a house and doubting that God would actually bless us with the best of the crop. Peace once again left me because I let doubts take control.

The Lord reminded that wanting was causing me anguish. My human desire to live in a house made me lose happiness and peace. Once I gave up my human desire, I was free from wanting. I revisited thankfulness for everything I already received from God. I realized living in a house, apartment, or being homeless was far less important than having my heart centered in God's will.

Vision for a house was a temporal vision. Heaven's home was my long term eternal vision. I left my bold prayers in Jesus' hand, and understood God didn't have to jump to answer prayers. He had the right to say no because He knew what was good or bad for my family. My prayers would be answered if a house was in His plan. My prayers would be answered if the house would be used for Godly purposes to glorify His name.

My longing subsided as I submitted my desires to God. I stopped following cravings and committed my ways to the Lord. My earthly desires should have never been placed in a higher position than my relationship with God.

We were on a standstill in God's merciful hand four days from being homeless in Alaska.

Prayer Fulfiller, I submit my human desires into your hands. A house of bricks does not compare to the future Afterlife. I wait for a great surprise Heavenly Home with pearly gates you are preparing for me. Amen.

Additional reading: 1 Corinthians 2:9, Hebrews 11:6, 1 Thessalonians 5:17, James 4:3, Matthew 6:9-13, Psalms 37:4.

Self-reflection: Who rules your heart, God's will or your human desires?

Two Days From Being
Homeless In Alaska

"Instead of shame and dishonor, you will enjoy a double share of honor. You will possess a double portion of prosperity in your land, and everlasting joy will be yours." Isaiah 61:7

We had two days to vacate the extended stay hotel. I could have been frantically looking for rental vacancies. Instead, I waited on God to make the impossible, possible, even though we're two days from being homeless in Alaska.

The Lord tested my faithfulness and submission. Once my heart was lined up with His will, He began working on the details of our lives. God tested my thoughts and examined my heart. God worked in my interior life before working on my exterior life. He waited on me to change inside before He could change the circumstances on the outside. Once I partnered with His Spirit, He answered my prayers.

It was a day of expectations. We knew our lives were going to change in two days. "*Ring!*" I hurried to pick up the phone at the hotel room. "Emilia? It's Lisa from Kachemak Glacier Housing. I need you to stop by the office to sign the lease. You and your children have been approved for a house unit." I raised my eye brows trying to contain the excitement. "*Uh... wha? Huh?* Thank you, we'll be right there, Lisa!" I hung up the phone. "C'mon guys, yep! Let's go! We've been approved for the house!" I gathered the kids out of the hotel room. Other guests could hear our loud *Woot! Woo! Woo-hoo! Hooray! Yay! Yeah*, as we walked out of the hotel thanking God for the super miracle!

We hurried to the office to sign the lease. The landlord gave me the address of the "surprise" house. We were supposed to meet him in front of the place. We found the street and waited for the landlord in our car. "No... *no no no no no*... Are you sure you have the right address, ma?" Anna's smile turned upside down upon seeing the wrecked house we're going to rent.

The house was not exactly what I prayed for, but if God wanted us to live there, then we could make something out of it. The place was very old, with trash and a wrecked vehicle parked on the yard. The shingles were coming loose. The paint was disintegrating. It looked like termites in the wood were having a wonderful feast because I saw large holes from the outside! But as I looked more carefully at the house, I noticed it was not vacant.

I called the landlord, "*Uh...* ...we've been waiting outside the house, but something seems to be wrong, because I see people still living in it, and maybe I have the wrong address?!" He explained I was on the South part of the street, and the correct house was on the North! Hopes were renewed as we headed to the North side.

I parked the car in front of the correct house and immediately we're on cloud nine. I prayed boldly for a house with abundant sunlight coming through the windows, a washer and drier, wood floors, a two story home with a garage, and with a mountain view. Surprisingly, God double the bold prayer. The house was brand new, and Kachemak Glacier Housing was just finishing the landscape as we arrived by planting flowers and trees on the yard. It was architecturally designed as a duplex model with soaring ceilings and plentiful natural light. It offered attention to detail such as a solid surface countertop, double car garage, and manufactured wood floors in common areas and carpeted bedrooms. Also, it had energy efficient and energy star appliances, such as washer and drier, accommodating lower monthly utility bills. It was above and beyond all our expectations.

Mike, Anna, and Max explored the house inch by inch. On the other side of the bedroom window, God rekindled my eyes with the view of Alaska's Chugach Mountains. I was tearfully blessed and amazed that God made the impossible, possible! He provided a beautiful house and a mountain view!

Alaska was our land of "milk and honey." God brought to fruition the vision I've received many years ago when I sat in the airplane's cockpit and gazed my young eyes at the glacier icy waters of the Gulf of Alaska. God made the impossible, possible! I asked my daughter to pinch me because I was on cloud nine praising God.

God gave me double for my trouble. I've learned to count it all joy when I met trials, because the testing of my faith produced steadfastness in the Lord. God took time to answer prayers because He was cleansing my soul before bestowing blessings. But in the end He answered my bold prayers and blessed me beyond expectations.

Two days later, we moved to our new home. Like Joyce Maynard quote goes: "A good home must be made, not bought." And, God was the maker and the provider of our home!

Blessor, thank you for your miracles. I prayed for blessings, peace, and provision. I prayed for sadness to diminish and trials to lessen. Then I realized your blessings came through pain and sufferings which were your mercies camouflaged by your love. Thank you for giving me blessings as a fruit from trials. Amen.

Additional reading: James 1:12, Deuteronomy 7:13, Psalm 30:5, Genesis 22:1, Judges 2:22, Job 7:18, Psalm 17:3, Hebrews 2:18, Hebrews 3:9.

Self-reflection: Have you gone to God and seen blessings fall in your life one by one? Have you written a prayer journal recording your daily blessings?

The Anabaptist Foyer

"Because of the sinful things they say, because of the evil that is on their lips, let them be captured by their pride, their curses, and their lies." Psalm 59:12

I was captivated by the Anabaptist denomination for many years. One reason being their emphases on family community. Also due to their commitment to subversive non-violence through the peace teachings of Jesus. However, I was never able to join their community since the closest Anabaptist church to my home in the East Coast was three hours away.

Joining an Anabaptist Church was on my prayer list for the longest time. Upon arriving in Alaska, I searched for an Anabaptist church on the iPod. I was elated to find out it was minutes away from the hotel.

As I drove for the first time to visit the church by the O'Malley precipitous mountain peaks, Mike shouted in the car, "Mama, look! It's *a...a...a* bear!!" In fact it was a black bear running awkwardly across the road.

We arrived at the quaint church which sat on top of a hill. We quietly accommodated ourselves in the back of the building. Behind the pastor's pulpit, was a large glass window with panoramic views of the city and Mount Susitna, also called the "sleeping lady." Later I was told of her legend. Mount Susitna resembles a recumbent sleeping lady, named Susitna, who vowed to sleep until her beloved would come back from battle. Susitna still sleeps!

After the service, church members warmly welcomed us at the foyer. "What brings you to Alaska?" that was the question of the day. I suddenly got chocked up, *"Uh... Wha? Huh? uh...* I was...*hum,* it's a long story." The look in everyone's eyes demanded a short answer, but any short answer would have diluted the greatness of what God has done for us. I decided to remain quiet, instead of taking away from God's glory.

I chose to give my testimony another day, instead of sharing fragmented short sentences, such as: "I moved because my son was accepted at a close by university, or due to cooler climate, or my illness, and so on." That would make the move sound like the makings of my hands instead of God's hands. My lips could have been caught into the pitfall of pride. And, pride always leads to downfall.

I didn't want to take God's work frivolously. The Bible teaches this lesson through king Nebuchadnezzar in 2 Kings and the book of Daniel. The king was prosperous and possessed the greatest empire in the world, Babylon. He was exceptionally blessed by the Lord. However, after God blessed him with all riches, his pride got inflated, as the Scripture mentions: "Twelve months later he was taking a walk on the flat roof of the royal palace in Babylon. As he looked out across the city, he said, 'Look at this great city of Babylon! By my own mighty power, I have built this beautiful city as my royal residence to display my majestic splendor.'" Daniel 4:29-30.

King Nebuchadnezzar took credit for everything God had done for him. As a consequence he was driven away from his people and lost everything. He ended up eating grass like cattle. His pride led him to utter disgrace.

After seven years of suffering, the king raised his eyes to Heaven. As a consequence, his life, honor, and kingdom were restored as mentioned in Daniel 4:37: "Now I, Nebuchadnezzar, praise and glorify and honor the King of Heaven. All His acts are just and true, and He is able to humble the proud." The king learned humbleness the hard way. God brought down the king's proud heart. God's purpose wasn't to destroy the king's life, but to draw him back into fellowship with Him. Through his new found humility, king Nebuchadnezzar found wisdom.

The Bible teaches us to glorify God. That means to acknowledge His kind hands in our lives. The Lord should always be on our lips and hearts. Also, we should be cautious not to fall into pride.

Path Maker, you work in mysterious ways, making a way through impossible ways. I desire to honor you with all my heart. I praise you for the miracles you performed in my life. Let my lips worship you as you have your way in me. Amen.

Additional reading: 2 Chronicles 26:16, 2 Chronicles 32:26, Job 20:6, Job 33:17, Psalm 10:4, Proverbs 8:13, Proverbs 11:2, Exodus 6:30, Exodus 13:9, Job 12:20, Job 15:6.

Self-reflection: What is the relationship at the above verses between pride, downfall, and God's glory? What are the fruits of your lips?

Souvenirs

"Don't store up treasures here on earth, where moths eat them and rust destroys them, and where thieves break in and steal. Store your treasures in Heaven, where moths and rust cannot destroy, and thieves do not break in and steal. Wherever your treasure is, there the desires of your heart will also be." Matthew 6:19-21

My father travelled weekly to different countries because of his career as a pilot. He'd head back home dressed with a navy blue four striped gold blazer uniform with gold stars, holding a gold ribbon captain oak leaf sprig hat in his hand. On the other hand, he'd carry the flight crew luggage, which he'd open on the bed first thing upon arriving in his bedroom. My mom, brother, and I would gather around the bed and anxiously wait to see what kind of souvenirs he'd purchased from oversees.

Due to my father's love for cultural diversity, our home was decorated with artifacts from different countries. African masks made of wood used in ritual dances in Zimbabwe, Uganda, and Nigeria hung on the staircase wall. The living room had oil paintings from the Eiffel Tower and the *Café de Paris*. The door knobs of our house were from Holland, brought one by one in my father's suitcase.

Our move to Alaska made me think of dad's flight crew luggage. It gave me a sudden craving for souvenirs. The kids and I window-shopped at the 4th Avenue Market Place. It featured retail shops with Alaskan native mementos such as Alaskan dolls, totem poles, mukluks, and much more. I was tempted to purchase a few knickknacks, but fortunately, the temptation didn't last, because I've learned long ago that things don't fulfill. The Lord soon pointed out I should not make any hasty choices. Our money was budgeted to the penny and it all belonged to the Lord, as He appointed to spend it for our survival.

As a child, I learned material things didn't fulfill the quenches of the soul. I understood things were a quick attempt to fill the empty black void of the heart. Once a souvenir was purchased, it would be put away, out of sight, out of mind. In order to keep satisfying the desires of the flesh, a consecutive item would have to be bought, but the emptiness of the soul would never be met.

The perpetuation of self-indulgence was a rollercoaster leading to a life of spiritual emptiness. It was a dead end consumed by a force of nothing.

I discovered that human nature has a tendency to value wrong things in life. Humans value diamonds without shine, which are empty of eternal worth. At times, we are blind to real glittering diamonds designed by God, which are deposited in our hearts. They are diamonds that outshine worldly things due to grace.

God's grace is better than any material keepsake. God's grace is unconditional and filled with provisional mercies. God's grace is what He granted as I transformed my earthly desires to His higher desires, which was to love everything of Him.

As I allowed God to be all, the love of money, the love for possessions and worldly treasures became null and void. I found my all in Jesus. Nothing else fulfilled me as my relationship with Him. Nothing else was as complete and perfect. In Him I found happiness, comfort, and console. The more I surrendered myself to Him, the more complete I became.

Emptying desires from earthly treasures helped me focus on the here and now. It helped achieve satisfaction with everything which was bestowed upon me by God's hands. It led me to a perpetual state of innermost satisfaction and peace. But once my flesh would suddenly crave for things which I could not have or were a mirage of satisfaction, suffering would blind my soul and evict peace. I concluded that wanting caused pain, but living with God's grace caused peace.

The best souvenirs after all were not purchased by money in my wallet. The best souvenirs were given to me freely. God was the giver

185

of souvenirs which didn't collect mold or dust. God's souvenirs were treasures in Heaven being collected during my journey on Earth. Every day I added a new spiritual souvenir in my Suitcase to Heaven.

Hosanna, you are my everlasting God who grants perfect gifts. You satisfy my hungry heart with your eternal grace. Amen.

Additional reading: Luke 12:15, 1 Timothy 6:10, Matthew 16:26, Matthew 6:33, 1 Timothy 6:9, James 1:17, Ephesians 2:8, Matthew 10:28.

Self-reflection: Based on the Bible verses above, what is your conclusion in regards to material possessions in the life of believers? Are you seeking the things of this world or are you seeking Heavenly gifts to satisfy you?

First Day Of School

"You parents—if your children ask for a loaf of bread, do you give them a stone instead? Or if they ask for a fish, do you give them a snake? Of course not! So if you sinful people know how to give good gifts to your children, how much more will your heavenly Father give good gifts to those who ask Him." Matthew 7-11

Max loved his first summer vacation in Alaska, but the first day of school made him anxious. It was a big new experience. His life changed radically since we moved from the East Coast to Alaska. He had to face a new teacher, students, and environment.

Mike, Anna, Max, and I waited outside along with the rest of the kids for the elementary school to open. Max was clingy as he observed the other students cautiously. Suddenly, an approximately eight hundred pound moose with large antlers appeared on the school entrance. He produced a heavy grunt sound. The yard supervisor opened the school doors at once: "Everybody in! Get inside!" he said. In a few minutes all the children were safely inside. "The moose grunted, welcome to Alaska's Elementary School!" I said laughing to Max who was amazed at the uniqueness of the first day.

We walked Max into his classroom to meet the third grade teacher, Ms. Smith. Max wrapped his arms around my arm. His tiny body began to shake. He looked down and his face turned pale. Ms. Smith came to assess the situation. I explained we just moved from the East Coast and he had to catch up on reading and math.

Ms. Smith turned her attention to the rest of the class. She handed out a worksheet with some math and writing to be completed in the classroom. Max sat on his desk. He looked fearfully at the questions and didn't touch the paper. I sat down next to him upon noticing he wasn't able to complete any of the questions. I explained to Max everything was going to be fine, but his anxiety continued to escalate.

Max began to shake uncontrollably. I grab his little sweaty palms and we walked towards the door. As we approached the door, Ms. Smith confronted us: "Is everything ok?" I looked at her with concerned eyes and said, "I'm sorry Ms. Smith, but I need to speak to Max out in the hallway. He is very anxious because it's his first day of school and he is not being able to answer the questions on the worksheet."

Max's knees and hands continued to shake. His face was one of a child close to passing out. Ms. Smith kneeled down next to him, looked deeply into his eyes and said with a special sweetness in her voice: "You know Max, I'll tell you a secret: my son couldn't read at your age as well. So, I'll tell you the same thing my son's teacher told him back then: 'I will teach you to read and write little by little, but for now, just turn your worksheet around and draw me the most beautiful picture you ever drew in your life.'" Max arms immediately stopped shaking. In a flash of a second, he acknowledged the empathy Ms. Smith displayed him. He mirrored her calmness and was filled with hope. With a new found confidence, he smiled big and said: "I can do that!!!" he ran back to the desk and drew a beautiful happy picture.

God always gives His children the best! Sometimes we don't understand what is best for us. I thought the school was going to be a bad school according to the ranking of elementary schools in the United States, but God was not looking at surveys. God was looking for a treasure to advance Max's path to education. He found Ms. Smith to be the treasure. She was the pearl in the clam. She was filled with love and compassion, which was exactly what Max needed at the time. By the end of the semester, Max was able to read!

Wondrous Lord, your love is absolute. Blessed be your name! There's no one that comforts like you! On my knees, my secret petitions fall on your ears, and with open arms you receive my devotion. Amen.

Additional verses: Psalm 127:3-5, Mark 10:14, Matthew 18:10, Proverbs 22:6, Deuteronomy 11:19, Proverbs 20:11, Matthew 7:7, Matthew 21:22.

Self-reflection: Do you make choices according to surveys or God's path for your life?

Submission

"Dear brothers and sisters, when troubles come your way, consider it an opportunity for great joy. For you know that when your faith is tested, your endurance has a chance to grow. So let it grow, for when your endurance is fully developed, you will be perfect and complete, needing nothing." James 1:2-4

I suddenly realized Mike ended a part of his life. One stage was over once he graduated from high school and another was ready to begin. A new chunk of life events were going to unfold because he was accepted at a university. And so, an interconnectivity of events began to evolve.

"Mom, God speaks to me! I don't know how to explain it, but I think He wants me to do something special," Mike said with a reflecting mature expression. "I understand, Mike. Listening and talking to God is very much like having a friend on the phone. You can't see him on the other side, but you know that he is listening. You know, I'm looking forward to see what God has for your future. I'm sure He has something special!" I said to Mike before his first day at the university.

Mike was thrilled to attend college. His future was looking bright! God was blessing him. He visualized himself completing education in four years, joining university clubs, and making new friends. He was awarded financial aid and scholarships. He thought nothing could go wrong!

Five days after Mike's first day in college, financial aid office called explaining he needed additional money to cover the total cost of tuition. I couldn't come up with the sum, and it seemed Mike would have to drop out of college.

Mike became furious at the college, God, and me. "Everything in my life goes wrong. God teased me!" Mike folded his arms, sat down, and scowled mumbling words of despair. He was inconsolable and allowed himself to be sucked into a black hole of self-pity. Meanwhile, I searched for cheaper colleges in the area. I looked at private loans and scholarships. I desperately searched for God's answers in order to help Mike, but peace left our home.

I waited on God's still voice. I reflected on my own path. God opened doors and closed doors for His glory. After years of training to be a ballet dancer, I developed epilepsy and had to stop dancing. So I studied music in college just to have that door also shut due to a sudden relocation. Later, I went into nursing school, hoping to be a nurse in ministry. That door also closed due to my neuromuscular disease.

Ballet, music, nursing, and more pales in comparison to what I have now, which is a deeper relationship with the Savior. I wanted to trail different paths, but He wanted me in Wisdom College where suffering 101 was the pre-requisite for graduation. The Lord transformed disappointments into a closer walk with Him.

Many dreams were shattered, but I raised my head to the Lord, and He always had a better path prepared for me to fulfill. When God closed a door, He opened another door, but while I was in between two doors, I was never able to see the whole picture. Those were the moments I had to trust God the most. I had to look beyond my situation, knowing that everything had its purpose.

Mike ended up lashing out his anger on the broom. He spun it around and around until he got whacked on the head. Blood began to flow down his eyebrow. He didn't yell in pain. He simple said: "Huh, God just whacked the self-pity out of me. I needed that!" Suddenly, a new sense of peace flowed within him. He opened his hands to God and submitted to His path.

Mike wanted to be in the service of the Lord, so his trail had sudden and unanticipated turns. After he was done with self-pity, I sat next to him and said: "I know it seems you are being destroyed, but God is remaking you into a better you. You need to submit dreams and plans to the Lord, and only then you will be at peace and secure!"

Mike submitted his plans to the Lord acknowledging that God was watching over the situation and was going to guide him the rest of the way.

James 4:13-17 shows we must be consistent in our walk by submitting our dreams to our sovereign Lord because the future is uncertain. Our lives are frail if left to our own devises, but God has a supreme perfect will for us. "Instead you ought to say, 'If the Lord wills, we shall live and do this or that'" (see James 4:15), which demands we humble our plans into submission to God.

Every plan we have should involve God from the very start. If we ask God to endorse our plans, then we are asking God to submit to our desires. We should get behind God's plans by seeking His kingdom first and His righteousness (see Matthew 6:33). Submitting to God is not an action of praying for what we want. Submitting to God is the intention behind the act of praying. It's the humility that comes with spending time with Him throughout the day and accepting the outcome of His plans for our lives.

Submission to God is acknowledging that His thoughts are greater than our thoughts and His plans are greater than our plans.

Three days later: "Mike? This is Donna from the financial aid office. We're able to come up with the rest of the money for tuition and you may resume your classes tomorrow." Mike went back to class praising God. He repented for being angry at God. He learned to overcome arrogance. His actions became shaped with submission to God's plan.

Supreme God, I submit all my plans to you. I invite you to be involved in everything that matters from the very beginning. I seek your Kingdom first in all your righteousness. I bow down to your will. Amen.

Additional reading: James 4:13-17, Proverbs 6:6-8, Acts 18:21, 1 Corinthians 4:19, 1 Corinthians 16:7, Psalm 39:4-6, Philippians 2:19-24, Psalm 90:10.

Self-reflection: Have you invited God to be part of every area in your life?

The Green Play Dough

"And yet, O Lord, you are our Father. We are the clay,
and you are the potter. We all are formed by your hand."
Isaiah 64:8

Mike was nineteen years old when asked to teach a Sunday school class at our Anabaptist church. I really didn't know how his young jolly personality would take the task, but he carried himself with the usual amusing smile which lit up the room.

Church members sat in a circle waiting for Mike to begin the lesson. He reached into his pocket and pulled out a green ball of play dough. Silently, he looked down and his fingers began to rake, flatten, squeeze, punch, and roll the play dough. Everyone's serious expressions were on him, wondering if he was taking the task of teaching Sunday school as a big joke. Mike didn't mind if everyone stared at him with puzzling eyes, and continued to knead the play dough until the green ball was as smooth as possible.

After some time, Mike began to teach:

"Christians are like this green ball of play dough. In the beginning we're thick, misshaped, full of cracks, and imperfect. Then God pinches the dough of our lives, rolling us in between His fingers to improve our souls. As God begins to knead us, our rough edges turn smoother. We become more rounded in God. He adds scents and colors, which are His special gifts. Of course, there'll always be some cracks between the play dough, because we'll never be perfect as Christ is, but as we walk in

His likeness, the road to perfection will make us more like Him. And, that's how God is working in me...

When I was a little boy I knew of the existence of God. He was a common word used in my household and a common belief that bonded our family together. When others asked me if I was born again in Christ, I would say yes because my mother was, therefore I thought I was covered by her faith.

When I entered my teenage years my father went to prison. The shadow of his crime haunted me. I was ashamed and angry at him even though I still missed him. In my anguish, I began to meditate. God's presence became real to me and I understood the meaning of being born again. I began to soak in His presence constantly.

When I turned sixteen the pain I carried because of my dad's crime lessened and I floated away from God. I just lived my day to day carefree.

God didn't let me off the hook so easily. When my mom got sick, I had to return to God's presence. I had lost my father to prison and I was about to lose my mother to illness. I was being put to the test again. But I miserably failed because I became bitter and snappy.

When my family and I joined your Anabaptist church, I finally understood the full meaning of being a born again Christian. A born again Christian is not a person that is born out of another born again Christian. To be born in Christ is to be touched by God. It's the birth of a beginning into His kingdom. It's the assurance that whatever test I might encounter in life, I can depend on God to take me through it by His grace, forgiveness, and love.

In the end, being born again is letting God be the big Hands that knead, roll, and squeeze me. Again, being born again in Christ is letting Him be the big Hand in my life while I get shaped into a more perfect green play dough ball."

Soul Shaper, shape and conform me into your character. Make me a worthy vessel filled by the Holy Spirit. I submit and surrender my will to your desires. Amen.

Additional Reading: Exodus 4:11-12, Psalm 139:14-16, Mathew 16:24-26, Luke 8:39, 2 Timothy 1:8, Revelation 12:11, Matthew 10:32 Psalm 71:15-18, Psalm 119:46.

Self-reflection: How is God molding you? Do you proclaim to others how much Jesus has done for you? How did you come to know Jesus?

Infectious Love

"For even the Son of Man came not to be served but to serve others and to give His life as a ransom for many."
Mark 10:45

I opened the bedroom window on a Sunday morning and the ground was covered with several inches of our first Alaskan snow. We're extremely excited but thought the church would close due to snow accumulation. After all, we lived in the East Coast, where schools and churches report being closed with only one inch of snow.

"Hi pastor, is church going to be open for service this morning?" Anna asked the pastor on the phone. "We don't close for snow... this is Alaska!" the pastor informed.

As I began driving to church, I noticed the roads were not salted or plowed like in the East Coast. Driving was like skiing with the car without ski poles on the fresh white snow. I had very little control of the vehicle. I decreased the speed to leave plenty of room to stop behind other cars. The car wheels began to slide here and there, so I eased off the brake. I prayed for the safety of my family and me.

Thick flakes fell non-stop from the sky rustling and whirling in the wind causing a total white out. I didn't know which lane was mine. I didn't know which lane was next to me. It all became a guessing game. I thought we could reach the church eventually if I drove carefully and slowly.

I was driving on flat ground, but as I attempted to drive uphill towards the church, the car simply skidded and got stuck. I tried to get it unstuck by turning the wheels sideways, but the blanket of soft white turned into ice, and then my little car began to slide downhill towards the car behind me, regardless how much I pushed on the accelerator. "Lord, help us," I prayed in a panic. Mike quickly got out of the car and pushed the car uphill in the midst of the freezing heavy traffic. His snickers were slippery which made him slide to the ground. The car rolled underneath him. A man seeing our great distress left his car and helped Mike up. He stopped the car from rolling down. Immediately they pushed the car up and around the corner.

It was impossible to reach the church. I turned back to flat ground and headed back home. The usual twenty minute drive from home to church turned into a two hour drive of tension and prayers. Exhausted but thankful for "all is well that ends well," we arrived back home.

The next day, I wrote the pastor an email mentioning what happened during our drive. He called me on the phone and said: "You should search on eBay for studded tires to drive on Alaska's snow." I was confused. "Studded tires what?" A few days later the pastor contacted Garan and Kira from church who kindly offered to find the tires. Immediately I purchased the special tires with metal studs which enhanced the traction for the slippery roads of Alaska's snow and ice.

Our first Alaskan snow incident reminded me of an occasion when we moved to Brazil in 2002. It was the first time as an adult that I lived outside of the United States. I moved to find safety for my children after my divorce. Yet, I felt overwhelmed by the clutches of a major metropolitan area like São Paulo. I was already a single mother of three young kids. I left United States with only a few bags to begin a new life along with forty million *Paulistas* residents, dealing with the hustle and bustle of the fast paced city life.

I had to provide a new home, school, and safe haven for my children in a short period of time. It felt overwhelming but the Lord kept whispering behind my ears: "Depend on me. I'll lead you one step at the time." With that in mind, I didn't overload my thoughts. I kept in step with the Holy Spirit who guided and provided us with everything needed.

A month after our arrival, we moved to a high-rise apartment. The kids were playing in the playground of the building. Anna was trying a new trick on the monkey bar. Suddenly, we heard a big bang. Her hands slipped off the equipment and she hit the ground face down. Anna's eyes rolled back and she passed out.

I wanted to call 911, but that was Brazil and not United States! I didn't have a list of Brazilian emergency numbers. I didn't know where the hospitals were and I still didn't have a car. I felt lost and alone, but God reminded me once again He would take care of us!

Thankfully, Anna was alert again, but I had to make sure she didn't suffer a contusion or concussion. "Lord, guide me. I'm lost in this big city," I prayed.

The gatekeeper of the high-rise building saw our distress and took upon himself to help us. He called a cab and asked the driver to take us to the nearest emergency room. The cab driver was ungroomed. He had a two-day beard. His hair had not seen a comb in days. He lacked a few teeth in his mouth. The struggles of poverty were obvious by the looks of his face.

At first, the cab driver looked like some others I've seen in his line of job. But I found out he was no ordinary cab driver. He was more like an angel. I explained to the cab driver what happened to Anna. He said with a big toothless smile: *"Não se preocupe com nada. Deus cuidará de sua menininha!* (Don't worry about a thing. God will take care of your little girl!)" He began to speed on the streets of São Paulo as if he was a NASCAR driver, making sure Anna would get to the emergency room for medical care. As we arrived at the hospital, I asked him the price of the fare. The cab driver insisted vehemently, *"Não se preocupe, você não precisa pagar. Que Deus abençoe a senhora. Se você precisar de qualquer outra coisa, apenas me pergunte!"* (Don't worry about it, you don't have to pay. God bless you and if you need anything else just ask me!)" The cab driver showed us love and empathy. He was able to understand we needed help because he knew suffering first hand. At that moment we were interconnected.

Even though I was a total stranger, the cab driver practiced empathy through "love your neighbor as yourself," as Jesus taught. He gave us a free ride while he was poor himself. He loved us with open arms and with no reservations. His love was warm and infectious. My kids and I felt at home with a complete stranger sitting on the back seat of his taxi.

Through Jesus practice of "love your neighbor as yourself," Anna walked out of the emergency room as good as gold. The gatekeeper helped us. The taxi driver helped us. The hospital x-ray and procedures were completely free of charge.

The Brazilians displayed an infectious Jesus' love. The Alaskan man, who immediately got out of his car to help Mike through the struggles of the snow, displayed Jesus' love. And, Anabaptists from church, who generously offered to help us with the studded tires, displayed an irresistible Jesus' love.

I was blessed to be the recipient of generosity, but not everyone follows Jesus' sacrificial teachings. I learned that some of us love others with open arms, while others love others with closed arms. Some will go half a mile, some go the extra mile, and some will just point to the direction of the next mile.

Jesus' teachings are clear. He loved us with open arms. He said in Matthew 5:41, "If a soldier demands that you carry his gear for a mile, carry it two miles." We should help others even if involves some form of sacrifice. That's acting like Jesus! He went the extra mile for us by dying for our sins on Calvary.

Sacrificing Savior, thank you for giving your life as a ransom for many. Give me grace to love my neighbor and walk in your footsteps. Help me to go the extra mile for all those in need. Amen.

Additional reading: Matthew 22:39, John 12:26, Galatians 5:13, Mark 10:42-45, Colossians 3:12, Ephesians 2:10, Mark 10:45, Proverbs 11:25.

Self-reflection: Do you go half a mile, the extra mile, or point the direction to the next mile to help your neighbor?

One Another

"Be devoted to one another in love. Honor one another
above yourselves." Romans 12:10

It took one year for my youngest daughter Anna to draw a portrait for
my birthday. She was able to capture the structure and features of my
face with technical precision. She observed every detail including the
shape of my head, the size of my eyes, chin, the expression of my smile
and more. She learned to see me in ways others could not see me. She
noticed when I was happy or sad. She understood me! Every pencil line
in the big canvas was a line of love. She took her time to do the best
job she could. Her only motive was to love me deeper than ever before.

Anna's ways constantly reflects the qualities of God. She has
this sparkling genuine love about her that springs forth everywhere.
Everything she does promotes peace and harmony. Everything she does
is for one another. She tends to strip herself from self-seeking and puts
others first at all cost.

Just as Anna learned to see me how others could not see me, we
should learn to see others beyond what hides behind their smiles. Many
of us hide pain behind our masks. We show the world what we think
they ought to see. We hide our real emotions and let pain involute
inside us. We lose touch to what is real or not. We even wonder to
ourselves at times if our smile is genuine or fake. Smiles many times
don't correspond to what is really going on inside our souls.

Anna was born with a gifted perception of recognizing a genuine
smile. She can tell when one is hiding pain behind a smile of dystrophy.
When she sees a smile hiding behind pain, she is able to embrace and
love deeper.

The Bible mentions love one another thirty eight times. Jesus demonstrated that we should love one another as He did. We should learn how to see beyond the surface of a facial expression, and encourage one another by building each other up in ways that promote healing in the body of Christ. Our love should reflect communal harmony, hospitality, humility, forgiveness, patience, compassion, and kindness.

All perceiving Lord, help me serve others as a life style. Strip me from self-seeking. Show the people you want me to be good to today. Show me how to glorify your name through loving others. Help me to habitually serve and be all that you want me to be. Help me love others who hide pain behind their smiles. Amen.

Additional reading: Zechariah 7:9, John 13:14, John 13:34, John 13:35, Romans 12:10, Romans 12:16, Romans 13:8, Romans 14:13, Romans 15:7, 1 Corinthians 1:10, Ephesians 4:2, Genesis 16:13.

Self-reflection: When Church service is over people gather for coffee, tea, and snacks. The most asked question is: "How was your week?" Church members usually share what they've done and haven't done during their week. We smile and greet one another in love. However, have you ever ponder what's behind everyone's smiles?

Heavenly Treasures

"Don't store up treasures here on earth, where moths eat them and rust destroys them, and where thieves break in and steal." Matthew 6:19

Mike stopped at the university's bookstore to sell his used books after finals. He was looking forward to having money in his forever empty wallet. He wanted to buy a new video game. I waited for him at the university's parking lot. Minutes later, he walked towards the car with a giant smile while holding a brand new backpack in his hand. I thought to myself: "how responsible, he bought himself a new backpack instead of a video game!" Mike's old backpack was patched up by Anna, who re-stitched the straps a few times over.

Mike told me he received one hundred dollars for used books and bought a new backpack for Max which cost seventy dollars! I was flabbergasted. "Did you buy yourself something? Didn't you want a new video game? Don't you want a new backpack for yourself?" I asked surprisingly. "My backpack can be re-stitched one more time. I thought Max would be happy with a new backpack. Besides, I still have some money left. Maybe we can all do something together, like going to the movies..." he said happily.

Mike always placed others before himself. His preference was to store up treasures in Heaven, where the safe is unbreakable and the reward is eternal. He realized at a young age that all things under the sun decay. He chose to be a heavenly hoarder of heavenly fortunes.

Mike has been a constant example of servitude to others. I always observed him helping people without holding anything back. He reminded me of Jesus' words: "It is more blessed to give than to receive." (Acts 20:35)

The Christian life should be all about giving. Giving is pure if there are no ulterior motives of receiving anything in return. Giving is love in action. Giving is a true representation of what lies deep in the heart of the giver. Giving should be done generously without a grudging behavior.

The act of giving may take many forms. Giving may be in the form of a hug, smile, or complement. Or it might as well be in the form of a listening ear, an empathic heart, or a shoulder to cry on. Or it could also mean giving a special gift, a special moment, or a donation.

Nevertheless, the biggest gift of all was given by the Greatest Giver, who gave us eternal life! "For God loved the world so much that He gave His one and only Son, so that everyone who believes in Him will not perish but have eternal life." (John 3:16)

My Eternal Life Giver, help me to share all the good things with others. May I offer what I have willingly and wholeheartedly. Help me to store treasures in Heaven. Amen.

Additional reading: 1 John 3:17, Deuteronomy 16:17, 1 Chronicles 29:9, Proverbs 3:27, Proverbs 11:24-25, Proverbs 21:26, Proverbs 28:27, Malachi 3:10, Matthew 6:3-4, Mark 12:41-44, Luke 3:11, Luke 6:30, Acts 20:35.

Self-reflection: What do you value the most: giving or receiving? How do you give of yourself to others?

Winter Solstice

"God rescued me from the grave, and now my life is
filled with light." Job 33:28

We experienced our first winter solstice in the Arctic Circle. It gave us
the chance to appreciate Alaska's Northern lights. It appeared during
the cold midnight hour, and it danced in the sky like a colorful umbrella
of beauteous light.

Winter Solstice was the shortest day of the year with only five hours
of sunlight. The dawn was late yet the sunset was early, accompanied
by extremely cold temperatures, giving Alaskans a vortex of seasonal
blues.

The blues were noticeable in the local residents. Some seemed to be
suffering from Seasonal Affective Disorder. They craved for daylight
and appeared to display low energy levels accompanied by sadness.
The population seemed to have a tendency to over sleep and over eat.

Seasonal Affective Disorder can lead to depression and feelings of
hopelessness. Some Alaskans displayed a pessimistic attitude towards
life and seemed to think the long winter would never cease. They tended
to withdraw to their homes and socialize less. The seasonal mood is
related to lack of sunlight, and the curative therapy is administration of
a light box that emits more lumens than a regular lamp. Light, then is
the cure for Alaskan's winter blues.

Nevertheless, humans don't have to live in the North Pole to have
depression associated with lack of light. Depression is real whether
you live in cold weather or if you are surfing on the best Barbados'
waves. Depression is like a soul going through winter solstice every
day. It overtakes the spirit creating a hole of internal darkness.

Depression is having misery as your shadow without finding an escape route. Depression is like a bridge that welcomes you to quit and jump. Depression is walking in the fog not finding a way out. Depression is looking at the mirror and seeing hopeless as a reflection. Depression is the death of the soul. Depression is the absence of Light.

Depression is what I felt after finding out about Tom's crime. Depression is what I felt when we divorced and our lives fell apart. I sat on the bathroom floor hugging myself because my world turned upside down. I thought I would be with the man I loved for the rest of my days. I pictured Tom and I raising our kids together while enjoying the farm until death do us part. My dreams were over and I was not able stop my tears. My spirit felt crushed. I had known physical pain, but the crushing heartache made my soul spin into grief. If I was hurting physically, I could have distracted myself. I could have pushed my headache away, but somehow my mental anguish refused to be pushed aside. Pain gnawed and grinded away at my past happiness.

My emotions were trampled and my heart was stomped on. Dreams spun with the wind. Sadness was worse than physical pain.

Misery drove me to depression. I've been through much but had never been depressed. I used to push my pain away and keep going for the sake of others. I suppressed my every tear, my every ache, and kept on walking with the Lord. But not that day while I sat on the bathroom floor in a pool of my own tears. I gave myself permission to embrace my anguish. I didn't want to eat or read or do anything asides from enveloping myself in a pool of self-pity. I allowed myself to have- depression.

No words comforted me. I was in a pit of oblivion. It felt I was in a place of no return. I hoped to die in my sleep. I was disappointed upon waking up to find out I was still alive.

Nevertheless, depression is the absence of Light. Depression is also a selfish monster. I had children to take care of and they needed me to be whole. My soul needed healing, and healing I found in the Heavenly pharmacy, bottled by God's insights.

It took soul searching and seeking God to find out my soul became unhealthy because my priorities were misplaced. I became depressed because God took away my dreams of marriage. As God's child, I protested! Why would God do that? Well, because He can! I lost the dream because my attachment for the dream suddenly took higher priority in my heart than my attachment to the Creator. I sought the earthly dream more than the life God was creating for me.

Once God help me realize all things were part of His divinely orchestrated plan, my depression was lifted, as the fog is lifted from the mountaintop. Just like that, a miracle! I could see things clearly again, and I boldly venture in the path of being a single mom with the grace of God (see Romans 8:28).

Depression was the absence of my light, while God turned my darkness into His Light.

God is the lamp of mankind. God redeems our souls from depression and helps us to enjoy His Light when we allow His face to shine upon us. God delivers us from sadness and helps us walk before Him in the light of life. God is our armor of light whether we suffer from Seasonal Affective Disorder or depression from the loss of a dream. That's because He heals our inner anguish by sheltering us underneath His wings. God is our healer and the best prescription for depression.

Father of Light, my soul is cast down and I see only darkness, but I know my only hope is in you! Give me a good future and hope. Shine in my darkness. Wrap me in your garment of Light. Be the Light in my path. Lead me out of depression and turn my darkness into Light. Make my rough places smooth. Go before me, and help me not to be dismayed. Deliver me out of afflictions. Amen.

Additional verses: Romans 13:12, John 9:5, John 3:18-20, Luke 11:33-35, Matthew 5:13-16, Matthew 6:22, Isaiah 60:19, Isaiah 50:10, Isaiah 42:5-7, Psalm 56:12-13, Deuteronomy 31:8, Psalms 40:1-3, Psalm 42:11, Jeremiah 29:11.

Self-reflection: Would you put your trust in the Lord of Light to end longsuffering by letting Him give you long daylights of summer rays? Will you accept God's light as the curative therapy for your depression?

Advent

"Silent night, Holy night,
Son of God, love's pure light
Radiant beams from Thy holy face,
With the dawn of redeeming grace,
Jesus, Lord, at Thy birth,
Jesus, Lord, at Thy birth."
-Joseph Mohr

Advent is an old tradition observed by our Anabaptist church. We commemorate the coming of Emmanuel in Bethlehem, as well as the return of the Messiah. It's a time of anticipation because we celebrate our Alpha and Omega King. We light up one candle a week during four consecutive Sundays until Christmas day.

On the first Sunday our congregation lit the first candle. We read Isaiah 41. It reflected the prophecies regarding the coming of the Messiah, who delivered us from our transgressions. The second Sunday another candle was lit, which brought into our minds our need for having a Savior. The third Sunday signaled our expectation of Jesus' coming. Finally, the fourth Sunday marked the "Joy to the world, the Lord is come!" (Isaac Watts)

The first Advent of Jesus came to pass in a silent and holy night. Baby Jesus was in a manger while courageous Mary and Joseph were beside Him. Unlike the first Advent, during the second Advent, Jesus will appear with thunder and glory. It will be a holy day but definitely not a silent day. There will be a blast of trumpets and lightening flashing in the sky. It will be a good day for Christians, but a day which will lead many to eternal damnation if they don't know Jesus as a Savior.

When Jesus was born in a manger, He came as a gracious and loving Savior. He grew up to do astonishing miracles of love. Even though Jesus was a man of miracles, love, and peace, His enemies crucified Him hoping His name would disappear from the face of the earth. Instead, Jesus' name didn't fade away throughout time. His life, glory, and everlasting power were magnified evermore throughout the world. His name became inerasable!

Jesus birth, life, and resurrection marked the beginning of the most astonishing walk of faith in human history. Jesus became a contrast to the history of mankind because His social behavior defied the norm. He didn't come to rule like Caesar. He was not born to dominate, conquer, and dictate. He was born to give life eternal!

Jesus was a revolutionary King. While other kings in the Old Testament fought wars, Jesus fought for love, peace, forgiveness, and salvation by presenting eternal life to all mankind.

As our church continued to celebrate the Advent of our Alpha Jesus, His expected Omega Advent became a reminder that we shouldn't grow weary of spreading the Good News of the Gospel to those who don't know Christ.

Alpha and Omega King, thank you for loving me in the midst of my sin grime. I have the assurance that you are coming because your promises never fail. Thank you for your eternal and endless mercy. Amen.

Additional Reading: 1 Thessalonians 4:17, Isaiah 7:14, Isaiah 9:6, John 1:14, Matthew 1:21, Luke 2:21, Luke 2:9-12.

Self-reflection: Have you given your life to the Alpha and Omega King?

Contentment

"That is why I tell you not to worry about everyday life—whether you have enough food and drink, or enough clothes to wear. Isn't life more than food and your body more than clothing? Look at the birds. They don't plant or harvest or store food in barns, for your heavenly Father feeds them. And aren't you far more valuable to Him than they are? Can all your worries add a single moment to your life? ...So don't worry about these things, saying, 'What will we eat? What will we drink? What will we wear?' These things dominate the thoughts of unbelievers, but your heavenly Father already knows all your needs. Seek the Kingdom of God above all else, and live righteously, and He will give you everything you need." Matthew 6:25-27, 31-33

Our church sang the hymn "He leadeth Me: O Blessed Thought," by Gilmore and Bradbury. Every word reflected Anna's daily conduct. She gently sang the song next to me: "Lord, I would place my hand in thine, nor ever murmur nor repine; content, whatever lot I see, since 'tis my God that leadeth me."

Anna was about to have her seventeenth birthday. Due to unexpected bills, I couldn't give a gift that represented her merits. I explained the Lord was meeting our expenses but there was no money left for anything special for her commemorated day. She did not frown or complaint, but was a mirror of the hymn's lyrics. Without murmur or repine, Anna was content with the lot she was given, as long as God was leading her. She said sweetly: "I'm fulfilled with God and already have everything

I need. Once you have God, you become free from wanting and turn out to be satisfied."

Anna didn't rely on birthday gifts to feel extra loved or more satisfied with life because of her personal relationship with the Lord. She sought Jesus in everything and He fulfilled her in every way. She didn't live by the tyranny of cravings but by submitting her life to the will of God. She didn't let sin cast a vote in the way she went about her life. She threw herself wholeheartedly into the hands of the Lord, who unchained her soul to do things God's way (see Romans 6:12-14).

Conversely, the world is filled with unfulfilled and lonely people, who crave for something or someone to give them happiness. However, happiness is not sustainable without God in our hearts.

A heart without God is like a decelluralized ghost organ. It's a bloodless heart which can only be transplanted without rejection through God's regenerative power. Only He can pump a heart with rich sustainable blood.

Anna received the rich royal blood of Christ in her veins. She is fierce in taking up her cross and following Jesus. She has received the complete fulfillment of God's promises with satisfaction guaranteed. She knows Jesus' cross is not a mirage, but her salvation. She found true life and abundance of heavenly delights in the Savior. She has received gladness, courage, virtue, safety, and everlasting life due to her commitment to the Lord.

Satisfying Savior, I want to surrender myself completely to you. Help me let go of the things I hold onto with tyranny. I commit all desires to you, and invite your will into my life. Thank you for the doors you open, but I also thank you for the doors you have closed, for although it was a path I wanted, you closed the doors for my own good. Amen.

Additional reading: Job 36:11, Proverbs 19:23, Philippians 4:11-12, Hebrews 13:5, Ecclesiastes 3:12, Luke 21:1-4, Ecclesiastes 7:14.

Self-reflection: Is Jesus living in your heart? Will you submit your desires to the One who has a good plan for your life?

Chameleons

"And who is a liar? Anyone who says that Jesus is not
the Christ. Anyone who denies the Father and the Son
is an antichrist." 1 John 2:22

I learned in my sociology class in college that all humans have a
presentation of self. It's a conscious or unconscious method people
exhibit in order to influence the view of others around them. I thought
of my father while that topic was being taught. He had a different
presentation of self everywhere he went. At home he acted like a dictator.
He was cold, strict, and easily angered. While with acquaintances he was
funny, friendly, and charming. His presentation of self was a dichotomy
to his real self. I believe deep inside, my father was suffering profoundly,
causing his pain to spill all over into a social survival mechanism. He
reminded me of chameleons because of their distinctive characteristic
of changing skin colorations and patterns as a camouflage for different
social functions.

My father had many roles and acted differently in each of his role
status. His roles were: an airline captain, husband, father, social friend,
church goer, and so on. He tried to keep his roles separated since it
seemed difficult to mix and match the roles with his chameleon like
presentation of self. He acted in compliance to each expected role,
behaving according to the given position. My father stayed within the
boundaries of each role which caused each different social group to see
him in a different light.

Christ on the other hand was not afraid of mixing His diverse roles.
He had different roles as well. He was the son of Mary, carpenter,
teacher, healer, Son of God, resurrected Christ, and Savior. He came to

proclaim the Good News which required His roles to be combined and interlaced into one role.

Jesus presentation of self was not of a chameleon. He was who He was and didn't have to act with a different persona to different people. He was the same everywhere He went. He was Jesus with Mary, Jesus with the apostles, Jesus with the Pharisees and Sadducees, and Jesus with His followers. His presentation of self was impeccable. Not even once He denied God's mission. He wore God everywhere He went even to the cost of His great sacrificial pain on the Cross. Jesus presentation of self was of a perfect Son of God.

Christians should have the same presentation of self as of Jesus. Many of us are Christians on Sundays, saying our "praise the Lord" in front of believers, but as soon as Sundays are over, we live a non-Christian lifestyle from Mondays through Saturdays. God wants more of us than weekend church visits. He wants us to be bold in Him, but many of us are afraid to show Jesus in our lives to our co-workers, friends, and even families, for fear of being rejected or ridiculed. Many of us circle around Jesus cross but never really kneel at the foot of the Cross.

Jesus should be our presentation of self. We should shine for Him even on Twitter and Facebook, but many Christians keep Christ out of social networks. They don't want to mix and match their roles because they exhibit a chameleon like presentation of self.

Apostle Peter was a chameleon. He loved Christ and followed Him when it was convenient. However, when Peter felt fear and pressure, he denied Christ by pretending he didn't know Him. Peter was vehemently faithless (see Mark 14:66-72). If we denied Christ and keep Him out of the different roles in our lives, we act just like Peter.

We should wear Jesus twenty-four-seven. He should be our identity. We should be vehemently faithful to our Savior, without being afraid to show our love for Him to the world.

Genuine Jesus, you are the same yesterday, today, and forever. I don't want to be a chameleon. I want to shine for you as a father, mother, sister, brother, husband, wife, friend, employee, and a boss. Let my

presentation of self be always the same to everyone so others may see
your light in me. Amen.

Additional reading: Hebrews 13:8, Revelation 1:8, Psalms 119:163,
Psalms 52:2, Proverbs 12:17, John 8:44, Colossians 3:9, Proverbs 12:22.

Self-reflection: Have you been denying Christ outside your church?
Would you ask Jesus to manifest Himself in you so that you may have
the boldness to be all that He wants you to be?

Single-Parent

"Oh, how great are God's riches and wisdom and knowledge! How impossible it is for us to understand His decisions and His ways! For who can know the Lord's thoughts? Who knows enough to give Him advice? And who has given Him so much that he needs to pay it back? For everything comes from Him and exists by His power and is intended for His glory. All glory to Him forever! Amen." Romans 11:33-36

I've been a single parent for almost fourteen years. During that time I made a commitment to my children to put them first in everything. I didn't seek a relationship after my divorce. My ex-husband incestuous crime against my oldest daughter left our family deeply wounded. I sought God's help to love my children tenderly in order to mend their broken crushed hearts. Our home became God's gentle sanctuary where emotions were sorted out and acknowledged.

I didn't open my heart to any man. I devoted myself to God in every possible way. He was my Father, companion, and guide. He strengthened me during every trial. I emptied all my thoughts, concerns, and prayers into God's throne. He satisfied my need for companionship. With Him I was alone, yet not alone.

Nonetheless, once we moved to Alaska things changed. I thought I was happy and single until I was confronted with God's changing wind. The course of my heart was altered by a new challenge. I noticed I was settled as a single woman until my kids grew older because God didn't introduce anyone to my heart. Abruptly, God switched the course of my life. Though I didn't understand God's reasoning at the occasion, as time went on all began to make sense.

I began having conflicting emotions once we joined the Anabaptist church. I asked Mike and Anna if they really wanted to join the church as an attempt to run away from my own inner battles. Mike said with great conviction he wanted to remain with the Anabaptists.

We attended the Anabaptist church for the second Sunday. At the end of the service, Pastor Jones looked into my eyes and randomly said: "I'm single and have no kids." I was embarrassed and retrieved from his presence.

Days later, Anna and I were at a grocery store. Pastor Jones walked right in front of us. My cheeks flushed. I was mad at myself for it. I was out of my comfort zone. "Maybe God was up to something," I thought. After all, out of almost four hundred thousand residents which I didn't know in the city, the Lord made sure the only person I officially met crossed my path. "Are there coincidences with the Lord?" I asked myself.

A seed of infatuation was planted in my heart. I opened myself to the prospect that God could lead me into something more than being a single-parent for the rest of my life. At the same time the idea terrified me. I didn't want to hurt my children and I wasn't sure how that would affect my relationship with the Lord.

"Would my devotion to God change with a man in my life?" I wondered. After all, there was something organic about being single. I was in balance with my soul. I served God and God only. I knew He was always there to love and embrace my every need.

Singleness gave me freedom to love my neighbor expecting naught in return. I gave of myself to others because I loved to give. Everything I've done was with open hands through an altruistic heart. I sacrificed without looking back to see if there would be a thank you in return.

The solitude of singleness gave me a greater connection with the Almighty. I had peace that flowed in and through me. I cared solely about what God thought of me. My behavior was exclusively to please Him above anyone else in the planet. I submitted entirely to God's will without questions asked.

Singleness made loving others easier because I didn't expect anything in return. At the same time, it felt safer and kept my heart cloistered from being hurt again. In a way I realized it was a selfish approach to love. I loved others without risking my emotions. I didn't have to endanger my heart again by throwing it into the fire of affliction. I didn't have to make myself vulnerable because I wasn't giving my heart to anyone. I locked my heart in a dark airless coffin. I was making myself impenetrable because I didn't want my heart to be broken again. Singleness was my answer to self-preservation. It made me feel safe, but it was selfish.

God was working on my love walk when He planted a seed of infatuation inside me for Pastor Jones. God began to show that my fear to love a man was a pointer that I needed to be healed from my brokenness.

It was nothing short of divine intervention that I just moved to Alaska and was faced with a new dimension of trust in the Lord. As my mind continued to struggle with the possibilities of inviting a man into my heart, God whispered in my ears Romans 8:28: "And we know that God causes everything to work together for the good of those who love God and are called according to His purpose." At once my soul was restored to peace and a calm delight.

Lord of Surprises, I don't understand your decisions but I want to follow your path. Show me how to love vulnerably as you love me. I want to be open for whatever you wish. Amen.

Additional reading: Psalms 119:105, Psalms 1:1, Proverbs 5:6, Psalms 16:11, Psalm 118:6, Philippians 4:13.

Self-reflection: Do you question God's ways? Do you accept new situations? Do you see all the pieces of your life working together for your good?

Chaste

"'For your Creator will be your husband; the Lord of Heaven's Armies is His name! He is your Redeemer, the Holy One of Israel, and the God of all the earth. For the Lord has called you back from your grief—as though you were a young wife abandoned by her husband,' says your God. 'For a brief moment I abandoned you, but with great compassion I will take you back.'" Isaiah 54:5-7

My infatuation for Pastor Jones shook my heart. I questioned myself: "Why should I want a companion, if the Lord is my Holy Husband?"

Years ago, after the dissolution of my marriage, I found myself scared and alone. Suddenly the world seemed like a big place for my three children and me. One night I prayed to the Lord: "I'm afraid of being by myself, take me as you bride. Envelope me with your perfect love!" God answered my prayer and enfolded me in His protective arms. He became my perfect loving provider.

The Lord cared for me with perfect divine agape love. His love was self-sacrificing, thoughtful, and sublime. His love was flawless. He was kind, not jealous, nor rude. He kept no records of my wrong doings, but forgave my every sin. Jesus never gave up on me, and heard my every cry. He rejoiced with my smiles. He delighted with the progress of my sanctification. He provided all my needs and I never wanted. His love never disappointed and He never left me.

I devoted myself to Him in body and spirit. I became chaste and focused on doing God's will without having a romantic relationship.

Nevertheless, God introduced Pastor Jones in my life. The challenge confused me and I desperately sought God's chamber for new insights.

"Lord, if you want me to have a companion, then I pray that this man will seek you first in order to find me. May he open the door, pull out a chair, and give me his jacket if I get cold. May this man be my knight in shining armor, amen."

Jesus soon whispered in my ear: "Look no further, I am He, your perfect one, who gives you all you need!" I realized I was chasing for something I already had. My perfect Jesus! He was not only my Knight in Shining Armor, but because I walked with Him, I wore His armor. Soon, the Lord showed me He places a man and woman together for their spiritual growth, and for His glorification, and not for a Cinderella happily ever after.

Hollywood and Disney movies portrait marriage as a final destination. A happily ever after! Humans tend to buy into the idea of "castle love," while in reality that kind of love is based on "endorphin fantasies." Reality is that no relationship is a final castle destination because only Heaven is our final destination. We expect a partner to fulfill our empty hole, while only God can do that.

The Lord was not necessarily interested in changing my relationship status into "Cinderella is in engaged to a prince." He introduced Pastor Jones in my path in order to polish my patience, longsuffering, perseverance, and trust along the path of sanctification. Most of all, the Lord was interested in teaching me a kind of love that never fails. He was developing in my spirit a kind of love whereas the *you* preceded the *I*.

My God, Husband of my soul, I thank you for being my redeemer and the true everlasting love of my life. You are with me day and night. You never abandon or forsake me. Help me not to fail love. Help me to love selflessly without desire to possess. Amen.

Additional reading: Romans 5:8, John 3:16, 1 John 4:10, 1 John 4:8, 2 Peter 3:9, Galatians 5:22, Johns 13:35, Colossians 3:14, Ephesians 1:1-23.

Self-reflection: Do you fail loving others because you desire to possess more than to give?

More Beautiful After Being Broken

"You keep track of all my sorrows. You have collected
all my tears in your bottle. You have recorded each one
in your book." Psalm 56:8

I left church filled with conflicting emotions after seeing Pastor Jones.
"Why would I get into a relationship after everything I went through
with my ex-husband?" I asked myself. My thoughts tormented me and
I asked God to show me if my thinking needed rearrangement.

There was a part of me which didn't want a relationship with any
man due to fear. There was a part of me that wanted a new relationship
due to hope. And, there was a part of me which didn't want to have a
new relationship because it was easier to continued being single under
God's protective umbrella.

I wanted to be content with what God had given me, but somehow I
felt incomplete and broken. Tormented emotions were a pointer I had to
deal with the pain of my divorce. I internalized all my tears for fourteen
years, because I wanted to take care of my kids first, and simply didn't
have time to take care of myself.

I never spoke to anyone about the ashes of my divorce. I left the ashes
in God's hand and moved on. I stopped being depressed by trusting God.
I kept going but at the same time, I bottled all my pain, pushed it down
and tried the best to forget about it. I put away all tears in a locked wall
safe, but tucking pain away didn't mean that brokenness didn't haunt
me. I still felt pain in every pore. My hopes and dreams with my ex-
husband were all shattered. I let the loss of my marriage make me feel
insecure and abandoned as a woman. I felt broken in ways which lead
me to think no man would ever want me again. I felt utterly rejected.

I stopped seeing myself as a woman, and saw myself not as a *she* but as an *it*.

The brokenness of my marriage came as a surprised. My husband and I used to be bright together. We laughed and played at every possible occasion. Many times he made me feel I was in heaven, but after I found out who he really was, I sought God's safe haven. After my divorce, God became the one and only I could trust and feel safe.

After meeting Pastor Jones, I realized God wanted to heal my broken heart for I could not be in a healthy relationship without being healed first. God kept all my tears in His bottle and wanted to heal every tear drop. He began wiping each one away through His loving hands. Every broken piece of me was a delicate piece He intended to mend.

I was like a broken Japanese ceramic bowl called *Kintsukuroi* which is repaired with lacquer mixed with gold. The bowl becomes more exquisite after being mended because it recognizes its history. Likewise, I felt broken and demoted after my divorce. Perhaps others thought I was not worth being repaired but God thought differently. He considered me a beautiful broken ceramic bowl worth repairing and wanted me to be more beautiful after been broken. God picked up all of my little pieces, gathered all tears, and gave me true life after being dropped and shattered. He began to glue my little bits with gold lining, making me more pristine in appearance and more beautiful for His sake.

God never ignored my pain, but used every pain for my ultimate good. I like to say every tear was a growing pain. It hurt but it made me taller in His grace. I cried out all tears to make more room for more of His grace.

At last, I became grateful for being broken by my ex-husband. He was part of my story. Even though he hurt me, he also helped me grow spiritually. It was not a mistake I married him. It was not random bad luck. It was not God's oversight. As a matter of fact, my ex-husband was crafted by God for my life. God created a unique journey and took me to unforeseen places I've never expected to go. He penciled a story I never imagined to be mine. Through our marriage God granted me beautiful children. I gained more from losing my husband than retaining the dreams I once had. It'd have been easy to say pain broke my life, but when I look closely, I know pain gave me a new consecrated life.

Tear Collector, my heart is broken. My tears are locked inside and I don't know how to cry. I'm afraid to let my emotions go. Set my soul sailing and help me let go of hidden pain. I kept all sadness under lock and key. Please set me free. Amen.

Additional reading: Isaiah 38:5, 2 Kings 20:5, Revelation 21:4, Job 16:20, Isaiah 25:8, Isaiah 55:8,9, Psalm 56:8, Psalm 62:8, Hebrews 4:16.

Self-reflection: Are you approaching God's throne of grace boldly and receiving His mercy by letting Him collect your tears? Are you ready to let God heal your broken heart?

Yes, No, Maybe So

"'For I know the plans I have for you,' says the Lord.
'They are plans for good and not for disaster, to give you
a future and a hope.'" Jeremiah 29:11

When the kids were little I drove ten hours to get to Anaheim, California. They were very excited because we're heading to Disneyland. However, thirty minutes after leaving the driveway, little five years old Mike began asking: "Are we there yet? Are we there yet?"

Mike became extremely impatient because he wanted instant gratification. He didn't want to be in the car for ten hours. His excitement to visit Disneyland kept him from enjoying the present moment. He didn't enjoy seeing the beautiful mountains, the cows along the road, and all the beautiful scenery around.

I wanted to sing in the car with the kids and have fun along the way, but Mike's anxiety stole the present moment and discolored the joy of the drive. His questions were like echolalia in my ears: "Are we there yet? Are we there yet? Are we there yet?"

The truth of the matter is that adults also act like Mike when he was a child. Patience is not a natural human attribute. We are a society that loves instant gratification. Patience is truly a gift from God and a virtue from the Holy Spirit.

Years went by and I remembered one day driving Mike to college. He was bigger and taller, but this time, I was the one acting childish. I found myself acting like his five year old self. The drive was beautiful. I drove on top of God's Alaskan fluffy soft snow blanket. White flakes fell from the sky making no sound. The trees were covered with crystal snowflakes. Snow formed snow houses, snow roads, snow trees, and snowmen. Yet my mind was not on the beauty of the drive because I was asking God: "Are we there yet? Are we there yet? Are we there yet?"

I was impatient because I wanted God to make my path clear. I wanted Him to answer my prayers right away. I was distressed because Pastor Jones flirted with me for four months but never asked me out. I was puzzled by this and wanted him to make a move. But nothing! The waiting annoyed me. My anxiety discolored my present joy. I stopped celebrating my blessings. I found myself fighting lack of contentment.

Jesus convicted me. He put me back where He wanted me to be. My anxiety was the thief of my happiness. God showed me that patience is not living in the future. Patience is enjoying the present while God works His plans for the future. Trusting in God means to let go of the "what ifs" and embrace God's promises. Faith is trusting that God is either going to say yes, no, or not yet. If God says no, acceptance is acknowledging His answer leads to a richer plan.

I understood that God has a good reason for every no. Nonetheless, He always makes up for the no with a better yes along the way.

While I waited on the Lord to answer my prayers, I learned to be content during His "not yet."

All Knowing Jesus, thank you for your open doors, but also thank you for your closed doors which lead me to a better path. Help me let go of earthly attachments and be only attached to your better will for my life. Amen.

Additional verses: Isaiah 41:10-13, Joshua 1:5,9, 1 Peter 5:7, Psalm 56:11, Psalm 9:10, Psalm 94:19, Psalm 138:8, John 14:27, Isaiah 26:3, Isaiah 40:28-31, Philippians 4:19, Matthew 6:25-34.

Self-reflection: Are you casting all your cares on Jesus? When doubts fill your mind, do you seek answers in God's promises? Are your anxieties discoloring your present moment?

Cactus Pedals

"Don't act thoughtlessly, but understand what the Lord wants you to do." Ephesians 5:17

It was a beautiful Alaska day. Snow slowly melted after a cold and long winter. The sun radiated over the whole city, but I could not admire the scenery because my heart was dismayed again. My emotions were tight up in knots because of Pastor Jones. Infatuation had stricken me ill. I fought the torment emotions. I had daisies in my thoughts. My mind recited: "he loves me, he loves me not," which made me nauseous to my own logic.

I gazed at the city's view from the mountain top. I pondered on the many miracles Jesus performed in my life. He poured blessings after blessings yet my troubled thoughts discolored my gifts. I wanted to be happy for being single once more. I wanted to embrace all God had given me without longing for a relationship with Pastor Jones, but the wanting was not going away, even after prayers and petitions.

I asked the Lord for a new insight. He pointed out that I was pulling dead "he loves me, he loves me not" cactus' pedals. My behavior was a pointer I was acting like a hopeless romantic, craving for a love story. My attraction for the pastor turned into wanting love and not a path of God. Somehow, I blinded myself into thinking he was what God wanted for me, because I had a hole in my heart, which I expected a man to fill. I was searching for a missing piece of myself, hoping to find it in a man, but it was a love war that could never be won.

My quest for love was having a toll on me. I was chasing feelings which could not be satisfied because feelings are never constant. The more I chased love the more it ran away from me. That's because I fell in love with love, not necessarily Pastor Jones. I didn't really know him! I never had a deep conversation with him. I fell in love because of the way he gazed at me, but he never told me he liked me! I thought he implied it every time we saw each other. Yet, he never really declared it!

I'd placed Pastor Jones in a high pedestal. I made an image of him of a wonderful, loving, and almost perfect Christian man. I made "being in love" my destination on earth and I prayed my story would end up at a wedding somewhere! But I should have known better because I've been married before. But no, I had to re-learn this lesson and realize once more that no man, no husband, should ever be my ultimate destination on earth. If God would so desire to place us together, it would have been for His sake only and not for my heart to be complete. A union would not have meant the end of my cravings for love, but the beginning of another great test, which would be the test of marriage. That is because the only destination ending in a complete and fulfilled heart is God Himself.

I was seeking being loved by a man thereby dismissing the fact I was already loved by Jesus. Every other avenue to love would have never been truly satisfying. That's because only Jesus is the true source of true love.

Nevertheless, my quest did not end there. I kept running after the mirage of human love. I continued praying to have a relationship with Pastor Jones. However, my prayers were not meeting my expectations. I didn't know why God put him in my path, but I knew that every day became an arduous test of faith to have what God wanted me to actually hold in my heart. And, what he wanted me to hold was not what I desired. God had a reason for what was happening, even though I couldn't understand it at the time.

God of love, give me a new understanding in the new path you set before me. Show me the hidden truths of true love. I give you my tormented thoughts. Help me have peace and joy while you're working in me. Amen.

Additional Reading: Matthew 22:37-40, Proverbs 14:12, John 7:24, Luke 9:23, Matthew 6:33, Galatians 5:22, John 20:29, Psalm 34:18.

Self-reflection: Does anxiety make you want everything to happen right now? Or do you trust that everything in your life will happen in God's timing?

Cravings

"Now we see things imperfectly, like puzzling reflections in a mirror, but then we will see everything with perfect clarity. All that I know now is partial and incomplete, but then I will know everything completely, just as God now knows me completely." 1 Corinthians 13:12

I had a dream I got stuck in malfunctioned elevator with broken cables. The elevator started to drop exceedingly fast. I held the rail inside the elevator. I was terrified at first, but suddenly a bright light illuminated the whole elevator. The light began pulling me up to the sky, while the elevator kept going down. I thought to myself: "I don't need to worry, I am going to Heaven!" The bliss of peace was indescribable. I woke up felling a heavenly daze.

I believe my dream was a reflection on how I felt towards Pastor Jones. At times I thought we had some kind of connection, but other times I felt the opposite. I couldn't understand at the time what God was doing. That's because on earth God does not grant our eyes perfect clarity, so faith without sight can be exercised.

The ups and downs of infatuations were like my elevator dream. It was symbolic that a free fall would harm and break my heart, yet God would uphold me. One moment I felt positive, the next I felt negative. I did not know how to get my emotions in order. I was confused and asked myself: "Did I fall in love just to have my heart broken again? Why do I feel so miserable? Am I running after cravings or God's will?"

Being in love felt like a curse not bliss. Yet, God showed me being in love was one of the cravings which He invented. Cravings to be loved, cravings to be wanted, cravings to be touched, cravings to be needed, cravings for chocolate were all part of God's design.

My dream represented the elevator moving down passing by all the various floors. Each floor represented the entrance to a craving. But the problem was that the cravings could not be satisfied in any of the floors because they were a mirage. I sought after a mirage of love, thinking it was real, but I could never reach satisfaction. I would come back empty handed seeking for more. I tickled for the things I craved for but the itching never fully went away. All seemed to end up in unfulfilled wants and dreams. Until, I finally realized some of my cravings on earth will only be satisfied once I enter the gates of Heaven. Others yearnings I had were fulfilled in this planet as a sample of what Heaven will be like.

My lessons on falling in love were not yet complete. I still prayed and hoped for a relationship with the pastor. God was still at work in me!

Lord of Heavenly hopes, I leave my earthly cravings and unfulfilled desires into your hands. I want to open my fingers and give you all longings that were not designed by your will. Shed light in my heart. Strengthen my emotions as you strengthened my spirit. Heal my broken heart and bandage my soul. Test, mold, and make me into your will. Amen.

Additional reading: Psalms 37:4, Psalms 37:1-40, Psalms 16:1-3, Romans 8:28, Matthew 6:21, Proverbs 16:9, Matthew 6:33, Proverbs 3:5-8, Proverbs 3:6.

Self-reflection: "Remember how the Lord your God led you all the way in the desert these forty years; to humble you and to test you in order to know what was in your heart, whether or not you would keep his commands. He humbled you, causing you to hunger and then feeding you with manna, which neither you nor your fathers had known, to teach you that man does not live on bread alone but on every word that comes from the mouth of the Lord." (Deuteronomy 8:2-3) God gives longings and causes us to hunger. He places in our hearts yearnings and desires. God has a special reason to give us appetites. He tests, molds, and humbles us to see what is in our hearts. Do you follow God while you are being tested with your longings or are you prone to wander away from God?

Falling In Love With The Real One

"Turn to me and have mercy, for I am alone and in deep distress." Psalm 25:16

After months of eye gazing I decided to make a move on Pastor Jones. After all, he was not making his feelings verbally known. I told him *I liked him.* He looked deeply into my eyes, holding onto every word I said. But his lips said it all, "I'm not interested in a romantic relationship. That is not going to change. My relationship to you is that of a Christian brother and friend. I can't be more than that." I kept my head up but my heart sank. I felt distraught.

I didn't expect that outcome! I was so sure Pastor Jones had the same feelings towards me. His body language seemed clear he liked me, but his words so contrary to it. We gazed at each other for months, but I realized we were looking outward together in opposite directions. The truth was the truth though! He did not like me back.

I sought the Lord day after day, learned to hope, and prayed for the desires of my heart, but the doors were shut right before my eyes. I felt a sudden gut-wrenching emptiness of loneliness and rejection. It was worse than experiencing physical pain!

I couldn't make sense of God's will at that moment. It wasn't adding up. God had just healed my broken heart from the previous marriage and my heart got broken again! Why God permitted me to fall in love with Pastor Jones and not have a relationship with him, I didn't know. Nevertheless, God had taught me again and again we cannot have anything that is contrary to His will.

I'd been faithful to the Lord. I sought Jesus in everything I did, but God did not permit the relationship. I didn't know why God denied the desires of my heart. I wanted smiles but received tears. I wanted love but received rejection. Yet in the midst of suffering, God wiped my tears. God embraced me when I felt downcasted. He walked with me through my pain and pushed me deeper into His loving embrace. God gave me more of Himself and more of His wisdom while I was going through pain.

At first, it was not easy to let go of my feelings for Pastor Jones, especially seeing him every Sunday at church. It's easy to let go of something else, but infatuation? I wanted to hold it tight in my heart. But God wanted me to let it go because it wasn't good for me. God wanted me to give up my heart's desire.

My attachment became contrary to what God wanted for me. I became attached to being in love but God wanted me to find something other than that to be attached to. I needed to fill the empty space in my heart with God, my permanent attachment. My feelings of infatuation for the pastor were a false attachment I needed to let go of, even to the cost of more pain. It became an unhealthy attachment which I became dependent upon. Somehow my infatuation for him filled my empty broken heart for a while. I made myself believe I couldn't live without being in love. But that wasn't true, because the only One I couldn't live without was God!

I made a decision to sacrifice my longings for what God wanted for me, which was a healthy free heart. I wanted love from a man in this life and became consumed with my desires. I wanted my life on earth to fulfill me, while all the while, my true fulfillment could only come from God Himself. He was the One who I needed to fall in love with. He was my real version of love. But my eyes could not see clearly while I was consumed with my infatuation towards Pastor Jones. I fell in love with a lesser, fake model of love. That's because all earthly love comes from a worldly life filled with deficiencies and imperfections.

My love for God had to be defined by Him first and foremost. I learned to stop letting my heart be defined by my infatuation for a man. That kind of love was like a destructive slavery. I was trying to get my worth by the retribution of a man's love instead of Jesus' love. All the while, Jesus was trying to let me know that my worth came from my relationship with Him and not a relationship with a man.

At last, the Lord gave me distinctiveness to be loved and completed by Him again. He showed me that my body and soul was created to love and to be loved by Him first.

I've learned that my heart should be so consumed with God that a man should seek God completely in order to find me. I've learned that God will place that kind of man in my life if He so desires, but my heart should never be misprioritized because a man will only be a loving companion, not my ultimate version of love.

Psalm 46:10 "Be still and know that I am God" echoed in my heart. God spoke to me in my stillness. The more I sought Him in my quietness, the more He became my Real version of Love and the easier it became to give up the version of love God did not intend for me.

Finally free from worldly infatuations, God liberated me from the bondage of worldly wants. I learned to be content and single again. However, I learned to be vulnerable and unselfish in regards to love by unlocking my heart, but ultimately came back into the arms of the Lord.

More empowered by His grace, I returned to His safe embrace.

Soul comforter, I am still before you. You are my home and resting place. I often don't understand the perplexities of my desires. At times I can't trace your path or see the road ahead. I often don't get the desires of my heart. Yet, I submit my questions into your supreme plan. I don't want anything to occupy my heart that is not from your wise hands. I want your approval for everything. Thank you for embracing my pain with your loving embrace. Amen.

Additional reading: Hebrews 13:5, Psalm 10:17, Psalm 37:4, Psalm 139:13-16, Jeremiah 29:11, Psalm 139:1-4, Psalm 34:17-20.

Self-reflection: Are you letting the Lord direct your path in regards to relationships? Do you thank Him when He closes the doors as much as when He opens the doors?

Hope

"Having hope will give you courage. You will be protected and will rest in safety." Job 11:18

Mike was always a bright light in a dim room. People were automatically transformed by his happy spirit. He constantly smiled and joked around, but things suddenly took a turn in his life. I expected him to continue acting that way because I assumed it was part of his jolly personality. But I was wrong.

He changed when he was let down by others he looked up to. For three months his life was in disarray. He lost hope for the future. He lost love for his friends. He became tired of all human beings. Finally, he lost his faith in God and drifted away from Him.

He snuggled into a self-pity bubble. He resorted to playing video games all day. Anna and I listened, prayed, and comforted him to no avail. A sad cloud hung over his head wherever he went because he was disappointed with everything.

Mike stopped relying on God's hope and began relying on human hope. He wished his troubles would go away. "God never answers my prayers. He never gives me what I want. Christians are unfair. There is no God," Mike would say again and again in anger. He hoped for happiness but received trouble. He wanted pleasures but received displeasures.

He gave up on God and gave worldly hope a chance. But the problem is that worldly hope doesn't quench the thirst. Once one desire is fulfilled, the next desire stands at the doorstep. Worldly hope lies because it promises false nirvana for nothing in the world truly satisfies.

Mike forgot Biblical hope. He ignored the fact that God's hope never lies and never disappoints. God's hope rescues us in every possible way. Unlike worldly nirvana, it's a hope that is attainable. God's hope is the expectation that something wonderful is going to happen under God's guidance.

Nirvana hope says: "I hope I'll lose ten pounds in a week." However, Biblical hope is more than floozy wishful thinking which relies heavily on luck. It is something Christians can count on. It's a certainty yet not realized. It's hope based on faith. And, "Faith is the confidence that what we hope for will actually happen; it gives us assurance about things we cannot see." (Hebrews 11:1)

Hope in the Bible is God infused, therefore trials and tribulations cannot rob us from the faith that is in Christ Jesus. If we hold onto the hope that is in God, then there's no drifting away because we are holding onto solid ground. It is a secure assurance that we can trust our lives in Christ because He holds our future. Since our hope lies in God's hands, there's no need for relying on luck or wishful thinking.

At some point in time Mike stopped holding onto the hope he professed in Christ (see Hebrews 10:23). He tried nirvana hope, but after three months of soaking in insecure grounds, he decided to go back to the God of all hope. He woke up one day saying: "I'm done thinking about myself. I'm done with self-pity." Mike returned to a life of prayer, and helping others.

Mike's friends didn't apologize to him, but something inside him changed. He chose to forgive without evidence of repentance from friends. He chose to hope in God without evidence of situational change. His struggles strengthen his character. He began to wait for his future-well! Mike was suddenly renewed by an overflow of God's infused hope.

God gave Mike power to fight hopelessness. As a consequence, he shone once again around every part of the room with his contagious smile.

Blessed Hope, I'm confident that miracles will happen in my life. I'm sure you will heal my broken heart. I'm sure you will help me forgive those that hurt me. I'm sure you will be there for me when life comes tumbling down. You mend me. When humiliated, you comfort me. When judged, you support me. You are never tired of loving me. Putting my hope in you never disappoints me. Amen.

Additional reading: Romans 5:3-5, Romans 15:4, Hebrews 10:23, Romans 15:13, 1 Corinthians 15:17-20, 1 Peter 1:3-4, Romans 8:24-25, Hebrews 11:1, Isaiah 49:23.

Self-reflection: Are you banking your life in worldly hope? Have you been alienating yourself from God and others?

Rejection

"Moreover, I will make my dwelling among you, and
my soul will not reject you." Leviticus 26:11 (NASB)

It was time for our church annual campout. We were supposed to meet
at Lake Etkna in Alaska by the end of the day. My kids and I arrived
at the camp and waited for our group. Three hours later we were still
waiting. We drove around the campground several times. We asked the
park ranger if he spotted our group. "I haven't seen anyone from your
church," the ranger replied.

No one showed up! We headed back home without participating
in the campout. Later we found out our church changed the retreat
to another campground location since all the sites were full. I was
disappointed no one waited at Lake Etkna to ensure we would join the
rest of the group. My sense of belonging was violated. I felt rejected.

"What about my family? How could they not wait for us?" I
wondered. It's not the first time I felt ostracized. I tended to expect
certain relationships to reciprocate what I put in. In this case it was the
body of Christ, other times, best friends. I tended to allow relationships
to define my sense of belonging. I expected friendships to be perfect and
unbreakable. However, that was an unreasonable expectation because
everything in this planet brakes or shrivels away. Why did I expect my
relationships with people to be any different than our broken world?

Everything in this planet is imperfect, but I wanted everything to be
perfect because I'm a perfectionist. I give my blood, sweat and tears for
a cause, friend or stranger, and somehow expect others to do the same,
or at least have some reciprocity, but I'm always let down.

My unrealistic expectations set me up for disappointments. I looked for love and came back empty handed. However, the blame was on me! My disillusion with people was a warning sign that something was wrong with my thinking. It was a pointer to unhealthy attachments to people. I needed rearrangement. I needed God to change me.

I gave my brokenness to God and waited for Him to transform emotional wounds into spiritual growth. I realized my need to be loved had to be sustained by God and not friends. I needed Jesus to define my sense of belonging and my place of true fulfillment.

I began acknowledging that rejection was an anti-Christ spirit. God loved and appreciated me. He wanted my love to be rooted in His love and acceptance instead of being rooted on people (see Ephesians 3:19). That meant having my identity grounded in Christ before and foremost anything. Once I changed my focus from people's love to God's love, I began feeling rejection-proof, knowing He would never abandon me.

Jesus' reaction towards rejection helped me deal with my sense of exclusion. Jesus was despised and rejected by men, yet His complete identity came from God. He didn't feel sorry for Himself because others abandoned Him. As a matter of fact, He was the stone that the builders rejected but became the chief cornerstone (see Psalms 118:22).

Jesus was scorned: "Only in His hometown, among His relatives and in His own house is a prophet without honor." (Mark 6:4) Even though Jesus was rejected in His hometown, He didn't park in His sorrow. He continued with God's work which was far more important than receiving His identity from people around Him. He didn't let rejection keep Him from fulfilling the plan of salvation, even if it meant saving those who hurt him the most.

Jesus knew who He was. His identity was not disturbed when others shouted insults at Him. He was secure in Himself: equal to God, the Lord, the Way, the Truth, the Light, the Bread of Life, and the Light of the World!

The only way to overcome my rejection problem was to follow Christ's example. When they hurled insults at Him, He did not retaliate; He suffered but made no threats against others. Instead, He entrusted Himself to God who judges justly (see 1 Peter Ch.2:23). He overcame rejection by putting His complete trust in God and by fixing His eyes on Him.

The roller coaster that once defined my relationships finally came to an end, as I found emotional stability in Christ. I placed my hope, trust, and dependence on Him. My peace no longer was disturbed because someone was not nice or didn't respond to my love. I became grounded in God's stability because my attachments were not dictated by people's reaction towards me.

My entire dwelling became the Lord and He never rejected me!

Loving Lord, you never cut me off. Even when others abandon me, you hold me close. I am your child created by your hands. Make me deeply grounded in you so no human rejection is able to shake the foundation of your will for my life. Mend broken relationships with the light of your wisdom and grace. Amen.

Additional reading: Isaiah 53:4-6, Romans 8:31, Luke 6:22, John 1:11, Leviticus 26;11, Isaiah 41:9, Psalm 94:14, Psalm 77:7, Psalm 27:10.

Self-reflection: Have you been wounded by rejection? What is your coping mechanism to deal with rejection? Do you receive your identity from other people or do you receive it from Christ? Have you forgiven those who made you feel rejected?

The Package

"Trust in the Lord with all your heart; do not depend on your own understanding. Seek his will in all you do, and He will show you which path to take. Don't be impressed with your own wisdom." Psalms 3:5-7

I sat next to Anna. Next to Anna sat Mike. It was a Sunday morning at our Anabaptist church. A few minutes into the service Matt showed up for the first time. He squeezed in between Mike and Anna. Matt was Mike's university friend who had just come to know Jesus. I looked at Anna and nudged her a bit with a *ah-hah* smile. Her packaged was delivered via prayer express.

Two months prior, Anna prayed: "Lord, if you want me to marry someone, I pray for him to be Asian, Christian, smart, kind, and violinist; if not, I would like to remain single." When Matt walked into the church, Anna thought God's answer was delivered in total.

A few months later, Matt gave Anna a book which told a story of God's visions in the life of a couple. Simultaneously, Anna began having a vision that Matt and she were to be eventually married. She prayed and waited on the Lord. Finally, they had their first date. However, the following week, the vision disintegrated. She saw Matt through the rosy lens of love but when she saw him for who he really was, she was disappointed and broke up with him.

She became confused and asked me: "Why did God give me a vision we're to be married and suddenly everything fell apart? I was so sure, and now I feel empty and without direction! I feel futureless. Why did God allow me to dream of an empty future?"

None of the questions were easy to answer. All I could do at the time was to listen and give Anna a shoulder to cry on- until I went to bed. My night was out of the ordinary. I fell into a deep sleep. I couldn't wake up because my body felt heavy. It was as if gravity was stronger than usual and I was being magnetically pulled closer to the ground. I had vivid dreams and woke up at noon, which was unusual.

My dream was of Mike running halfway into my bedroom during the morning. After waking up I thought it was a silly dream. After all, in reality, Mike never walked in my bedroom in three years since we've been living in our house. "Why would I dream of that?" I thought.

I began morning as usual and while I was brushing my teeth I heard running in the house. I asked Anna what was happening. She said Mike just ran halfway into my bedroom. "*Wha? Huh?*" I asked perplexed. "Are you ok, ma?" Anna questioned my surprised expression.

The dream about Mike became reality about an hour after I got up from bed. "Why would God give me a prophetic dream?" It took me a couple of hours to understand what the Lord was trying to convey through my dream. It all began to make sense.

God gave me a dream about Mike running into my bedroom. Nothing more, nothing less! The dream came true. There was nothing to add to it. However, if my heart had hidden desires, then my emotions would have interfered with the prophetic dream. I'd have wakened thinking God gave me a vision about Mike running into my bedroom, *plus* giving me breakfast in bed, and *plus* cleaning the room. My hidden desires could have augmented God's prophesies to satisfy my yearnings. My imagination would have been extended from a simple prophesy into a hopeful illusion.

Similarly, God gave Anna a vision about Matt. God gave her a short lived relationship with a smart Asian man who played the violin. However, Anna augmented the vision into what she desired in her heart. She extended the vision into a hopeful illusion and made Matt the final destination of God's plan for her life.

God tested Anna's ears to see if she was walking in step with the Holy Spirit. She learned to see God's vision for what it was and not for what she desired it to be. Everything served God's plan to enhance Anna's spiritual walk. She felt futureless, but God promised to restore her heart. She understood her life was being divinely orchestrated. She learned not to force her desires to come to fruition because she continued to trust God to make a new way from her old pathway.

Supreme Guide, I don't want to backslide or fudge with the truth. Let me stand firm with the facts you give me. Let your truth be my truth. Thank you for the tests and temptations. You give me opportunities to advance in your Kingdom. I want only what you will for me. Amen.

Additional verses: Numbers 12:6, Habakkuk 2:2-3, Isaiah 43:18-19, Jonas 2:28, Psalm 89:19, Jeremiah 23:16.

Self-reflection: Do you augment God's visions by making it fit your desires?

There Is A Balm In Gilead

"There is a balm in Gilead to make the wounded whole
Sometimes I feel discouraged and think my works in vain
But then the Holy Spirit revives my soul again.
There is a balm in Gilead to make the wounded whole
There is a balm in Gilead to heal the sin sick soul."

"When Jesus heard this, He said, 'Healthy people don't
need a doctor—sick people do.'" Matthew 9:12

"There is a balm in Gilead" is a beautiful old African American hymn which invigorated my soul while I felt ill due to neuromuscular disease. Its lyrics were inspired by prophet Jeremiah who sought healing for his people. I envisioned Jeremiah speaking out loud: "'The harvest is finished, and the summer is gone,' the people cry, 'yet we are not saved!' I hurt with the hurt of my people. I mourn and am overcome with grief. Is there no medicine in Gilead? Is there no physician there? Why is there no healing for the wounds of my people?'" (Jeremiah 8:20-22)

Prophet Jeremiah asked God to restore his people because he felt powerless during the horror of the Babylonian invasion in Jerusalem. It was a dreadful time. In his despair, Jeremiah stood on a hilltop, located outside the city, and gazed towards Gilead. It was a location famous for producing medicinal balms to heal wounds. There he cried out to God: "Is there no medicine in Gilead?" He petitioned for a curative ointment. His prayer was ultimately answered, for out of Palestine came our Great Physician, Jesus.

I also cried out for the Balm of Gilead whenever neuromuscular illness acted up and whenever I found myself in despair. Jesus was my medicinal balm and always renewed my strength. My Great Physician was the hope for all sufferings, as He is for all of us who call upon His name.

However, when I felt better, my cry to the Lord diminished. I dealt with health problems more independently, as if saying to the Lord: "I've got this!" Unperceptively, I'd shove the Lord aside from sunshiny days. My faith would relax and spiritual growth tended to stagnate.

One day I was reminded that the Great Physician was there for me as my twenty-four-seven doctor. The Great Physician was there for well-checkups and not only for medical emergencies.

It all happened once we moved to Alaska and I visited an ophthalmologist. As soon as the eye doctor looked inside my eyes, he said I needed a laser iridotomy right away or I could lose my vision at any moment. My intraocular pressure was extremely high, and he diagnosed me with narrow-Anglo glaucoma.

After the laser surgery, I ended up ill from the medications side effects which affected my muscular disease. I was at rock bottom again. The crisis brought back memories of the worst days during illness. As my muscles became weaker and painful, my faith muscles began its usual workout. I trusted God once more for healing.

"There is a Balm in Gilead" song reverbed in my heart. Once again, Jesus restored my health to a tolerable level and also convicted me of lack of dependence on Him when things were going my way.

After many ups and downs of trusting God during bad times, and relaxing faith during good times, I've learned that the Lord didn't want me to go to the top of Mount Gilead only when I was falling apart. God was not to be used as a crutch, or as 911 emergencies. He wanted me to dwell in His presence even when life was filled with cheerful sunshine.

Dear Great Physician, faith in you thrives during sickest moments. Help me have the same measure of faith during good days. Forgive me for going to you only when I'm sick and in need. I want to set my face towards you during good times as well as during bad times. Amen.

Additional reading: James 5:14-16, Matthew 10:1, Ecclesiastes 3:1-2, Psalm 41:1-3, Job 5:17-18, Acts 9:34, Matthew 8:15.

Self-reflection: Do you use God as a crutch during bad times or do you still seek Him during good times?

Miraculous Healing

"And a woman was there who had been subject to bleeding for twelve years. She had suffered a great deal under the care of many doctors and had spent all she had, yet instead of getting better she grew worse. When she heard about Jesus, she came up behind Him in the crowd and touched His cloak, because she thought, 'If I just touch His clothes, I will be healed.' Immediately her bleeding stopped and she felt in her body that she was freed from her suffering." Mark 5:25-29

The bleeding woman probably dragged her body around in discomfort in order to accomplish the things others took for granted. It must have been difficult to get out of bed and go on with daily activities. Perhaps she had some kind of dysfunctional uterine bleeding. Whatever the cause of the illness, the constant bleeding left her depleted of blood from the circulation. She had to be iron deficient, causing pallor, fatigue, and weakness. Undoubtedly, she walked on the streets breathlessly. Her heart probably palpitated fast every time she walked uphill. I imagine she thought every day could be her last.

Disease was this woman's lonely companion in her path of despair. She couldn't understand her condition. No one quite understood how she felt. Doctors couldn't help her. Her illness was not curable by balms. She suffered without hope until hope came her way as she touched Jesus' cloak.

This woman's desperation caused her to squeeze through the large crowd leading to Jesus. She thought to herself: "If I just touch His clothes, I will be healed." She probably stretched her weak arm giving away the last energy she had. Upon touching Jesus cloak, she was instantly healed. Jesus tells her: "Daughter, your faith has healed you. Go in peace and be freed from your suffering." (Mark 5:34)

Can you just imagine Jesus saying to you "go in peace and be free from your suffering?" It must have been an unforgettable moment in this woman's life. Suddenly, the woman's weak physique was renewed. She had a new sense of strength. She could breath, walk, and live a life free from physical suffering. Faith gave her a ticket to a new healthy body.

I could relate to this woman. Neuromuscular disease drained me to a point I was almost too weak to stay alive. I was ready to go to Heaven with Jesus. I dragged my body to do activities of daily living. And, it was truly hard.

Like the hemorrhaging woman, I needed a physical miracle. I wanted to touch the cloak of Jesus. I wanted to be instantly healed and bouncing off the walls. I wanted His power to flow into me in order to end weary days.

I have given up on doctors, drugs, and hospital emergency rooms. I was tired of being a guinea pig and hearing doctors say: "There's nothing I can do to help you." I had two options: the first was to let myself die in the arms of Jesus, and the second was to touch the cloak of Jesus. And I chose the cloak!

I read Psalm 118:5, 17: "In my distress I prayed to the Lord, and the Lord answered me and set me free. I will not die; instead, I will live to tell what the Lord has done... he did not let me die."

As I read Psalms, the Lord fortified me and did not let me die. Since I moved to Alaska, my health slowly began to improve. I haven't done anything different other than the usual, asides from giving up waiting for answers from doctors.

The day my kids and I moved to our new house in Alaska, we had to clean and unpack. I was able to keep moving the whole day. By the time I went to bed, I've done physical work just like during the days I was healthy. I went to bed, pinched myself, and wondered: "Am I alive? Is this Heaven? Am I dreaming?"

I never thought I could have any quality of life left, yet the Lord began restoring my health, but it was a lengthy process. I still felt sudden leg weakness, occasional night breathing problems, and neuropathy. Yet, I was nowhere I used to be.

Two years went by since the day we unpacked and moved into our new house in Alaska. I haven't seen any new specialist but I did see my Great Physician Jesus. His cloak gave me healing power, and little by little He renewed my strength and began to invigorate me. I was alive, walking, breathing, moving, talking, and thanking the Lord for His miracle of restoration. I thought it was my end. I thought I was going to die. But Jesus whispered: "this is only the beginning; you still have more mountains to climb!"

Can Jesus heal today? Yes, He greatly restored me and I'm here to tell you this story. He renewed me for His sake and glory. He repaired me to display His power and continue His work in me.

Jesus heals some, but not others. Even the woman who Jesus healed from bleeding surely became ill from some other ailment and died. The Bible doesn't mention if this woman was healed from future illnesses. All we know is that she eventually died, because everybody dies. And we know that everyone that was healed by Jesus eventually died either by natural causes, accidents, or secondary illnesses.

Jesus heals to display His power of love so we may have faith in Him and recognize His presence. We also know if Jesus doesn't heal our infirmities on Earth, He will heal us permanently by giving us new bodies in Heaven. Bodies which will be imperishable, never die, never get sick, and never feel pain.

JEHOVAH-RAPHA, my healer, I praise you and exalt you for the miracles you bestowed upon me. Thank you for your healing cloak. Thank you for answering prayers and giving me victory. May I proclaim your glory for your name's sake. Amen.

Additional reading: Peter 2:24, Luke 18:1, Matthew 28:20, James 5:14-15, Isaiah 53:5, Mark 11:24, Matthew 9:35, Luke 6:19.

Self-reflection: Jesus Christ wants to heal you. Will you receive His anointing power of healing? Would you approach Jesus' throne boldly and confidently to receive your physical healing?

Vacation

"Come to me, all you who are weary and burdened, and I will give you rest. Take my yoke upon you and learn from me, for I am gentle and humble in heart, and you will find rest for your souls." Matthew 11:28-29

For the past two years I've been praying for a vacation. My life has been a testing place and not a resting place. I begged God for a break from the storms. The Lord kept some of the storms away but cloudy days continued.

Every time I'd have a little test I'd go back to God asking Him for a sunny vacation. I didn't necessarily ask Him for a Club Med vacation. I just wanted rest from trials.

The Lord always answers prayers. It might not be on my time frame, but nevertheless prayers were answered. It might not be how I want it answered. It might not be a sudden answer. But the Lord always knows best. So, the answer to my "vacation prayer" came little by little, almost unperceptively.

Suddenly, I noticed the snow falling from the sky more than ever before. I have been blessed by the sun on my face upon waking up in the morning. I thanked God for the warmth of my blankets during Alaska's dead of winter. I praised Him for the light coming through the windows of the house in the beginning of spring. I have enjoyed my family's stability and love. Halleluiah, God answered prayers and I have been on vacation from trials.

Are you in the midst of the coldest and stormiest waters of your life? Have you been facing rogue waves, frigid gales, and ice formations on and around your life boat? Have you been asking God for a break from the storms? If you ask the Lord, He will give it to you, if you seek Him, you will find your answer, and if you knock, He will open the door (see Matthew 7:7-12). The Lord gives His children only good things. We might be tested from time to time, but after the storm comes the sun.

Faithful Lord, I praise you for granting me rest and peace. As I count my blessings, love for you grows deeper and my faith stronger. Amen.

Additional reading: James 1:17, Luke 6:38, 1 John 5:14-15, James 4:3, 1 Thessalonians 5:17, Hebrews 11:6, John15:16, Matthew 21:21.

Self-reflection: Has God answered your prayers without you noticing it?

Fasting

"Jesus replied, 'Foxes have dens and birds have nests,
but the Son of Man has no place to lay His head.'" Luke
9:58

I engaged in eight days of complete fasting as a teenager. I craved being fortified by a closer relationship with the Lord. During fast, I prayed for a homeless man and a blind woman I assisted weekly. I abstained from food while I focused on prayer. Fasting caused my physical cravings for food to be emptied while spiritual cravings for God to be full. My soul was purified because I denied natural desires of the flesh to gain God's greater spiritual clarity.

Fasting helped me let go of everything around which didn't come from God. Fasting took me to a place where I was physically living at my parents' house but spiritually dwelling with the Lord. Fasting elevated me to a higher altitude of communion with God.

As the days went on hunger for food disappeared as hunger for the Lord intensified.

During the eight days of fasting, the refrigerator at my parents' house was full of food. I could have opted to end fasting at any time and go to the fridge, but I remained in God's presence. However, there was a later time in my life in which my fridge was empty and fasting was not an option. I became poor and hungry. It occurred when I moved out of my parents' house. I went through a period of lacking. I rented a room in an attic of a dirty one hundred year old house. The door of my room didn't close all the way. The walls were not sealed and bugs crawled through the cracks. I was constantly cold. I made three hundred dollars a month working part-time, assisting a lady who had a stroke.

After paying the rent I had little money left over to buy food for myself. I literally lived off of bread, tea, and an occasional can of tuna.

As a teenager, fasting was a choice, but living on bread, tea, and tuna was not. Through time I began to understand the Lord had a plan for every lesson He prepared for my life. Fasting and lacking humbled me. It helped me empathize with the needy and hungry in a greater sense. The emptying of the stomach cleansed and purified me by giving the opportunity to fill my heart and mind with Jesus' empathy towards the starved.

Fasting and lacking reminded me of the word "blessons," which are lessons that leads to blessings. My life's "blessons" taught me that homeless individuals are invisible people who are often avoided, but Jesus loves each one of them and wants to give them hope. Blessons showed me that it is my job to show them mercy in their time of need. It is my job to provide them with some measure of comfort and God's love. For when I look at them, I say to myself: "It could have been me!"

Jesus came to engage in the brokenness of the world. Not just to offer us a home in Heaven. We can't just go to the streets and present Jesus' forgiveness and salvation to the hungry and starved when it's convenient. Jesus came to show us how to respond to their need- now! Jesus came to show us how to engage in their pain- now! Jesus came to show us how to fill their stomachs- now! Jesus came to show us how to love them- now!

Jesus was able to empathize with the needy for He was not born in a hospital. Jesus was not born in Mary and Joseph's home. Jesus was born homeless in a barn with animals. Baby Jesus didn't have a beautiful fancy crib with mobiles and toys. Jesus was away in a manger asleep on the hay. Jesus suffered as a homeless Savior, from birth to death.

As a homeless man, Jesus gave us everything! He gave us hope, love, and salvation. He demonstrated how to live in community with one another by serving the hungry, homeless, and hurting. Jesus calls us to share His love, compassion, hope, and bread. Jesus invites us to have empathy to those who hurt: "Suffer with them as though you were there yourself. Share the sorrow of those being mistreated, as though you feel their pain in your own bodies." (Hebrews 13:3 NLT)

Merciful Jesus, enlarge my heart to the needy. Forgive me for being a bystander when I see brokenness all around. Help me to reach others through your love by sharing my bread with the hungry and homeless. If I see the crippled, lame, and blind show me how to bless them as you bless me. Amen.

Additional reading: Leviticus 25:35-36, Isaiah 58:7, Luke 14:13-14, Matthew 25:34-40, Isaiah 58:5-8, Matthew 6:19-20, Luke 10:30-37.

Self- reflection: Can you think of ways in which you can show Jesus' love and compassion towards the needy?

Jehovah-Rophi

"If a soldier demands that you carry his gear for a mile,
carry it two miles." Matthew 5:41

Our church decided to get involved with a non-profit Christian
organization called Agape Inc. which recruits volunteers to care for the
needy throughout Alaska. I joined the force and volunteered my nursing
skills. Soon Agape Inc. called me requesting I give a lady named Lyssete
a ride to the doctor.

I drove towards Lyssete's apartment and found her waiting outside
on a bus bench. She looked fatigue, frail, and ill. I helped her into my
car because she could barely walk.

The drive to the doctor's office was heartbreaking. Lyssete murmured
breathlessly: "Ask your kids to pray for me." Mike and Anna, who were
sitting in the back seat of the car, began pleading God for her feeble
body to make it alive to the doctor's office. It looked like she could die
right in my vehicle.

After five hours at the doctor's office, Lyssete was admitted to
acute care due to terminal cancer. We tagged along with her because
we simply couldn't walk away from her pain. During that time, Lyssete
whispered her life story etched with sorrow. "I was homeless in Florida
and my family abandoned me," she said with a weak voice. She made
her way to Alaska and was accepted into an Alaska subsidized housing
apartment a few years back. She was living in grave poverty since then.
She only possessed an air mattress, a frying pan, and few utensils.

Lyssete was critically ill for some time, but didn't have Medicaid.
She couldn't go to a doctor due to lack of money, which caused the
cancer to grow undetectably. A few days before I met her, she came

across a pamphlet from Agape Inc. She went to the neighbor's house to call them. Soon after that, Agape Inc. made an appointment for her to see an oncologist in which I was to take her. Nevertheless, she still didn't have a way to pay for the doctor's visit.

Lyssete remained grateful during her struggles even after hearing her terrifying diagnosis. She did not murmur. She possessed a beautiful smile and a peaceful spirit. She sought Jesus for guidance. Soon her faith in the Lord began to open new doors. Miracles lined up one by one. The hospital provided complete financial coverage until she was accepted for Medicaid. She was on the operation table the next day, and it was through divine intervention that Dr. Holden, her surgeon, was a member of our Anabaptist church. He performed the surgery but not before praying with Lyssete for a successful operation. Another church member bought her a walker because she used an old luggage with wheels to sustain her feeble body. God also provided Lyssete with material provisions. By the time she returned home, she had a bed, table, sofa, and new support system. Other members of the church opened their hearts to help, pray and love her.

Lyssete became part of my life. I was just going to give her one single ride to the doctor's appointment, but God had another plan which was more than just a ride. God called my children and me to go the extra mile. He invited us to go to unexpected places and do unforeseen acts of radical love toward Lyssete. God guided us towards a divine love that heals broken hearts and mends fragile souls. In the end, I was more blessed than I blessed. It became clear that it was better to give than to receive.

What we've done was nothing more, nothing less, than following Jesus' footsteps. He was called Jehovah-rophi, the Lord who heals. Jesus healed bodies through love and benevolence. "Jesus traveled through all the towns and villages of that area, teaching in the synagogues and announcing the Good News about the Kingdom. And He healed every kind of disease and illness. When He saw the crowds, He had compassion on them because they were confused and helpless, like sheep without a shepherd." (Matthew 9:35-36)

Jesus was and is an inexorable lover and healer of shattered people. He never took a vacation from serving others. He went the extra mile and cured bodies riddled with illness even during the Sabbath (see Matthew 12: 9-14).

Jesus invites us to carry the soldiers' gear two miles. He wants us to be a relentless blessing to others everywhere we go.

As we carried Lyssete's gear the second mile, we were blessed to see her smile in the midst of her pain. Jesus was healing Lyssete's lonely heart through love. Her cancer was drawing her closer to Jesus. She was suffering bravely with perseverance towards the Holy Throne of God.

Gentle Jehovah-rophi, touch my heart and soul so I may love others. I don't want to grow weary of serving the needy. Enlarge my soul to understand how they feel, so I may serve with greater compassion. Help me to respond to their pain. Amen.

Additional reading: Galatians 6:9, 1 Peter 4:10, Acts 20:35, Galatians 5:13-14, Mark 9:35, Matthew 20:28, Luke 6:38, Matthew 25:35-40.

Self-reflection: Do you get weary of doing good? Would you ask Jesus to enlarge your heart to love others with radical agape love?

Hard Times

"It's not important who does the planting, or who does the watering. What's important is that God makes the seed grow." 1 Corinthians 3:7

My kids and I left a local eatery. On our drive back home, Mike asked me to drive around a few blocks because he thought a person was lying dead on the pavement. After driving around a few blocks, we found a woman who seemed dead. I parked the car and decided to investigate. "*Ma'am*, are you alright?" she didn't move. I asked her again with a louder voice and she finally mooned and said she was sleeping. Actually, she was drunk and homeless.

On our drive back home we saw several homeless individuals sitting on the sidewalks. One homeless man moved my heart more than others. He made an impression on me while I came upon a long stop light. He opened his cardboard sign right in front of my window. The cardboard said: HARD TIMES. My heart squeezed because I didn't have anything to offer the homeless man. I had no food in the car. I had no cash. I didn't even have a Bible to give him.

The sign HARD TIMES steered my thinking and I decided to learn more about homeless individuals in Alaska. I found out that they fight substance abuse issues, domestic violence, mental illnesses, and HIV/AIDS. Some homeless are young and some are war-veterans. According to local news, homeless experience beatings, rapes, and robberies out in plain view. Some die of hypothermia during Alaska's cold spring and some die frozen during the winter.

The homeless man holding the cardboard by my car window was having HARD TIMES. I think he meant his difficulties were not being overcome by his efforts to improve his life. Hardship ruled his days. As a consequence, he sought strangers to respond to his despair. He must of thought: "Is there anyone who can turn my hopelessness into hope?"

My heart filled with compassion. I knew I couldn't save the homeless from their misery. However, instead of just observing their pain, the Lord led me to plant a seed of Jesus' hope every time I came in contact with a homeless person. After all, "Not all of us can do great things. But we can do small things with great love." (Mother Teresa)

God touched my heart after seeing the homeless man holding the "HARD TIMES" cardboard sign. As a result, every time we headed to the streets, my children and I distributed lunch bags to homeless people containing a sandwich, cookies, juice, and a pamphlet with God's promises. We couldn't save the homeless from their plight but God could use our willingness to love them through random acts of obedience. As a result, we could offer a measure of hope to those undergoing hopelessness.

Nevertheless, hopelessness is not a plight of the homeless only. We all suffer from it from time to time. We may experience a consuming darkness which makes us forget that light exists at the end of the tunnel. We may get lost within ourselves.

Our despondent hearts drive us to give up. We ask ourselves: "Why bother if nothing will ever work out?" We become pessimistic, thinking we will never be happy. We tend to think we will never get what we want, our relationships will never work out, and so on. We begin doing things we thought we would never do before. We fall into sin. We become detrimental to ourselves. We finally believe we are cursed and everyone is against us.

As a result we isolate ourselves in our sad world and stop engaging with friends. We don't try anything new. Hopelessness becomes a whirlpool of gloominess.

Lyssete told me she suffered from hopelessness once. It was one year ago when she lay in a hospital bed with stage V colorectal cancer. Her sweet eyes looked deeply into mine as she shared her story of hope:

- "Ten years ago, I was homeless in Florida. One day I reached rock bottom. I had no reason to live. I felt cursed, poor, and forgotten. I wanted to give up, but then a stranger reached out to me and gave me a bottle of water. He said: 'Jesus loves you.' His words gave me strength. My life was turned around at that moment because I realized Jesus loved me and I was not forgotten. That glimpse of hope helped me turn off my suicidal thoughts."

I had tears in my eyes while Lyssete shared her story. It was a confirmation that God uses our random acts of obedience to turn a person's life around. The person who gave Lyssete the water bottle has no idea that his simple act of obedience saved Lyssete's life.

Lyssete lived to tell others her story of hope, for hope is a good thing! Hope heals and strengthens the soul. Hope shows there's no pit too deep that God can't scoop us out of. Hope is a lamp for those who trust God. Though the light may be dim, if we fix our eyes on His hope we will not be disappointed. Those who trust in Him receive renewed strength because His hope is genuine and does not fail.

Hope Giver, you are a lamp in my night, guiding me out of sorrow. Your anchor holds me when the seas storm betides me. You whisper comforting words in my times of trials and troubles. You chase darkness away healing my wounds as I pray. Amen.

Additional verses: Proverbs 24:14, Jeremiah 29:11, Titus 3:7, 1 Corinthians 15:19, 2 Corinthians 4:16-18, 1 Peter 1:3, Romans 12:12.

Self-reflection: What's giving you a sense of hopelessness? Are you worrying, isolating, and avoiding everything? Do you find yourself looking everywhere to pin hope into something or someone to fill your void? If so, do you come up short? Would you make God your solid source of hope?

Mike And The Beggar

"Right now you have plenty and can help those who are in need. Later, they will have plenty and can share with you when you need it. In this way, things will be equal."
2 Corinthians 8:14

As I was about to turn on an interception, a homeless man was begging on the street corner. I parked the car at a gas station. Mike walked out of the car and gave him something to drink. Then Mike looked in the beggar's eyes and shook his hands firmly wishing the man a good day. The beggar's body language lid up. He seemed happier because Mike shook his hand than for receiving a juice pouch. Later, I asked Mike, "Why did you shake the man's hand?" he said: "everyone needs to be acknowledged and valued as equal."

In our society we have two kinds of givers. The first kind gives to the needy because it makes them feel better about themselves: "I love to give and God loves the giver!" And the second kind of giver, gives to the needy because they empathize and understand the needs of the one that lacks. They think more about the beggar receiving than the act of their giving.

I admired Mike when I saw him shaking the beggars' hand. He empathized with the homeless man and saw him as equal. He reminded me of my grandfather's teaching: "you should eat at a king's table in the same matter as you eat with a beggar sharing a snack at a street corner." After all, the Lord doesn't treat one person better than another for He shows no partiality (see Romans 2:11).

The Lord is directing Mike's footsteps. It's possible that Mike could be wealthy someday. It's conceivable that the beggar could become wealthy as well. We never know God's purposes, so it is also doable that Mike could become a beggar someday. That is because "The Lord sends poverty and wealth; He humbles and He exalts." (1 Samuel 2:7) It all comes from God's hands because He tests our hearts to see what's inside.

God tests us during poverty but He also tests hearts during times of wealth. Many times the poor gives more than the rich, while the rich retains their wealth by obsessing with more riches. Financial prosperity will not make a man superior in God's eyes than a beggar asking for money. God does not give preferential treatment to different social classes. To Him there's only "spirit class," for He looks at the motives of the hearts and not the wallets in our pants.

Jesus said: "I tell you the truth, slaves are not greater than their master. Nor is the messenger more important than the one who sends the message." (John 13:16) All humans are the same in Christ. When humans are buried, they go to the same place. A wealthy man will be six feet under identically as a beggar. Their bodies will deteriorate in the same way. The only difference is that light will only be given to the ones that were baptized into Christ and have put on Christ.

Just Savior, help me to imitate you by loving my neighbor as myself. Give me grace to mirror all your teachings. Amen.

Additional verses: Galatians 3:28, Romans 2:11, John 13:16, Genesis 1:27, Galatians 3:26-29, Mark 12:31, Colossians 1:16-17, Leviticus 19:33-34, Acts 10:34.

Self-reflection: Do you practice Christ's egalitarianism?

Putting Others Ahead Of Yourself

"We who are strong must be considerate of those who are sensitive about things like this. We must not just please ourselves. We should help others do what is right and build them up in the Lord. For even Christ didn't live to please Himself. As the Scriptures say, 'The insults of those who insult you, O God, have fallen on me.'" Romans 15:1-3

There was nothing else I would rather do than go out and celebrate 4th of July with my kids by watching fireworks at the park strip. Although my muscle disease was much better, it decided to act up that day. I needed to rest.

After Independence Day, Lyssete phoned to take her to a chemotherapy appointment. I was still recovering but at the same time I was the only one that could drive her to the oncologist. I felt terrible. I was ill, but she was in a worse position than I was.

At the end of my rope, I prayed God would let me borrow His strength, smile, and love in order to care for Lyssete. I was like a car running on empty needing God to fill my tank to the brim.

The morning of Lyssete's appointment came. I was still not feeling well. I needed to tap into Jesus miraculous healing balm. I dragged myself out of the door. Mike and Anna joined me as my reinforcements. They helped me by getting Lyssete out of her apartment. Mike wheeled her into the oncology center, Anna carried her belongings, and little by little God renewed my strength by giving me courage to go another extra mile. Jesus lent me His smile and helped me put her pain ahead of my own.

The day was over, Lyssete had her chemotherapy, and we helped her back into her apartment. I drove home thanking God for refreshing me with His miraculous grace.

It might seem on the outside I'm always confidant and willing to step into whatever God wants me to do. I am aware He expects my commitment and not my convenience. But reality is that I'm not always altogether. I often have an urgent plea not to be what He wants me to be when my desires are not to serve Him. I get exhausted easily and my mind fills with thoughts of anxiety. At times I feel I don't have the strength to face one more day of doing what God wants me to do, especially when I'm ill myself. But His promises are real! In desperation I find that I can rely on God to strengthen me to the task ahead. And at the end of the day, my words, smiles, prayers, and compassion are never from me, but borrowed from Jesus to Lyssete and others. And to God all praises are due!

God often calls us to self-sacrifice. Apostle Paul talked about it in Romans 15:1, 2. We are called to give of ourselves for the sake of others and not to put ourselves first. We're called out of our comfort zone even if it means acting opposite to our desires. By doing so, we're doing everything for the sake of Jesus and being His imitators by bearing "the infirmities of the weak, and not to please ourselves." (Romans 15:1, 2) because "...even Christ pleased not Himself; but, as it is written, the reproaches of them that reproached thee fell on me." (Romans 15:3)

Great Strengthener, I do not fear, for I am with you! You renew my strength and help me. You supply me with all I need. Help me count all joy to serve you and others. Amen.

Additional verses: Matthew 7:12, 1 Peter 3:8, John 13:35, Romans 12:15, Romans 12:10, Isaiah 1:10, Philippians 4:6-8, Jeremiah 17:7-8, Matthew 11:28-30.

Self-reflection: Do you do everything through the *JOY* acronym order: *Jesus*, then *Others*, then *You*?

Divine Coincidences

"Furthermore, because we are united with Christ, we have received an inheritance from God for He chose us in advance, and He makes everything work out according to His plan." Ephesians 1:11

Mike, Anna, and I became Lyssete's regular caregivers. We drove her to oncologists, grocery stores, and when she'd feel better, we'd take her dancing to local church gatherings. She was beginning to improve and I thought she was going to beat cancer.

I checked on Lyssete almost daily because she lived by herself and spent most of her days in bed alone.

One afternoon, I called Lyssete but she didn't pick up the phone. I was concerned since that was unusual. I called the hospital to find out if she was readmitted. Since they haven't heard from her, I decided to call 911. The police went to her place to do a well-check. Meanwhile I drove to her apartment. I was praying not to find her hurt or dead on her bed or on the floor.

Upon arriving at Lyssete's apartment, I found out she took a sleeping pill and didn't hear the telephone ringing. "I just want to sleep because today is my daughter's birthday and I have no idea where she lives or how to find her. I want to send her a birthday card, but I don't even have an address for her," she told me in tears. As she continued sharing her sadness, my daughter Laura, who was the same age as Lyssete's daughter, called my cellphone asking for Lyssete's address. Laura wanted to send her a "get well" card.

Is it coincidence or God's plan that Laura called me at the perfect time to remind Lyssete that there's someone the same age as her daughter that thought of her during that memorable day? Is it coincidence or God who prompted Laura to ask Lyssete for her address just to wish her good health, even though Laura had never met her?

When Laura called me, Lyssete continued crying, but this time not because her heart was broken but because God used Laura to let her know He cared about her tears. The Lord in His sovereignty arranged a divine coincidence. God reassured Lyssete that even though things appeared out of control, He was in control of events that could not be understood by human mind.

Minutes later, Lyssete's tears were gone and a sweet peaceful smile returned to her face. God was making everything work according to His divine plan. Lyssete's broken heart was becoming an instrument whose music was becoming more and more in tune for God's glory.

Divine Jesus, thank you for arraigning divine coincidences to reassure you are in control. I praise you because you have a good reason for every NO and every YES. You intervene in my life with a supreme plan. Amen.

Additional reading: James 1:27, 3 John 1:5, 1 Thessalonians 2:7, Galatians 6:10, Galatians 5:14-15, 1 Peter 5:7, Romans 5:5-8.

Self-reflection: Have you noticed the Lord uses divine coincidences regularly to show you that He cares deeply and personally about everything in your life?

Birthdeath

"… and the day of death better than the day of birth."
Ecclesiastes 7:1

Months went by. Lyssete was no longer beating cancer. Cancer claimed her body. Every minute her condition declined. She was no longer eating. She only sipped water. Her body was rapidly dying. She was living in between two worlds.

Mike, Anna, and I stopped by Lyssete's apartment to check on her. She tried to speak to me. Her lips moved but her voice crackled. I read her the Spanish Bible, for Spanish was her native language. Mike played the piano. Anna and I sang. After a long time, we prayed for a victorious passing from this life to God's glorious Homeland. However, she didn't pass away. She patiently endured physical affliction.

I rubbed her hand and asked if she needed anything: "Don't leave me, *urrrr*, it's too hard," she said. It was difficult to understand what she was saying but we finally understood she wished us to bathe her before burial.

I wanted her to pass on so her pain would cease. "Please Lord, take Lyssete to your Kingdom. Spare her from this suffering. Take her now while I'm here so she doesn't have to die alone." But she didn't die. She remained stuck through the active stages of death.

Two days later she no longer could talk. She no longer could eat or drink. Her skin color changed. She'd take three or four rapid breaths and then she'd stop breathing for a while. Her Cheyenne stokes breathing continued. She lingered through the process of dying.

Again, I sat beside Lyssete's bed reading out loud the Spanish version of Psalms, when suddenly I choked up between words. Tears flowed down my face. I told her I loved her. She opened her eyes a bit and then I thanked God for her life. I looked around the apartment and memories of moments I spent next to her during the past nineteen months came to mind. I thought of how cancer took her through the peaks and valleys of pain. I recalled her faith and hope in the Lord. I recalled her laughter in the midst of sufferings. I recalled the many times she looked deeply and quietly in my eyes and said: "Thank you," with a sweet melodic voice.

"Why couldn't I hold my tears? Was I sad?" I wondered. I suddenly realized I was not sad. I was filled with awe because I was given the privilege of participating in Lyssete's *birthdeath*. She was experiencing the drifting end of her perishable body into the birth of her imperishable eternal body. I realized her passage from this life to the next was filled with ethereal beauty. Lyssete's *birthdeath* was actually better than birthday pains because it was going to lead her to Paradise. The Lord would come down from Heaven and she'd rise with Christ (see 1 Thessalonians 4:16). Heaven's symphonies were inviting her to the Permanent Home.

When Lyssete was born to this planet, she was born to a life of pain. That's because even the happiest moment of her life was tinted with echoes of sorrow. That's because this life is just a glimpse of the hereafter. Lyssete's happiest moments on earth were just a sample of what Heaven will really be like.

My tears ceased. I was suddenly happy for her. I sat by Lyssete's bed and remembered times I helped babies be born in hospital delivery room. Babies that were born to this life of pain with tints of happiness here and there. Then their mamas and papas would embrace their new addition to their families thinking they reached their destination to nirvana, but soon, they'd go home to find out that it was a mirage. Once again they'd begin journeying through the peaks and valleys of joys and sorrows of raising children. That's because everything in this planet is a mirage. Everything in this planet is unstable. One moment we are happy and the next sad. Everything in this planet fades. Everything in this planet is a lesser model of Heaven. Everything in this planet is a representative sample of the Celestial City which last forever.

Our birthday on earth is not our final destination for happiness. Our birthday on earth is not better than our day of death. Our birthday on earth is a voyage towards eternal punishment or eternal life for those who believe in Jesus.

Our journey on earth offers an opportunity to seek a closer relationship with God. Our journey on earth gives us a platform to be tested by God or seek the desires of the flesh. Satan will tempt us, but we determine the outcome of our destination. We either regress or press on. If we regress than there should be fear in death. If we press on towards the Lord's throne, there will be no fear of death, but victory.

Once we are snatched away from our bodies, death will either cause us fear or causes us to rejoice. Our life on earth is our only chance to prove our faith and seek things from above. Our life on earth is our only chance to pass the tests of life with the goal of eternal life with Jesus. Our life on earth is an invitation to heal us from our separation from God. Our life on earth is an opportunity to cleanse our souls as a preparation for Heaven. Our life on earth is our walking shadow to our real life in Heaven with Jesus Christ.

Our *birthdeath* with Jesus is our final destination to a city designed and built by God. Our *birthdeath* is better than our lives in this planet because it is the portal to Heaven for those who embrace the Lord. Our *birthdeath* is the end of our physical bodies with the promise of a perfectly new and transformed heavenly body. Our *birthdeath* comes with the inheritance of hope, peace, and joy through God's infinite love.

Our *birthdeath* quenches the thirst as Jesus said: "'Anyone who drinks this water will soon become thirsty again. But those who drink the water I give will never be thirsty again. It becomes a fresh, bubbling spring within them, giving them eternal life.'" (John 4:13)

Lyssete drank Jesus' water. She was getting ready to never thirst again. She continued with Cheyenne stokes respiration. Her face was filled with peace. Her soul was more luminous than ever as her bodily powers began to fail. She waited for the light of the Lord to come in. Her new Heavenly birthplace was ready for her. The Lord was getting her ready to partake from the pure river of crystal Heavenly waters.

All of Lyssete's earthly tears, which God collected in His bottle, were being prepared to be wiped away from her eyes. All of her earthly sorrows would dissipate. All of her physical pains were being prepared to be no more. Her final destination was Paradise with Jesus. She'd receive an everlasting communion with God. Her final days in this planet were a preparation to receive an eternal and unperishable new body. Her inheritance was going to be incorruptible and undefiled.

During Lyssete's earthly days, her heart was captured by the love of God. At any moment the Light would come upon her from Heaven above. Winter leaves were drying up on the ground as Lyssete's eternal spring was about to flourish in her new home. Lyssete's day of death was going to be better than the day of birth.

"The Lord is my shepherd I lack nothing. He makes me lie down in green pastures, he leads me beside quiet waters, and he refreshes my soul. He guides me along the right paths for his name's sake. Even though I walk through the darkest valley will fear no evil, for you are with me; your rod and your staff, they comfort me. You prepare a table before me in the presence of my enemies. You anoint my head with oil; my cup overflows. Surely your goodness and love will follow me all the days of my life, and I will dwell in the house of the Lord forever."
Psalm 23 NIV

Additional verses: Matthew 18:10, John 14:2, Revelation 5:9-13, Revelation 21:4, Acts 4:12, John 17:3, John 14:6.

Self-reflection: Jesus said in John 14:6: "I am the way, and the truth, and the life. No one comes to the Father except through me." Will your final destination be paradise with Jesus? Would you turn your face to Jesus before your bones turn to dust?

Suitcase To Heaven

"Since you have been raised to new life with Christ, set your sights on the realities of Heaven, where Christ sits in the place of honor at God's right hand. Think about the things of heaven, not the things of earth. For you died to this life, and your real life is hidden with Christ in God. And when Christ, who is your life, is revealed to the whole world, you will share in all His glory... Since God chose you to be the holy people he loves, you must clothe yourselves with tenderhearted mercy, kindness, humility, gentleness, and patience... Above all, clothe yourselves with love, which binds us all together in perfect harmony. And let the peace that comes from Christ rule in your hearts. For as members of one body you are called to live in peace. And always be thankful. Let the message about Christ, in all its richness, fill your lives. Teach and counsel each other with all the wisdom He gives. Sing psalms and hymns and spiritual songs to God with thankful hearts. And whatever you do or say, do it as a representative of the Lord Jesus, giving thanks through Him to God the Father." Colossians 3

During a period of eighteen months, Lyssete was in and out of the hospital. "I wanna go home!" she'd say every time. However, while she was hospitalized, she never redecorated the hospital room. She didn't get new color pillows or a new floral design bedspread. She didn't purchase new furniture or curtains. That's because she didn't become attached to the hospital room.

She was uncomfortable at the hospital. She was uneasy for a little while because it was the only way to treat her cancer. Lyssete didn't object to the unpleasant bed and the bland meals because she'd return to her own bed and cook her own meals upon being discharged. The hospital was nothing more, nothing less than a temporary place for cancer treatment. She was like a traveler at the hospital.

Do patients redecorate their rooms at hospitals? Surely not, because hospitals are a temporary place and not a final destination! Patients don't buy rooms at hospitals. Insurance companies cover the cost of room and board. Patients hope to be discharged. Patients hope to go back home. Patients are merely travelers at hospitals.

Lyssete didn't redecorate her life with things that were perishable, just like she didn't redecorate the hospital room. She understood that earth was her temporary adobe, just like the hospital room. She didn't become attached to her life in this world because she knew she was a traveler in this planet. She didn't try to make this world her final destination. She enjoyed her belongings, memories, apartment, but was not consumed by them. That's because she realized she couldn't carry anything that belongs to earth in her spiritual Suitcase to Heaven. The only things she could carry in her suitcase were God's lessons which caused her to grow, learn, and love more deeply.

The spiritual Suitcase to Heaven Lyssete carried was not a cheap broken old luggage. Lyssete's Suitcase to Heaven was the sturdiest of all the suitcases. She began packing it when she accepted Jesus as her Lord and Savior and continued packing until it became full. Her robust suitcase was made to deal with bumpy streets, curbs, stairs, escalators, buses, and planes. During the last days of Lyssete's life, her suitcase was packed and complete in Him with every good spiritual gift.

Inside Lyssete's Suitcase to Heaven were priceless life experiences. She lived from grace to grace under God's embrace. Little by little God cut new spiritual cloths into new beautiful patterns which made her more and more radiant for Christ. She became not of this world because through Jesus, she was not conformed by the patterns of this world. She was tested and approved by God through every trial.

Lyssete's sufferings were good for her because it taught her to set her face towards Jesus and learn beauty from every pain (see Psalm

119.71). She was refined into God's image and perfected by His will. He transformed her life of storms to a life filled with good hope. Every passing day of Lyssete's life was a preparation for her life to end, because Christ, who suffered for her sins would bring her to God, along with her spiritual Suitcase to Heaven (see Romans 12:2).

Nevertheless, Lyssete's Suitcase to Heaven was not quite ready for her final destination. She was still going through lingering death. Back at her apartment, she survived through the evening, but didn't know if she would survive to see daylight. But during the morning, she didn't know if Jesus would take her by nightfall. She realized the curtain of her life was soon to be drawn, but Jesus had one more miraculous surprise on earth to grant her.

"Ding-dong," the bell sounded repeatedly. Marta finally walked into Lyssete's apartment!

I was flabbergasted! I thought of the time when I met Lyssete. Her greatest concern was not getting healed from cancer. She wrote in a piece of paper her daughter's name and said: "Can you find Marta for me?" Her greatest concern was to find her missing daughter! Lyssete's broken heart was much more painful than her cancer. She didn't want to leave this planet without telling Marta how much she loved her. She wanted to see her at least one more time.

For months on end, I searched high and low for Marta. I talked to a detective, searched on the web, and called her grandfather in Puerto Rico to no avail. She was nowhere to be found except in our prayers. Lyssete needed a miracle, and God was not delivering that miracle through me.

Months went by and her daughter never left Lyssete's prayers and mind. Lyssete's only choice was to wait on the Lord for a miracle. She missed her daughter and wanted a loving reunion towards a paved way into the softening of hearts.

Never too soon, never too late, the miracle arrived as Marta walked towards Lyssete's bed and held her hand. Breathless and speechless, Lyssete opened her eyes and heard: "I love you mom!" Marta offered words of candor, reassurance, and love. Lyssete's final reunion with Marta granted her permission to set aside all of her troubles of this world and move onto the next. Lyssete's spirit began the final process of leaving her body, environment, and all attachments. I realized Lyssete's best gift of goodbye was to hear "I love you" from her daughter which she so longed to see one more time.

The Lord miraculously brought Lyssete's daughter back after missing for ten years. During Marta's absence, Lyssete developed her faith muscles. She trusted and depended on the Lord to take care of Marta and bring her back. God was in control and provided a miracle of peace and love in Lyssete's final moments, for there are no coincidences for God and His plans are perfect. And, it was His plan that Lyssete would add much patience in her spiritual Suitcase to Heaven while she waited for God's plan to unfold.

Marta was holding Lyssete's hand. Suddenly Lyssete's sparkling eyes lost its shine. Her temporary earthy physical adobe became empty. Lyssete left her body and ascended to the Lord. I was overwhelmed with joy for her. I imagined her happiness upon seeing our Savior. I knew she had no more tears, no more pain, and no more sorrows. Lyssete's trip on earth was over and she moved to her permanent address, Paradise.

A few hours later, I began washing Lyssete's body for burial along with Mike and Anna. Her body was pale and translucent due to livor mortis. Mike grabbed a brush and gently combed her hair singing her a last song: Amazing Grace. We dressed her in a pink outfit and Anna put Lyssete's favorite hat on. Lyssete's body was there with us, but Lyssete's spirit was not with us anymore. We were saying goodbye to the vessel God gave her while in this planet. She borrowed her vessel for fifty-five years. Now, from ashes to ashes, her vessel began to decompose. Her eyes were vacant and her mouth askew. We're washing her corpse, which looked like a doll, for she was no longer existent.

Mike, Anna, and I continued to sing and say goodbye to Lyssete's doll like corpse. She became a used model of a human being. Her body represented the nostalgic value of her history in this planet. No possible restoration could be made on earth to revitalize her body which was now void.

All of Lyssete's most valuable belongings stayed behind in this unstable planet. Lyssete didn't pack her clothes, money, or documents in her Suitcase to Heaven because those things belonged to earth and she only borrowed those things from God for her use while she was alive. She didn't pack any memories of her life because they belonged to the time that she was here. She didn't pack her daughter or friends because Lyssete only borrowed them from the Lord. Those were earthly attachments given to her by the Lord to help her spiritual growth. She didn't pack her body because it was also borrowed from the Lord, and now it belonged to dust.

Lyssete left everything behind on earth. Her sufferings ended as she was finally called by the Lord. Lyssete's spiritual Suitcase to Heaven was filled with all of God's glories which she accumulated during her journey here. The Lord was done fulfilling all of His plans for her temporary life. Her travelling days on earth were over.

Lyssete departed with her spiritual Suitcase to Heaven. She collected beauty from ashes. She transformed all trials and tests into love, mercy, kindness, humility, gentleness, tenderheartedness, and patience. The message of Christ filled her life in this planet, which gave her an incorruptible and undefiled inheritance in Paradise.

I imagined the Lord saying:

> "Well done, my good and faithful servant.
> You trusted me through tribulations.
> You obeyed me despite your trials.
> You've packed many spiritual pearls.
> Welcome to your eternal Celestial inheritance."

Finally, Lyssete opened her spiritual Suitcase in Heaven to be forever with the Lord she loved.

Additional Reading: Matthew 25, 1 Peter 3:18-22, 1 Peter 1:4, Hebrews 12:28, John 14:2, Revelation 22:1-5, Revelation 21:4, Luke 23:43, Hebrews 11:16, Revelation 21:1, John 3:13, Isaiah 61:1-3, Hebrews 11:6, Romans 3:23, 2 Corinthians 5:21, John 1:1-3, John 3:16.

Self-reflection: Traveler, I can only show you the way but you must make the journey to Heaven yourself! The curtain of your life will end someday, for life is just a moment! God will come visit you because it will be your time to go. Are you ready? What have you been packing in your spiritual suitcase? Your belongings? Your money? Your regrets? Your memories? Your successes? Your failures? The photos of your family and friends? Have you been packing things that you cannot carry to the next life? When Jesus comes for you, will He find your suitcase full or empty? If your suitcase is still empty, would you invite Jesus into your life by having your first real conversation with the Lord?

Father, I acknowledge that Jesus Christ is Lord, lived a sinless life, and resurrected from the dead. He died in my place so I wouldn't have to pay for the sins I deserve. I confess my past life of sin. Please forgive me and help me to avoid disobeying you. I'm ready to trust Jesus Christ as my Lord and Savior. I invite your Son Jesus to come into my heart, reside in me, and begin living through me. I ask you to fill my Suitcase to Heaven with spiritual gifts. In Jesus' name I pray. Amen.

THE END

All Scripture quotations, unless otherwise noted, are taken
from the Holy Bible, New Living translation NLT.
Names and places have been changed to
protect the identity of individuals.

Printed in the United States
by Baker & Taylor Publisher Services